Praise for *The Gifted Teen Survival Guide*

"Reading this guide is like having an expert on giftedness, an excellent teacher or mentor, and a best friend to talk with—all at the same time. The combination of great information and great writing makes it a 'can't put it down' book! I recommend it highly for all gifted teens."

★ Susan Daniels, Ph.D., professor of educational psychology and counseling at California State University in San Bernardino, and coauthor of *Living with Intensity: Understanding the Sensitivity, Excitability, and Emotional Development of Gifted Children, Adolescents, and Adults*

A truly excellent, thorough, and up-to-date book! It will help gifted teens understand themselves in ways that will change their lives."

★ James T. Webb, Ph.D., psychologist and founder of Supporting Emotional Needs of the Gifted

"This new edition is the best yet! It has a fabulous format that is very appealing to teens. I consider it a 'must have' book."

★ Margaret Gosfield, acquisitions editor, *Gifted Education Communicator*

"Mutual respect between authors and readers is apparent on each page of this book . . . it is the ultimate problem-solving guide for gifted teens."

★ Colleen M. Harsin, director, The Davidson Academy of Nevada

"Judy and Jim packed this book full of actionable steps along with real-life stories, facts, and examples from many gifted teens. These stories will help build self-esteem, confidence, and important qualities for any teen to succeed further in life."

★ Lane Sutton, age 14, entrepreneur, social media coach, and founder/writer of kidcriticusa.com

"Galbraith and Delisle skip the platitudes, deconstruct common misconceptions, and get to the heart (and brain) of real issues for gifted teens."

★ Corin Barsily Goodwin, executive director, Gifted Homeschoolers Forum, and author of *Making the Choice: When Typical School Doesn't Work for Your Typical Child*

"This comprehensive, insightful, fascinating book is the classic guide for gifted teens, and the new, updated topics are essential in today's complex society."

★ Bertie Kingore, Ph.D., educational consultant and author of *Developing Portfolios for Authentic Assessment, PreK–3: Guiding Potential in Young Learners*

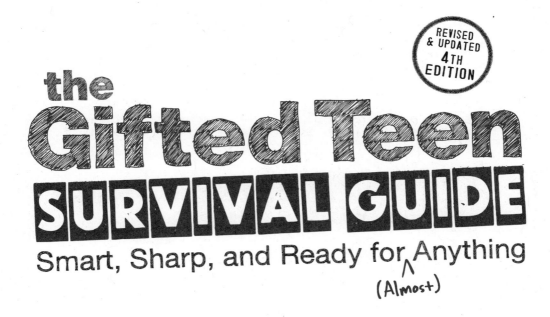

Revised & Updated 4th Edition

the Gifted Teen SURVIVAL GUIDE

Smart, Sharp, and Ready for Anything (Almost)

Judy Galbraith
& Jim Delisle

free spirit
PUBLISHING®

Library of Congress Cataloging-in-Publication Data
Galbraith, Judy.
  The gifted teen survival guide : smart, sharp, and ready for (almost) anything / Judy Galbraith & Jim Delisle.—Rev. & updated 4th ed.
      p. cm.
  Previously published under title: The gifted kids' survival guide: a teen handbook.
  Includes index.
  ISBN 978-1-57542-381-4
  1. Gifted teenagers—Juvenile literature. [1. Gifted children.] I. Delisle, James R., 1953- II. Title.
  BF724.3.G53G35 2011
  155.5087'9—dc23
                                                                                              2011020278

  eBook ISBN: 978-1-57542-683-9

Free Spirit Publishing does not have control over or assume responsibility for author or third-party websites and their content. At the time of this book's publication, all facts and figures cited within are the most current available. All telephone numbers, addresses, and website URLs are accurate and active; all publications, organizations, websites, and other resources exist as described in this book; and all have been verified as of May 2011. If you find an error or believe that a resource listed here is not as described, please contact Free Spirit Publishing. Parents, teachers, and other adults: We strongly urge you to monitor children's use of the Internet.

Note: The names of some students who appear in this book have been changed to protect their privacy.

Reading Level Grades 7 & Up; Interest Level Ages 11 & Up;
Fountas & Pinnell Guided Reading Level Z

Edited by Meg Bratsch
Cover and interior design by Tasha Kenyon
Illustrations by Vigg

10 9 8 7 6 5 4 3 2 1
Printed in the United States of America
S18860711

Free Spirit Publishing Inc.
217 Fifth Avenue North, Suite 200
Minneapolis, MN 55401-1299
(612) 338-2068
help4kids@freespirit.com
www.freespirit.com

As a member of the Green Press Initiative, Free Spirit Publishing is committed to the three Rs: Reduce, Reuse, Recycle. Whenever possible, we print our books on recycled paper containing a minimum of 30% post-consumer waste. At Free Spirit it's our goal to nurture not only children, but nature too!

Printed on recycled paper
including 50%
post-consumer waste

To gifted young people everywhere, and to those who work tirelessly to encourage, support, and challenge them. Your energy, intelligence, and contributions are an inspiration. It is my hope that you will follow your passions and make the most of your talents—for yourself, and for the world that so needs your gifts. ——*Judy Galbraith*

I dedicate this book to my friends and colleagues, Bob and Jan Davidson, founders of the Davidson Institute for Talent Development. Bob and Jan are the most generous, caring, and sincere advocates for gifted children that I have had the privilege to know in my 33-year career in this field. They have changed the lives of thousands of gifted young people for the better. Thank you, Bob and Jan. ——*Jim Delisle*

Acknowledgments

We'd like to thank the 1,381 respondents to our online survey about growing up gifted. Your candid, thoughtful, and informative responses were significant in shaping this fourth edition and helping it to be as relevant as possible for 21st-century readers. We'd also like to thank all the readers of our prior editions. The comments and questions you've sent us over the years have also helped shape this guide.

A special mention goes out to the hundreds of middle school students Jim taught in Project Plus, a gifted program in the Twinsburg, Ohio, Public Schools. Thanks to them, his career as an educator was transformed.

Both of us thank Meg Bratsch from the bottom of our hearts for being such a thoughtful, thorough, and gifted editor. You made working on this book fun, and your special affinity for gifted teens was particularly appreciated. (Readers, it might interest you to know that Meg was in gifted classes when she was growing up!) We also thank our creative and talented designer, Tasha Kenyon. Since neither of us can draw our way out of a paper bag, we truly valued your spirited design. And sincerest thanks to our illustrator, Vigg, for his witty and wonderful artwork.

Finally, we acknowledge the wonderful contributions of our essayists: Patty Rendon, Mike Postma, Chad Gervich, Susan Daniels, Zach Ricci-Braum, Amanda Rose Martin, Sarah Boon, Elizabeth Chapman, Paul Andersen, Morgan Brown, Kelsey Ganes, Alicia Bierstedt, Alec Bojalad, Olivia Fauland, Yuval Adler, Olivia Patrick, Alex Menrisky, Jalil Bishop, and Thomas Friedman. Your unique voices and perspectives have enriched this book tremendously.

CONTENTS - - - - - -

Introduction

Some schools today have strong, effective, exciting gifted programs in place. Countless teachers are dedicated to ensuring that *all* students, including gifted students, are given the chance to learn, grow, and succeed. In some communities, giftedness is encouraged, respected, and rewarded. If you are part of such a program, favored with such teachers, and nurtured by such a community, then you may not need this book, and the information in it may seem irrelevant to you. But if you have ever felt bored, unchallenged, confused, conflicted, frustrated, excluded, or unhappy with your school, your environment, your life, and/or yourself, and if you'd like to know how and why giftedness may have something to do with these feelings, read on.

How & Why We* Wrote This Book

This is not a book *about* gifted young people. It's a book *for* gifted young people. And it takes sides—yours. We wrote it with help from nearly 1,400 gifted teenagers from across the United States and countries around the world including Canada, the United Kingdom, Ireland, Iceland, Belgium, the Netherlands, France, Italy, Austria, Romania, Greece, Turkey, Pakistan, South Africa, China, Singapore, Chile, Australia, New Zealand, and even Atlantis,** who responded to a survey asking them to identify their questions and concerns about growing up gifted—and from hundreds more we've interviewed, spoken with, listened to, and heard from over the years. We drew on the expertise of forward-thinking educators, parents, and other experts on giftedness, and on current research and findings. And we thought deeply about our own experiences as educators of and advocates for gifted children and teens.

---

*See page 261 for our author biographies.
**That would be the Lost City of Atlantis, which obviously does not exist, but we liked the respondent's humor.

Unfortunately, gifted education in the United States and other parts of the world is often ignored or under fire. Many school districts, faced with shrinking budgets and cutbacks, have dropped their gifted programs altogether. Tighter budgets mean fewer qualified teachers and heavier workloads, and that in turn means fewer opportunities to give gifted kids the individualized and challenging education they deserve and thrive on.

The U.S. government's No Child Left Behind (NCLB) act gave rise to increased mandated state testing, which means teachers are pressured to "teach to the test" to ensure all students pass required exams. In theory, this is a good thing; no child *should* be left behind and not given an opportunity to learn important content. However, most regular classrooms today are *inclusive*—they include students with special education needs and learning difficulties—which means teachers often spend most of their time teaching material to the kids who struggle to learn. Gifted students who learn and progress through new material quickly may not be receiving an education that's appropriate for them. For some of these students, school is one dull day after another, a time when they seldom learn anything new and instead slog (or sleep) through unchallenging and repetitive information, assignments, and lessons.

Although many gifted students may be unchallenged in school, at least rich and famous whiz kids like Larry Page and Sergey Brin (founders of Google), Natalie Portman (Oscar-winning actress, Harvard graduate, and published science researcher), Mitchell Baker (she launched the Mozilla Firefox browser), and Mark Zuckerberg (founder of a little site called Facebook) have made it cooler than ever to be smart. You might think, then, that brainy, successful students are no longer harassed, teased, or resented, right? *Wrong.* While it's true that "geek has become chic" in parts of adult society, the message hasn't translated into some middle and high schools. Gifted students may earn the high grades (and even develop apps, write books, and record albums), but it's often still the kids who look a certain way and have large

"I DEFINITELY BELIEVE THAT THOSE INVOLVED IN ATHLETICS ARE VALUED MORE THAN OTHERS IN OUR SOCIETY. THEY ARE THE ONES WHO RECEIVE THE HEFTY SCHOLARSHIPS AND GET INTO THEIR FIRST-CHOICE SCHOOLS BECAUSE REVENUE FROM A SUCCESSFUL ATHLETIC PROGRAM IS KEY FOR A SUCCESSFUL COLLEGE OR UNIVERSITY." —*Erika, 17*

friend groups who get social status, and the athletes who continue to receive the awards, kudos, letter jackets, and full scholarships. Meanwhile, many smart kids who aren't part of those worlds seem to be pejoratively labeled geeks, nerds, dorks, or whatever the current (usually worse) word happens to be. They may be picked on and attacked, sometimes violently.

> "As a culture, we seem to value beauty and brawn far more than brains."
> ★ GREGORY ANRIG, FORMER PRESIDENT OF THE EDUCATIONAL TESTING SERVICE

About This Book & What's in It for You

The Gifted Teen Survival Guide presents facts, findings, ideas, quotes, insights, strategies, tips, quizzes, resources, and more about giftedness, intelligence, brain development, emotions, stress, expectations, time management, technology use, school survival, college preparation, career options, relationships, bullying, depression, philosophy of life, and other topics of interest and importance to gifted students today. How do we know? These topics were all identified as ones of interest by our survey respondents. To get an overview, skim the contents, scan the index, or flip through the pages and stop when you see something you want to know more about.

Over the years, gifted students have told us that problems with school and teachers are their number one concern, so we've included a hefty chapter about taking charge of your education through proper planning and action. Gifted young people have identified confusion about giftedness and relationships with peers as other pressing issues, so we've devoted considerable space to these topics. We offer solid advice on how to handle the elevated expectations parents often have of their gifted children, and fascinating new research into the brains and personalities of gifted people. We've also included several "Expert Essays" on key topics written by people with knowledge to impart from their fields of expertise. And perhaps most importantly, there are many observations and questions from gifted young people who took part in our survey and numerous "Gifted People Speak Out" essays contributed by gifted teenagers and adults, because it's reassuring to know that you're not alone and other people out there think and feel like you do. Throughout, we try to give you the tools you need to take control of your life, make good choices, and get what you want and need.

Tip: We suggest that you keep a journal—in a notebook or computer—as you read this book. Journaling is an excellent way to keep track of questions, insights, ideas, and feelings you have as you explore these topics. We've included a special notebook icon in places where we discuss ideas or topics that you might want to write about in your journal.

You should know up front that this book doesn't contain any quick fixes or easy solutions to your problems. Sometimes you'll already have ideas about possible solutions, and we hope you'll get the inspiration you may need to take action. In order to make the changes in your life, family, social group, and school that you feel are most important, you need to be willing to work, experiment, question authority, examine your own thinking, assess your goals and objectives, and persist in spite of setbacks, mistakes, and failures. We have made every effort to avoid preaching, moralizing, shoulds, got tos, and ought tos, although sometimes we can't help ourselves (after all, we're teachers and one of us is a parent). If you want to try some of our suggestions, that's great; we hope you will find them useful. If you don't find them useful, that's okay, too. Sometimes the things we say may appear self-evident to you, even boringly obvious. But before you dismiss a suggestion, *try it.* No matter how plain, ordinary, or simplistic it might seem. As a wise old adage says, "Nothing ventured, nothing gained."

Important

In writing this book, we've tried hard to focus primarily on those topics that are most relevant to teens who have been identified as gifted.

We wrote this book for gifted teens, but we hope teachers and parents of gifted kids will read it as well. We believe that it can give teachers and parents a clearer understanding of the gifted young people in their classrooms and families. We've both noticed that when a problem exists between teachers or parents and kids, it's often rooted in a lack of mutual respect. Parents or teachers may think, "You don't know anything because you're just a kid." Students may think, "My teachers don't care about me because I'm one in

100," or "My parents think that just because I'm gifted, I should be able to do everything on my own." Each side is guilty of assuming that the other has little or nothing to offer.

Note: *Throughout this book when we use the word* parent, *we are referring to any adult caregiver you have in your life—including a biological parent, stepparent, foster parent, grandparent, aunt, uncle, or other person.*

On the other hand, we've noticed that problems between teachers or parents and kids seem to diminish as respect and awareness of needs grow. We hope that this book will help teachers and parents become more respectful of the knowledge and abilities that young people have. We want adults to start asking, "What can I learn from you?" We also hope that this book will help students become more respectful of the wisdom and experience their teachers and parents have to offer. It all gets easier when the two sides stop arguing and working against each other. To that end, we have included several suggestions young people can use to get their needs met constructively, working *with* their parents and teachers whenever possible.

It's been said that life is a journey. We hope that your journey will be more than an exercise in survival. We hope that it will be challenging, adventurous, happy, and fulfilling. We hope that you will learn to accept your giftedness as an asset, if you haven't already, and use it to make the most of who you are.

Best wishes,

Judy Galbraith & Jim Delisle
help4kids@freespirit.com

chapter 1
Giftedness 101

Actually, it would probably be more accurate to write about Giftedness 701, since the topic has become complex enough to warrant a graduate-level course versus a freshman-level one. To begin with, there are countless definitions of the word out there. The U.S. government has a definition of giftedness, as does every state and many other countries. Most are similar in that they speak to giftedness as being in specific content areas—for example, being gifted in mathematics or science—or having greater intellectual capacity than others your age. Think of this latter definition as meaning that if your brain were a bucket, it would hold more water than do the buckets of most of your classmates.

But those are only two of the too-many-to-name interpretations of giftedness. Others have come and gone over the past centuries—yes, centuries—and have ranged from stingy (less than 1 percent of people qualifying as gifted) to generous, in which upwards of 20 percent of any population might be considered gifted at any one time. The term itself—*gifted*—doesn't seem to have a specific person you can point to and say, "Ha! So *you're* the culprit who gave us this label!" However, Lewis M. Terman, who helped develop the earliest IQ test in the early 1900s, the Stanford-Binet, is considered a grandfather of the gifted movement. After testing thousands of kids, he came up with all manner of distasteful and disrespectful terms to describe kids who scored very low—he labeled them "idiots" and "imbeciles." And those who scored 140 or higher on the test where the average score is 100—he called them "geniuses." Through Terman's continued work over subsequent decades (yes, decades) with the 1,528 "geniuses" he had identified, the term *gifted* came into use. It's stuck with us ever since, like it or not.

> "'GIFTED' CAN'T REALLY BE DEFINED, IN MY OPINION. IT MEANS SOMETHING SLIGHTLY DIFFERENT TO EVERYONE, WITH GIFTED PEOPLE BEING EVEN MORE DIVERSE IN THEIR DEFINITIONS THAN ANYONE ELSE." —*Noah, 16*

In looking over the many definitions of giftedness that have been espoused since Terman's time, they seem to fall into one of two camps:

★ giftedness is *something you do*

★ giftedness is *someone you are*

To the something-you-do proponents, giftedness is pretty much synonymous with achievement and production. They would say that your giftedness isn't real unless you can prove it by writing a symphony, recalculating pi, inventing a nonpolluting car, or writing a best-selling series of books about a school named Hogwarts. To these people, giftedness is truly an expression of advanced talents in almost any human endeavor; thus, you can be a gifted quarterback or cheerleader as much as you can be a gifted poet or neurologist. The one thing you *cannot* be in the eyes of the something-you-do crowd is an underachiever—you know, the smart kid who chooses not to do well in school or life. Giftedness is all in the actions, and if you choose to squander these talents by being mediocre or average, then bye-bye gifted label!

One of the first incidences of highly capable children being singled out for their abilities was in Constantinople in the 15th century. There, a palace school was created to educate boys, regardless of social class, if they met the admission qualifications: good looks, strength, and intelligence. These boys were groomed to be warriors, political leaders, and fathers, as it was thought that both inborn traits and learned talents would ensure success for these lucky few.

The Survey Says . . .

37% of respondents want to know why it's important to talk about giftedness.

38% want to know how to explain giftedness to friends.

32% want to know why some gifted students do poorly in school.

The someone-you-are adherents are a subtler, less judgmental crowd. They believe that giftedness is a set of inborn traits that allow you to experience the world with greater depth and increased awareness and sensitivity. Thus, when most people see yellow, you see goldenrod; things aren't dark blue, they're sapphire; and fuchsia is different from pink. The someone-you-are gifted individuals have an uncanny ability to note inconsistencies in logic; they appreciate sarcasm and irony (although others may never understand their jokes); and they are often the first ones to spot dishonesty or hypocrisy. From this vantage point, giftedness is not linked directly to academic achievement or life success, but to the inner workings of your mind. Should you choose to share these unusual insights and abilities through your work and play, so much the better. However, if your giftedness never manifests itself into anything that distinguishes you by your notable accomplishments, you are still gifted. In essence, giftedness is simply a part of your innate structure.

A Definition

Rather than spend time and space highlighting the many definitions of giftedness, we'll present you with our favorite interpretation of this sometimes-confusing, confounding word. It was penned by Dr. Annemarie Roeper, a Holocaust survivor who has worked with and studied gifted children for more than 70 years. She and her husband, George, began The Roeper School in Michigan in 1941; it stands today as one of gifted education's premiere institutions serving children from nursery school through high school. Here's Dr. Roeper's vivid conception of a word that causes such confusion:

> *Giftedness is a greater awareness, a greater sensitivity, and a greater ability to understand and transform perceptions into intellectual and emotional experiences.*[*]

In other words, giftedness is a mix of "something you are" and "something you do." A good example of this definition of giftedness is 17-year-old Nicole, whose mom tells this story about her daughter as a youngster: "When Nicole was five, she played soccer for the first time. I noticed that whenever she had practice, she did not pay attention to the ball *at all*. One day I said to her, 'Nicole, you don't seem to like soccer and it's okay if you don't want to play. But what exactly are you looking at when you are supposed to be paying attention to the ball and, instead, are getting hit by it?'

"'Oh,' she replied, 'I've been studying the geese formations. They seem to be in the wrong formations and I was wondering if it was some sort of danger signal and why are they doing this? I don't want them to go the wrong way for the winter. I'm worried about them.'"

We'll build on this definition of giftedness throughout this book, as we discuss how giftedness is a lifelong attribute and an invitation to strive and

> "I'M INTERESTED IN HOW DIFFERENT TYPES OF GIFTEDNESS ARE RELATED (E.G., WHY PEOPLE WHO ARE GIFTED OFTEN PLAY AN INSTRUMENT OR WHY THOSE WHO LIKE SCIENCE OFTEN HAVE TROUBLE IN ENGLISH."
> —*Carrie, 16*

---

[*] Roeper, Annemarie, "How the Gifted Cope with Their Emotions." *Roeper Review, 5(2)*, 21. 1982.

improve, not a laurel to simply rest on; as we review some of the ways that gifted people are more intense than many others their age; and as we try to give you as much direction as possible so that you see your giftedness as an asset to treasure, not a liability to dismiss.

Gifted vs. Talented

You might often hear the terms *gifted* and *talented* grouped together or abbreviated *GT.* Is there a difference between being gifted and being talented? Not really. It used to be thought that *gifted* referred to high academic ability while *talented* meant superior ability in visual or performing arts. But current research shows that academically gifted students are often also gifted in the arts, and vice versa. Whether or not you choose to discover or develop both your academic gifts and your artistic talents is up to you. For convenience in this book, we'll simply use *gifted* to encompass all forms of gifts and talents.

The Gifted Label: Burden or Blessing?

Every gifted person we know enjoys the benefits of being intelligent. They like being able to grasp difficult concepts, the constant flow of ideas that come so fast and furious they think their brain is dancing, and the ability to discern that virtually everything in life contains nuance, gray areas, and multiple points of view. Yet some gifted teens bristle at the label.

For some gifted teens, the worst thing about the label is the inner and external pressures they feel when there seem to be only two levels of performance: perfection or failure. For others, it is the absence of clarity the label provides, which goes back to the lack of consensus about what the term *gifted* really means. And to quite a few, the label feels elitist, implying that people without the label are somehow "less than" and *un*gifted.

"I ALWAYS HATED THE TERM 'GIFTED.' I MEAN, I WAS ALWAYS MORE OR LESS SET APART FROM THE OTHER KIDS IN SCHOOL, AND BEING LABELED GIFTED JUST MADE IT WORSE. IT GAVE THEM ONE MORE THING TO TEASE ME ABOUT." —*Mei, 19*

"I'M NOT SURE IF I AGREE WITH USING THE TERM 'GIFTED,' BECAUSE AREN'T OTHER PEOPLE BLESSED WITH 'GIFTS' THAT ARE NOT NECESSARILY A SMART MIND?" —*Peter, 16*

We really wish a better, universal term were in use, but there simply is not. And in our many years of experience grappling with this issue, we've found one thing to be true: more often than not, gifted teens *tolerate* the gifted label more than they embrace it. And, like the birthmark on your right shoulder or that cowlick at your temple that always messes up a perfect hair day, the less emphasis you place on these realities, the happier you tend to be.

"'GIFTED' IS SOMETHING THAT IS USED VERY LIGHTLY AROUND ME. I'M CALLED 'SMART,' 'TALENTED,' AND 'BRIGHT.' BUT IT'S VERY FEW TIMES THAT SOMEONE REFERS TO ME AS GIFTED. IT'S A TOUCHY SUBJECT, REALLY."
—*Gwendolyn, 13*

Instead of focusing on the gifted label itself, try thinking of the many advantages that the gifted label seems to provide. For example:

* You may have access to challenging programs, classes, and educational opportunities.
* You may be given more responsibilities and freedoms by adults, who assume your intelligence will guide you toward making wise decisions.
* You have the ability to tackle and surmount many types of academic challenges or problems that others may struggle with.
* You may run into adults who are gifted themselves and who take you under their wings as a mentor, teacher, or friend in a relationship built on mutual respect.
* You have numerous options open to you when it comes to selecting a possible job or career, as your interests and abilities may cover many diverse topics.

Of course, you can choose to dwell on the disadvantages that you may sometimes encounter—the unrealistic expectations, the schoolwork that can be mind-numbingly dull, the teasing and lack of friends who understand and accept you—but focusing on the negative is a great way to stifle your development. You paint yourself into a corner when you zero in on what's *not* working or who's *not* there. If nothing else, we hope the remainder of this book gives you both the fortitude and techniques for grasping the richness of your life as a gifted person.

So, is the label of gifted a burden or a blessing? Neither. It is simply an invented term that seeks to encapsulate your complex self in a one-word descriptor. Issues are bound to arise when something so multifaceted—you—is distilled down to one six-letter word.

Do you dislike the term *gifted*?

Can you think of a better term to use instead? If so, email us; we'd love to hear your ideas. Maybe you can get your term to go viral and catch on among your friends and in your school . . . and perhaps even among teachers, researchers, and authors (like us!).

Maddening Myths

Just as there are dueling definitions of giftedness, there are many stubborn misconceptions about what it means to be gifted. Here are 10 of the most common myths we've encountered over the years:

MYTH #1: Gifted kids have it made and will succeed in life no matter what. They don't need any special help in school or anywhere else.

FACT: Everyone needs encouragement—and help—to make the most of their abilities and succeed in life. In fact, many gifted teens experience intense emotions, perfectionism, and other traits that can sometimes make success a struggle.

MYTH #2: Gifted kids should love school, get high grades, and greet each new school day with enthusiasm.

FACT: Most schools are geared for average learners, not gifted learners, which makes it hard for gifted students to get excited about going. Some of the most talented students actually choose to drop out of school altogether.

MYTH #3: Behind every gifted kid is a supportive parent encouraging them to always do better.

FACT: Just because a person is gifted does not mean he or she has supportive or encouraging parents. In fact, sometimes the opposite is true.

MYTH #4: Gifted kids are good at everything they do.

FACT: Some gifted students are good at many things; others are exceptionally able at only a few things. The bottom line is that in some areas, gifted teens need to put forth effort and they may struggle just like everyone else.

MYTH #5: Teachers love to have gifted students in their classes.

FACT: Some do, some don't. Certain teachers feel uncomfortable with gifted students and get defensive or feel inadequate when they suspect their students know more than they do.

MYTH #6: If gifted students are grouped together, they will become snobbish and elitist.

FACT: Few will, most won't. What's especially pernicious about this myth is that some adults use it to rationalize decisions about not allowing gifted students to work or study together or not providing them with opportunities that meet their learning needs.

MYTH #7: All gifted kids have trouble adjusting to school and forming friendships.

FACT: Some do, some don't—just like other kids.

MYTH #8: Gifted students don't know that they're "different" unless someone tells them.

FACT: Most gifted kids don't need to be identified or labeled before they know that they're not quite like their age peers.

MYTH #9: Gifted kids are equally mature in all areas—academic, physical, social, and emotional.

FACT: That would be convenient, but it's not a reasonable expectation. On the other hand, it's not fair to assume that just because someone is advanced intellectually, he or she will lag behind in other areas.

MYTH #10: Gifted people are commonplace in some cultures and groups, but rare in others.

FACT: Giftedness knows no boundaries of sex, religion, socioeconomic level, sexual orientation, learning style, or physical ability. And equal numbers of gifted people exist among all cultures and racial groups, as you will see in the following section.

How Does Giftedness Differ Among Cultures?

"WHAT ARE THE DIFFERENCES IN THE GIFTED PROGRAMS IN SCHOOLS ACROSS THE U.S. AND IN OTHER COUNTRIES?"
—*Brady, 16*

Many cultures around the world and within the United States either do not recognize giftedness or view it as something very different than most schools do. Purdue University professor Jean Sunde Peterson interviewed a large group of U.S. classroom teachers about what they valued most and looked for in gifted students. Here are her findings:

★ Dominant-culture (mainly white) classroom teachers valued individual, competitive, conspicuous achievement—looking for verbal assertiveness, "standing out," and a strong work ethic in classroom work.

★ Latino teachers valued arts as a means of expression and humility most.

★ African-American teachers valued selfless service to community and personal hard work, especially if done by hand.

★ American Indian teachers declined to identify anyone as gifted, since they did not believe in standing out, although they respected individuals who could be comfortable in both white and Indian cultures.

★ Recent Asian immigrants valued adaptability, seeing the importance of education in North America.

★ Overall, most of the nonmainstream cultures valued "non-bookish" wisdom, not knowledge.

Keep in mind that the cultural values of one group are not better or worse than others, just different. But you might find it interesting that all cultures do not value, and thrive in, a highly competitive school culture that demands intelligence and talents be demonstrated. See the following survey quotes for examples.

"I'M BRITISH. WE'RE ALL GIFTED WHERE I COME FROM. AFTER ALL, WE HAVE NEWTON, THE BBC, MONTY PYTHON, AND PUBS AS A RESULT OF OUR BRILLIANCE."
—*Richard, 16*

The Survey Says . . .

Q: **"It's been shown that the definition of what it means to be _gifted_ varies by cultural and ethnic groups according to their values. How is giftedness defined in your cultural group?"**

"To be quite frank about it, in my culture (I am of Somali-Canadian descent) there is no real definition of giftedness. There is intelligence, somebody with great factual knowledge who can spew off facts and calculate figures. And there are those who are wise, who offer advice and are well-versed in inter- and intrapersonal skills." —_Amina, 16_

"In Ireland, being gifted or in need of additional educational support is defined as being in the top 5 percent of your age group. My family knows that I am gifted, however, they do not understand what that means. I try to explain it to them but they still don't understand." —_Niamh, 15_

"Giftedness is kind of taboo in my country (France), and most people aren't willing to recognize _gifted_ as a legitimate label." —_Ines, 16_

"In my culture (Vienna, Austria), giftedness isn't really present. So schools don't have any methods to identify giftedness. Sometimes teachers recognize that you are smart, but even then they treat you the same as before." —_Leonie, 17_

"Being that I am Armenian, my culture generally defines gifted as being capable of avoiding being killed by warring invaders. Among my family, giftedness is defined by how much scholarship money I can receive, so my parents are not required to pay for college." —_Narek, 16_

"I am from India, and most Indians are very competitive. So we always tend to try to do our best." —_Amaan, 11_

"I am Cuban and my family has always told me that all Cubans are gifted. On the flip side, we (as in my ancestors) have established ourselves from the ground up with nothing to start with in America. My mom has always told me that to get places, you must take yourself places and that is how Cubans have been so successful. I have been instructed to fully take advantage of every opportunity that presents itself to me." —*Laura, 18*

"I'm half Mexican, half Filipino. My culture's idea of being gifted is the same as the ideas of my black neighbors next door, the same as my white gifted teacher, and the same as the Indian family down the street." —*Mariza, 15*

"Most people think that Hispanics aren't smart, and that I must be the only Hispanic in gifted and talented and AP classes." —*Carlos, 14*

"Well, some people think that my ethnic group (African-American) will not perform as well as others, so my success means more to my people." —*Tyler, 18*

"In Thailand, where being gifted is more rare, you are *really* smart if you are 'gifted.'" —*Lawan, 11*

"Being that I am Asian-American and have very gifted parents, giftedness itself is not as important as one's work ethic and integrity." —*Sky, 13*

"Being gifted is a good thing. I'm part Chinese and they even have a special Chinese word for kids like us. It's cool." —*Henry, 13*

"In American culture, it seems as if giftedness is not valued as much as in other cultures." —*Garrett, 16*

Who Gets Left Out?

No matter how diligently teachers and administrators work to apply the gifted label to students fairly and accurately (so that these students can receive appropriate levels of challenge in their education), some gifted kids get left out. They aren't identified because they don't satisfy certain criteria. If you don't fit the description, you may miss out on opportunities that might enable you to demonstrate and enhance your giftedness.

10 Famous "Failures"

1. **Tori Amos** (Grammy Award–winning singer and pianist) at age five was the youngest person ever to be accepted to the prestigious Peabody Conservatory of Music. At age 11, she was kicked out for being "uncooperative."

2. **Pablo Picasso** was so disinterested in school as a young boy that the only way his family got him to go was by letting him bring a live chicken to class so he could draw its portrait.

3. **Albert Einstein** performed so poorly in high school that a teacher asked him to drop out, saying, "You will never amount to anything, Einstein."

4. **Whoopi Goldberg** (Academy Award–winning actress) struggled with ADHD and severe dyslexia as a student and dropped out of high school at age 17.

5. **John F. Kennedy** received constant reports of "poor achievement" in school and was a lousy speller.

6. **Steven Spielberg** (one of the most famous directors in movie history) was rejected by both the prestigious UCLA and USC film schools in California before finally being accepted into a small state school instead.

7. **Robert Jarvick** (medical doctor and researcher) was rejected by 15 American medical schools. He later invented the artificial heart.

8. **Agatha Christie** (renowned mystery novelist) said, "I was always recognized as the 'slow one' of the family." When she told her sister that she'd like to write detective stories, her sister replied, "They are very difficult to do. I bet you couldn't."

9. **John Lennon** received dismal school reports, such as: "Certainly on the road to failure . . . hopeless . . . rather a clown in class . . . wasting other pupils' time."

10. **Shakira** (Colombian singer whose albums have sold millions of copies worldwide) was rejected by her school choir in second grade because her vibrato was too strong. The music teacher told her that she sounded "like a goat."

Those who are most often passed over for inclusion in gifted programs include:

Gifted Boys

While it used to be true that girls were less likely to be identified as gifted, now that's true for boys instead—especially boys with a lot of energy. Some of these boys are wrongly believed to have attention deficit disorder, possibly with hyperactivity (ADD/ADHD). ADD/ADHD primarily occurs in males and, due to advances in research, its diagnosis has increased multifold in recent years. This is beneficial for those boys who indeed have ADD/ADHD and need special attention . . . but not great for those who instead may be gifted and in need of a different kind of attention.

People with Disabilities & Learning Differences

Also overlooked for gifted programs are those gifted males and females who actually *do* have a learning difference such as those related to ADD/ADHD, dyslexia, Asperger's syndrome, or autism; a physical disability; a mental health disorder; or an emotional or a behavioral difficulty. Their disability or difference may mask or hinder their capacity to demonstrate their giftedness in the most recognizable and acceptable ways. The traditional methods used to identify gifted kids would have failed to notice Stephen Hawking or Helen Keller, for example. Gifted people with disabilities have been called an "unseen minority." When teacher and parent groups are asked to imagine a gifted child, they rarely conjure up the image of a gifted child with a disability or learning difference. (See pages 21–31 for more on this topic.)

People Who Show Disruptive Behavior

They often aren't considered because some teachers associate good behavior with being gifted and bad behavior with being unwilling or unable to learn. Thomas Edison was considered a little hellion in school (and, in fact, he never graduated from grade school).

The Survey Says . . .

More than **62%** of respondents think that gifted boys have a harder time in school than gifted girls.

"Girls are able to sit for a longer time than boys, so boys have a harder time." —*Clayton, 11*

"Many teachers don't recognize boys as gifted and they slip through the cracks, and teachers think they have ADHD and want them medicated." —*Beth, 12*

People Who Perform Poorly on Tests

Some gifted students simply aren't good at taking tests. They may know the material, but the test situation is too stressful for them, and they perform poorly as a result. They may be penalized with low test scores due to a poorly trained test administrator, or they may have personal problems that prevent them from concentrating and performing up to their true capabilities. Since test scores are one of the principle methods used to identify gifted individuals, this clearly puts them at a disadvantage.

People Who Don't Get Good Grades

Some highly intelligent students may be left out of gifted programs simply because they don't get good grades in school. Yet grades don't necessarily have anything to do with giftedness. Some students may not be interested in a certain subject, they may lack motivation in school because it's not challenging enough for them . . . or they may be too busy running a Web startup from their basement to finish their homework! It's often these students who need gifted programs and opportunities the most.

People Who Are Homeschooled

Obviously, teens who are schooled at home are not in the school system and therefore aren't likely to be identified for a school gifted program. However, homeschooling for gifted children is on the rise, and while these students may not be formally labeled gifted by a school, that doesn't mean they do not fully deserve the label and all the support, advice, and opportunities that come with it outside of the school system.

People from Minority Cultures or Other Nonmainstream Groups

Students who fit this description may have gifts that are not measured by standard IQ and achievement tests, which are often biased to majority (white middle- to upper-class) students. Also, their gifts may lie in areas that are not celebrated or valued by the mainstream society.

"IN MY SCHOOL SYSTEM, GIFTEDNESS IS IDENTIFIED AT THE ELEMENTARY LEVEL IN ABOUT 5 PERCENT OF THE POPULATION, MOST OF WHOM ARE WHITE AND FROM MIDDLE TO UPPER SOCIOECONOMIC FAMILIES. I FIT IN THAT CATEGORY. I THINK GIFTEDNESS SHOULD BE DEFINED DIFFERENTLY FOR DIFFERENT ETHNIC GROUPS. THERE ARE SOME REALLY SMART KIDS IN MY SCHOOL WHO DON'T SPEAK 'SCHOOL ENGLISH' VERY WELL AND DON'T HAVE THE SUPPORT AT HOME TO WORK THE HIGH SCHOOL SYSTEM . . . MUCH LESS STAND A CHANCE OF SHOWING THEIR GIFTEDNESS IN SCHOOL." —*Taylor, 17*

Or, the idea of giftedness in their culture may differ from the way their school perceives it, so their families may not support their joining a school gifted program (as reflected in some of the previous quotes). Furthermore, some of these students may not speak English as their first language and so may be at a disadvantage expressing themselves and their gifts in school.

Expert Essay
"Start Seeing Gifted Hispanics"
by Patty Rendon

You're probably at a point in your life when you're pondering many complex questions—more questions than usual, that is—and some without easy answers. One such question might be: "Why are some very bright people of different ethnic backgrounds, such as Hispanics, so often excluded from gifted programs?" There is, of course, no easy answer to this question. But one reason may be that people—both within or outside their cultures—often fail to recognize the characteristics of giftedness among Hispanics. Sometimes there is a mindset that Hispanic students will not make good candidates for a gifted program. This erroneous assumption might be the result of cultural misunderstandings.

It is important for you to recognize the unique characteristics you possess, especially if you're a gifted member of a minority culture, so you can advocate for yourself. Deepening the understanding of your own needs will hopefully lead to a better understanding of these needs by your teachers, parents, and peers. Take time to research the lives of other gifted people in your culture, so that as you learn more about them you are also solidifying your own attitudes and beliefs about what it is like to be a gifted individual.

Consider the following gifted Hispanics who are leaders in their respective fields: Ellen Ochoa, the first Hispanic female astronaut;

ELL students, or English language learners, are the one demographic missing from virtually all gifted programs in the United States. For example, New Mexico is a U.S. leader when it comes to the number of Hispanics learning at advanced levels. However, even in New Mexico's schools—where over half of the students come from Hispanic backgrounds—just 36 percent of students in AP classes are Hispanic. Also, *three times as many* whites as Hispanics are enrolled in New Mexico's gifted programs.[*]

[*]According to the Santa Fe High School Portfolio released in September 2009 by the Santa Fe Public Schools Office of the Deputy Superintendent.

Roberto Clemente, Baseball Hall of Fame inductee; Jennifer Lopez, actress and singer; César Chávez, migrant labor leader; Sonia Sotomayor, United States Supreme Court Justice; and many others. Who are some gifted individuals you admire in your culture? Once you discover yourself and come to terms with your abilities, you can make a plan about how to lead others to advocate for your needs, too.

If you are Hispanic or a member of another minority culture, I recommend scheduling an appointment with your favorite teacher, counselor, or administrator. Inquire about the educational opportunities available to you through your participation in gifted programs. Inquire about leadership opportunities available to you, such as the Lorenzo de Zavala Youth Legislative Session for Hispanic teens (nhi-net.org). By working collaboratively with your school community, you will have the best team possible for ensuring success.

I wish you many blessings and a long fulfilling life.

Patty Rendon is the advanced academics coordinator at Region One Education Service Center in Edinburg, Texas, where she provides professional development for teachers of gifted and talented students. Her passion is to help others understand the needs of gifted learners.

2E: One Label, Many Facets

As we discussed previously, some gifted students have needs in two areas that seem to contradict each other: They are gifted *and* they have a disability or learning difference—in other words they are *twice exceptional,* or 2E for short. Like all labels, this one has its shortcomings, but it does call attention to students whose giftedness might otherwise be overlooked.

Twice-exceptional students may have uneven academic skills and may appear unmotivated. They may have processing problems with the way they see and hear, causing them to seem slow. They may have problems with motor skills that affect their handwriting. And because they are often frustrated with school, they may show disruptive behaviors and have low self-esteem. On the other hand, many 2E students score in the gifted range on ability, achievement, and creativity tests. They may have a fertile imagination and a wide range of knowledge about a variety of topics. And they may have a superior vocabulary and sophisticated ideas.

"MANY KIDS ARE BOTH GIFTED AND HAVE TROUBLES, AND THIS GETS IN THE WAY OF GIFTED TESTING. I HAVE ADHD AND SPENT ALMOST SEVEN YEARS SHOWING GIFTED TRAITS AND BEING CLASSIFIED AS GIFTED BY MY TEACHERS, BUT WAS NEVER ABLE TO MAKE IT INTO THE GIFTED CLASSES." —*Aliza, 14*

These students benefit when educators and parents focus on strengths, not perceived deficiencies. 2E kids also need opportunities to learn and to show what they know in ways that are more natural and effective for them. Following is more information on three of the most common 2E areas, as well as real-life examples.

Gifted & Dyslexic

Historically, the first students to be identified as 2E were those with learning differences such as dyslexia. They show high intellect and knowledge, yet find it difficult to get their thoughts down on paper. Their assignments, if done at all, can be riddled with grammatical and spelling errors, yet their thoughts and ideas are often high-level and perceptive.

Meet Hector, who is now 23. He was identified as gifted as a young boy, and yet, even then, there were signs that his path would not be an easy one. As Hector states: "First grade was a nightmare. Even though I could read words on flashcards (I had memorized their shapes), I could not read these same words when they were in sentences or paragraphs; all the letters and words ran together. I even remember doing 'mirror writing,' so that when I spelled my name it looked like this: *rotceH*." It's hard to say who was the most frustrated with this intelligent boy who couldn't read well: his teachers, his parents, or himself. Hector's teachers assumed that being gifted meant that your academic skills were flawless, not lacking. His parents—both educators—pleaded with school personnel to let Hector complete his assignments using more hands-on, demonstrative methods, versus only writing. And Hector himself began to doubt that his intellect was as high as people said it was—how could it be when he appeared to be dumb in so many subjects?

"FIRST GRADE WAS A NIGHTMARE. EVEN THOUGH I COULD READ WORDS ON FLASHCARDS (I HAD MEMORIZED THEIR SHAPES), I COULD NOT READ THESE SAME WORDS WHEN THEY WERE IN SENTENCES OR PARAGRAPHS; ALL THE LETTERS AND WORDS RAN TOGETHER."
—*Hector, 23*

Eventually, Hector was identified as having dyslexia, a learning disorder that makes reading and writing arduous and slow. His teachers wanted to yank him from his gifted program—where he was successful—to concentrate on his academic deficiencies in a class for children with learning disabilities. They insisted that Hector had to be either gifted *or* dyslexic—he could not be both. (The 2E label unfortunately did not exist when Hector was young.) Only after his parents threatened a lawsuit did Hector receive services for both his strengths and his challenges.

Now, meet Kate, who like Hector was diagnosed with dyslexia, but she was never identified as gifted. She was given an IQ test, and her score fell two points below the gifted program's cut-off score of 130. As much as the school gifted coordinator tried to convince Kate's teachers and principal that her high abilities were being masked by her dyslexia, no action was taken on her behalf. She was not allowed into the gifted program and continued to struggle throughout her schooling—not only as a dyslexic student, but also as a gifted student lacking appropriate learning opportunities.

Sadly, neither Hector's nor Kate's story is uncommon in schools today. So, if you are a kid like Hector or Kate, or if one of your friends is, try to find an advocate in school who will listen as you explain the world of the 2E teen. As with Kate, you might not always succeed, but just your attempt will show how dedicated you are in trying to make things right for the gifted kid who sometimes struggles with learning.

Gifted & AS

Although Asperger's syndrome (AS) was first identified in 1944 by Austrian physician Hans Asperger, its prominence in diagnosis only came about since the early 1990s. Listed on what is called the autism spectrum, AS often involves gifted teens who have particular traits and behaviors that set them apart from their classmates. For example, many AS teens have these qualities:

★ Their speech is often monotone, almost robotic.

★ They do not understand sarcasm or multilayered humor.

★ They possess an encyclopedic mind, especially with topics they enjoy, and talk about them endlessly.

★ Their eye contact is minimal, or they appear to look right through people they are talking to.

★ They don't pick up on social cues and do not participate in small talk.

★ They are hypersensitive to loud noises and certain textures, avoiding clothing or food that just doesn't feel right.

★ Their motor skills are often clumsy and appear immature for their age.

★ They often lack the ability to empathize; they overthink and underfeel.

As you might imagine, a teen exhibiting these traits in a typical middle or high school is often ostracized, bullied, laughed at, or avoided. What is often *not* seen in gifted kids with AS are their strengths, such as:

★ They are often logical thinkers, with particular skills in mathematics or other linear subjects.

★ They are highly verbal and knowledgeable about many topics.

★ Their long-term memories are often extraordinary, and they can recall even small details about previous experiences.

★ They're smart. Sometimes *very* smart.

So, the main gap that AS teens experience is in the social world—the very center of activity in most high schools. As adults, many AS students become successful professionals, yet they still struggle with their interactions with others. If they are isolated, it is not by choice as much as by habit.

Gifted People SPEAK OUT   "A Lesson in Perseverance"

by Anonymous

I have been diagnosed with Asperger's syndrome (AS). I have behavioral differences that people are going to pick up on, whether or not I reveal the fact that I have a neurological condition. Some of the more obvious examples include erratic eye contact, a slightly monotone speaking style, and limited facial expressions. I guess it's fair to say that I have finally and thoroughly come to terms with the condition. I'm not necessarily saying that I would refuse a medical cure to eliminate the obvious symptoms of AS, but I can live with the fact that I operate a little differently than most.

I have taken part in many public discussions about being diagnosed with AS. I've talked with parents about how they felt about the possibility of their son or daughter having the condition. One couple told me they were afraid of getting their child diagnosed due to the stigma that he would go through as a result of it, and they felt there was no reason to get the diagnosis in the first place since the child was really good in the math and science fields. I sometimes wish that were *my* case—that I could compensate for social deficiencies with an above-average skill in another area.

These guidelines . . . force me to discipline myself and concentrate on tasks and activities that are conducive to personal growth and development.

I suppose for me public speaking is that skill. However, this is looked upon as a rarity, because of the widely held misconceptions about common AS conduct. It is believed by many that kids who have AS greatly excel at math or science but aren't that gifted in writing, reading, or speaking. In addition, kids who have conditions on the autism line are thought to have frequent violent mood swings, engage in self-stimulating sensory behaviors, and be unable to feel emotions. I can say, at least from my own situation, that these can be accurate but they are not entirely factual across the board!

I graduated college with a major in special education, but I had trouble obtaining a job in my field, due to my awkwardness in interviews. For a while, I worked as an aide for a school system. It was something at least, even if it was beneath my true intellectual capacity. I went through a pretty serious period where I felt ashamed for a lot of things—not being able to find a teaching position, not being able to support those around me, being concerned about the future, and, most of all, being embarrassed about having the AS diagnosis hovering over me.

But through it all, I have created a set of standards for myself. Basically, what these guidelines do for me is force me to discipline myself and concentrate on tasks and activities that are conducive to personal growth and development. For example, I limit TV watching and frivolous activities on the computer. Following these standards is my own way of maintaining a sharp mind and living responsibly, something that is necessary for me to survive and succeed.

When you get right down to it, I am extremely lucky in so many ways. I live in a free country, I have all my limbs functioning properly, I can see and hear, I have high goals and aspirations—plus, I finally was able to get a teaching position! The frustration and disappointment that I've experienced in my life, I suppose, are to be expected for a while, but a good portion of it I brought on myself by not living as smartly or productively as I could have.

You want to change others' opinions about you and live your best life possible? Look into changing yourself and staying the course. That way, even if you don't think people get you—you will at least live free from doubt and uncertainty. In the end, isn't that worth a lot?

The author of this essay asked that his name and personal information not be shared.

Following is another essay on giftedness and Asperger's syndrome, but this one is told from a parent's point of view. Twice-exceptional teens often need help advocating for their needs, which is why caring parents, teachers, friends, and peers are so important to them.

Expert Essay
"Can You Imagine?"
by Mike Postma

Can you imagine being so smart it hurts? Can you imagine being that bright but having a disability that hinders your ability to think, feel, or express yourself? Now imagine that this obstruction never goes away, never subsides or dissipates over time. Can you imagine how painful it might be to want to jump out of your skin even just for a moment—a moment of freedom, a moment of acceptance, a moment of understanding—a moment that is never realized? There is somebody out there who can imagine this, someone whose life is a daily reminder of this ongoing paradox. Perhaps you know someone like this. He or she may even be close to you . . . in your school, neighborhood, or family. That someone is a twice-exceptional person.

Who am I to talk about this? Well, I was fortunate enough to have survived my adolescent years as a 2E student and become an educator of gifted students like you. Moreover, I now have a son entering his teen years who also has high intellectual potential that is both enhanced and encumbered by his life with Asperger's syndrome. The interesting thing is that I never saw myself as being "different" or having something that needed remediation. That is, until I raised my son and experienced flashbacks of my own childhood through the challenges that beset him on a daily basis. Challenges that I hope you will recognize in your fellow teens, or perhaps in yourself.

Being a 2E kid can mean a number of things. It can mean that you have social anxiety. It can mean you cannot decode the English language in the same manner as others, or, it can mean you struggle with being able to concentrate. It can mean a lot of things but the one common characteristic of the 2E student is the inability to express or communicate all his or her wonderful ideas to others. In addition, it means that there is a wide gap between how schools operate and how you learn.

Many gifted kids struggle in school due to the fact that it may not be challenging enough or meet their academic needs. Now imagine having that same burden with the *additional* problem that, due to a perceived disability, you are forced to spend your days in a special education classroom that requires you to do remedial tasks over and over again until you are about to explode. That is the experience of many 2E students. Furthermore, imagine the social isolation that comes with this label. It's difficult enough to be part of the "nerd herd" or "geek squad" as a smart kid, so can you imagine how alone you might feel if you also had trouble communicating, or even looking someone in the eye? Too many 2E students find themselves in this dark place.

Imagine . . . due to a perceived disability, you are forced to spend your days in a special education classroom that requires you to do remedial tasks over and over again until you are about to explode.

My son Ben was an intense child. You see, kids with Asperger's tend to be passionate about a few things and it is very difficult for them to shift focus away from those interests. Ben's interests were animals (especially snakes and dinosaurs), building things, and, as luck would have it, adventures. I remember the day when he first made his acquaintance with the local authorities—at age three. One morning, dressed in only a shirt covered in marker, Ben picked the lock on our back deck and found a path through the woods to a playground about a half-mile from our house. Thankfully, a neighbor contacted the police who returned Ben home to his panic-stricken mother.

While these stories are now great memories, our history with Ben and school is quite a different story. On more than one occasion, his needs were misunderstood by uninformed educators, ultimately leading to his fervent dislike of anything related to school. He continues to hold a truancy record that stands to this day. Friends are also a different story. One by one they seem to have drifted away from Ben. Today, at age 13, he has only a few friends that tend to be much younger than him because he can relate to them without fear of ridicule. And yet he still goes to school. He still hates it. He still has intense interests (although they have now shifted to video games and snowboarding), but what he doesn't have is his "parachute"—a close peer who understands him, accepts him for who he is, and sticks close to him through the good and the bad.

For 2E teens like Ben, friendship is the solution. And by friendship I mean empathy, understanding, and advocacy. As a gifted student you may know how challenging friendships can be. To befriend a 2E kid may be a special challenge. You may not always understand their thoughts, words, or actions, and they may embarrass you on occasion. Being a friend means sticking up for them; allowing them to be who they are; helping them navigate the complex teenage social world; and

Taking a chance to befriend a 2E student may just be the best decision you will ever make.

perhaps most importantly, defending them against peer bullying. Being a true friend is the most precious gift you can give a kid like Ben, and it is a gift that will give back. 2E people are renowned for their intense loyalty and will stick with you no matter what. Their senses of humor will keep you laughing, their unique perspectives will have you seeing things from a whole range of viewpoints, and their often-incredible creative abilities will keep you engaged day after day. Taking a chance to befriend a 2E student may just be the best decision you will ever make.

Mike Postma is in charge of the High Potential Program for Minnetonka Schools in Minnetonka, Minnesota, including the Navigator Program, a magnet school for highly gifted students. He is the father of four, including two children diagnosed with Asperger's syndrome.

Gifted & ADD/ADHD

Some gifted students are not exactly teachers' favorites. These students would rather complete their "seatwork" standing up; they may talk loudly and often, and frequently without raising their hand to do so; they get bored by easy tasks and either refuse to do them or complete them quickly and sloppily; they can be inattentive daydreamers, focusing on everything but the lesson being delivered by the teacher. When confronted with a student like this (who is often a boy, as discussed previously), some educators have an immediate, informal diagnosis: ADD (attention deficit disorder) or ADHD (attention deficit hyperactivity disorder). However, what we may really be seeing is this: a highly intelligent kid who is simply bored by the too-easy nature of school.

Actually, it's a perfectly understandable reaction to respond with indifference, daydreaming, or anger to a situation that is intellectually stifling. If day after day, year after year, you must relearn the same content rather than be challenged with new content, your mind is bound to wander off to more interesting locales—like replaying your favorite video game in your head, or composing a song for your band's next gig. If, however, you *do not* manifest these behaviors in situations where you are challenged and interested—indeed, you actively pay attention in these classes—then the ADD/ADHD label is suspect, at best.

Here's how to distinguish between ADD/ADHD and simple boredom and frustration:

★ If you can turn on and off at will your off-task behaviors, concentrating on topics of interest and challenge, then you probably do *not* have ADD/ADHD.

★ If you can explain to others why you do and do not focus on the lesson at hand, then you probably do *not* have ADD/ADHD.

★ If your ADD/ADHD-like behaviors do *not* interfere, overall, with your learning, then the label likely doesn't apply to you.

★ If your off-task behaviors decrease or disappear when you work with intellectual equals, then you most likely do *not* have ADD/ADHD.

Sadly, too many gifted students are given this label when a better alternative would be to examine the conditions under which they *do* pay attention. The source of your inattention may not be within you, but rather, it may be the unchallenging curriculum that you are offered.

Of course, ADD/ADHD is a legitimate diagnosis for some kids, including some gifted kids. Gifted kids with ADD or ADHD may face particular challenges in school. If tasks are repetitive or below their achievement level, these kids may tune out even more quickly than other gifted students. Consequently, they will miss out on vital information presented in the lesson and perhaps perform poorly on tests or classwork. As bright individuals, they are often more self-aware and sensitive than their peers and may feel their failures especially keenly and perceive themselves as inadequate. This can result in a lack of self-confidence and motivation. It's also possible that teachers may interpret their poor performance as laziness or having a slower learning rate and these students may be placed in a less challenging curriculum where they may grow even *more* bored and frustrated and perhaps act out. All of this greatly decreases these 2E teens' chances of being identified for gifted programs or accelerated courses.

"I'D LIKE TO KNOW MORE ABOUT HOW TO GET OFFICIALLY RECOGNIZED AS GIFTED AND REACH PEOPLE WHO CAN HELP HOOK ME UP WITH PROGRAMS TO HELP FURTHER MY EDUCATION."
—*Alexandra, 15*

What This Means for You

If you see yourself (or someone you know) in any of the previous 2E descriptions, the first thing you can do is find an adult, preferably at school, who believes in you and your abilities. Indeed, if this person already sees beyond your quirks or unusual behaviors and recognizes the intellect you possess, half your battle is won.

The next step is to document, from your point of view, the conditions under which you learn best:

★ Do you excel in written or oral reports?

★ Can you best show what you know by working alone or in groups?

★ Do you need specific formats and deadlines to succeed, or do you work best under conditions where you choose how the work is presented to your teacher?

★ Do you prefer repetitive work, even though it is easy, or more complex tasks, even though you may struggle through them?

Sharing these aspects of yourself as a learner with a teacher who is willing to listen will help you if you have some tendencies within the 2E range. Also, if you have been formally diagnosed with one of these conditions, you have legal rights to an education that is appropriate for your learning needs and strengths. A teacher or counselor you trust, as well as your parents, can help you find your way through the necessary processes that ensure you get what you need to succeed.

A Friend in Need

The previous advice also applies to anyone you know who you think might benefit from it. However, if you know someone who is 2E, the best thing you can do is be a nonjudgmental friend. Talk with this person one-on-one, invite him or her to participate in your groups,

"I AM INTERESTED IN HOW I CAN HELP PEOPLE THAT ARE NOT IN GIFTED PROGRAMS GET INTO THEM. WE NEED TO HELP THEM MORE, I THINK." —*Caleb, 13*

both in and outside of school; ask him or her to sit at your lunch table; and be supportive as he or she has to fend off the rudeness of classmates who choose to mock someone for a condition over which they have little control. The 2E individual may not respond to you with a firm high five or a gushing oratory of thanks, but know this: you are doing the right thing and making what is often a rough ride through school just a little less bumpy for a kid who needs, wants, and deserves to be accepted.

An Imperfect System

As you can see, clearly not everyone who is gifted is identified as such. Friends or siblings of yours may be gifted but haven't been spotted by the school's selection system. (If your test scores drop, you may be labeled *gifted* one year and not the next. Which doesn't make a lot of sense, but that's the way it is.) Some schools don't check for giftedness at all, so students in those schools are never identified. And some schools that formerly identified gifted kids don't anymore because their gifted programs have been eliminated.

What you need to remember, in the midst of all the confusion, inconsistencies, and inequities, is this: *The system isn't perfect.* People make mistakes. Right or wrong, most teachers aren't required to take training in gifted education. Therefore, many teachers know very little about giftedness and are not adequately equipped to identify gifted students.

What matters most is what *you* think of yourself and your abilities. Whether someone else believes that you're gifted is incidental and perhaps even irrelevant. It's up to you to decide how and whether you will use your gifts; it's up to you to determine the direction your present and future will take. Never let anyone else decide for you how smart and capable you are.

The Survey Says . . .

Q: Do you think your school has effective methods for identifying gifted kids? Why or why not?

"No, the parents have to request a giftedness test. If the parents are not involved then the student might never be tested." —*Amy, 16*

"It could be better. I think it just recognizes the students that use their special skill and not the students that have potential but don't use it. I know there are many more gifted students at my school, they just need help unleashing it." —*Javier, 17*

"No, because there are many factors (cheating, unfairness) that don't get calculated in the identification process. There are people who don't deserve to be in there, but are; conversely, there are people who should, but aren't." —*John, 17*

"No. My school district uses a matrix that does not always identify gifted students. The matrix is based mostly on performance, and many gifted students, such as myself, do not perform well on achievement tests. There is an appeals process, but it is mostly procedure. No additional or outside information—such as IQ score, above-grade-level testing, gifted and talented course evaluation, etc.—is taken into consideration, even if the available information contradicts the school matrix results." —*Bryce, 13*

"Yes, because they nominate you to take the test, and they mainly go by creativity, which in my opinion is what giftedness is mainly about." —*Michaela, 12*

"Yes, they have a peer nomination program, which helps identify kids who are slipping through the cracks." —*Ellie, 12*

"Yes. They do not only rely on the two tests taken, but also have parents, teachers, and the student write how the student is gifted and how it is apparent. The student also submits a portfolio, which allows some of their passions and giftedness to be seen. I believe it is more fair because some kids might be missed with tests because they are not good at test taking." —*Chiedu, 15*

Being gifted won't guarantee you a particular GPA or success in school. It won't automatically lead to a satisfying and meaningful career (or series of careers). It won't reward you with fame, friendships, and happiness. It won't make you kinder, more compassionate, and more caring than other people. Like everyone else, you're going to have to work at who you want to be and what you want from life. Still, being gifted *can* give you an edge. You just have to know when and how to use it.

> "BEING GIFTED GIVES YOU MORE RESPONSIBILITY. IT GIVES YOU THE TOOLS TO BE SUCCESSFUL THROUGHOUT LIFE'S COURSE. IT FORCES YOU TO BE DILIGENT, DEDICATED, AND PASSIONATE. IT OPENS DOORS TO DIFFERENT OPPORTUNITIES THAT YOU CAN'T HELP BUT WANT TO SEIZE."
> —*Rebecca, 17*

A Bill of Rights for the Gifted

Following is a bill of rights for gifted children written by Del Siegle, past president of the National Association for Gifted Children (NAGC). These rights apply to *all* the different types of gifted young people out there, including the Hectors and Kates (see pages 22–23)—and to you.

Gifted Children's Bill of Rights

You have a right . . .

. . . to know about your giftedness.

. . . to learn something new every day.

. . . to be passionate about your talent area without apologies.

. . . to have an identity beyond your talent area.

. . . to feel good about your accomplishments.

. . . to make mistakes.

. . . to seek guidance in the development of your talent.

. . . to have multiple peer groups and a variety of friends.

. . . to choose which of your talent areas you wish to pursue.

. . . not to be gifted at everything.

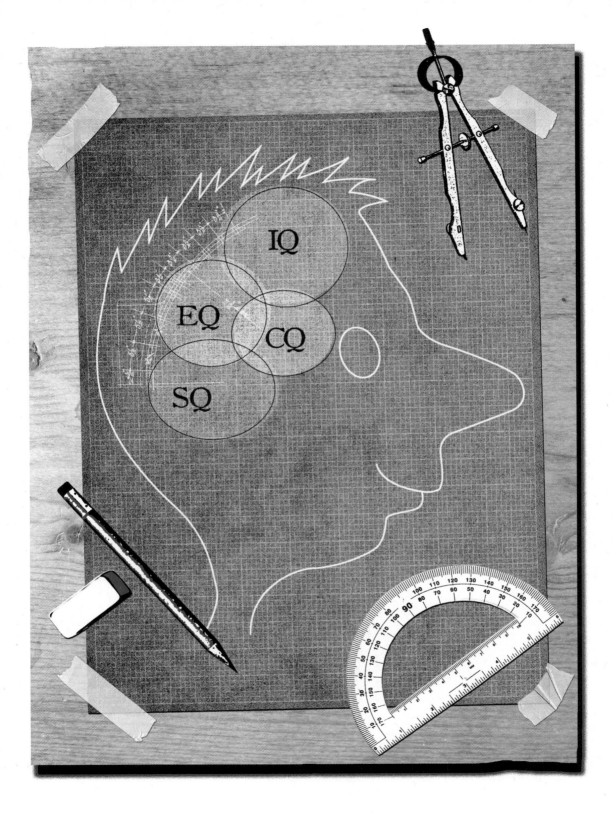

chapter 2
Intelligence Design

If you think that *gifted* has too many definitions, you'll really scratch your head over the term *intelligence*. It, too, is a term that means many things to many people. For instance, do you think knowing the meaning of the word *uxoricide* makes you smart? Well, someone apparently did, for this word appeared on an IQ test given to countless thousands of people (in case you care, *uxoricide* is the murder of a wife by her husband). Now, if you were on safari in the African Veldt and were being rushed by a stampeding elephant, do you think that being able to define words like *uxoricide* would halt the said pachyderm's pursuit of you? The point is: intelligence is hard to define because it is always—*always*—determined within a particular context. So, what makes one smart in Mozambique may not be the same traits or behaviors that get you noted as intelligent in Mexico or Maine.

> "ONE OF MY MOST PRIZED POSSESSIONS IS MY INTELLIGENCE, EVEN WITHOUT A GIFTED LABEL, THAT SAME INTELLECT WILL MAKE IT POSSIBLE FOR ME TO EXCEL IN COLLEGE AND CHOOSE THE CAREER PATH I DESIRE." —*Chris, 16*

Of course, some characteristics are considered assets in any locale. For example, the ability to solve problems, to think both logically *and* creatively, and to communicate your needs and thoughts clearly and meaningfully will get you far wherever you live. The context may change—as noted in the previous examples—but the underlying elements of intelligence are universal, at least among humans.

> "If the Aborigine drafted an IQ test, all of Western civilization would presumably flunk it."
> ★STANLEY GARN, FORMER PROFESSOR OF ANTHROPOLOGY AT THE UNIVERSITY OF MICHIGAN

The Survey Says . . .

66% of respondents want to know what IQ and achievement test scores do—and do not—mean.

70% want to know more about different types of intelligence.

50% want to know more about how to improve their critical-thinking, problem-solving, and decision-making skills.

Top Five Questions About Intelligence

Following are the questions about intelligence that we most often encounter in letters from students, survey responses, and Q&A sessions after our presentations and workshops.

1. Is intelligence inherited, determined by our environment, or picked up on our own?

The next time your mom wants to give you "a piece of her mind," remind her that she already has! It's generally acknowledged that genes (from both sides of the family) do count for at least part of our intelligence. What's not clear is how much is hereditary (nature) and how much comes from our day-to-day interactions with the people and things around us (nurture).

"With a good heredity, nature deals you a fine hand at cards; and with a good environment, you learn to play the hand well."
★ WALTER C. ALVAREZ, PHYSICIAN AND AUTHOR

Here's what we believe: You can't change your DNA, but you can enhance your environment. So read that book and attend that dance performance. Enroll in computer class at school (or cooking class at your community education center). Get on the Internet and explore the Louvre or Smithsonian websites. Go to the park. Exercise. Ask questions. Travel if you can, or talk to people who have.

2. If I don't use my intelligence, will I lose it?

Anyone who plays tennis, basketball, or chess can probably answer this question, because except for a few shining stars who didn't seem like they had to work at it, the key to any type of strong performance is practice, practice, and more practice. If you don't use your abilities on a regular basis, they won't disappear, but they will weaken. The same goes for brain power. If the most strenuous thinking you do all day is to choose whether to play *Angry Birds* or *Fruit Ninja*, don't be surprised if your mind turns a bit . . . soft and fruity.

3. Are some cultural groups more intelligent than others?
Simply asking this question might lead some people to think that you're prejudiced. But nothing's wrong with a question about bias—if you're open to hearing an honest answer. And the honest answer to this particular question is no. Just as we discussed earlier that giftedness knows no cultural bounds, neither does intelligence.

So why is this question asked at all? Because of our history, our culture, and our methods for determining intelligence. For example, some kids have the privilege of not worrying about where their next meal is coming from. They are free to focus on schoolwork and social activities that introduce them to a world beyond their own neighborhoods. When an intelligence test question asks them to define a *gazelle* or a *gazebo,* they can recall that they once saw the former at the zoo or the latter in a friend's backyard. This gives them an intellectual edge—or so it would appear on a traditional test.

But if you asked them what a *joggling board* is, or how to deal with a bull moose encountered on the way home from school, or how to prepare a cedar log for carving, or how to use the stars to navigate across the ocean, you might be met with vacant stares.

Intelligence is not doled out to some cultural groups any more frequently than it is to others. It's just that the way many people measure intelligence has a distinctly white, middle-class, middle-American tone. Blacks, Hispanics, Asians, whites, Native Americans: each group has its own traditions, wisdom, and areas of expertise; each has something to teach others. Smart people of all backgrounds would be wise to listen and learn.

4. Can intelligence get in the way of having a good time?
Sometimes gifted people are accused of always being "on": always thinking, questioning, explaining, and being too intense. Although these behaviors were probably considered cute when you were two, they might drive people nuts now that you're a teenager. Unfortunately for you, trying to keep your mouth (and your brain) toned down might be as difficult as putting

toothpaste back in the tube. You might not be able to distinguish between topics that light up the room and those that put people to sleep.

If this is an issue for you, consider the following options:

★ Slow down, talk less, and listen more. (It's possible that you do sometimes talk too much. This isn't a crime, but it can make it difficult for others to get a word in edgewise.)

★ Take a look at the people you're spending time with. Maybe you need to find another group of friends—people who appreciate your vocabulary and your intelligence.

★ Lighten up occasionally. Leave room in your life for jokes, humor, spontaneity, goofing off, and having fun.

5. Am I still gifted even if there are areas I don't feel very intelligent in?
Psychologist Howard Gardner has a very popular, intriguing model that you may have heard about called "multiple intelligences." Gardner believes that, instead of intelligence being any one single element, it actually takes many forms—eight, currently.* These eight intelligences are:

★ Visual/spatial (sometimes called "art smarts")

★ Verbal/linguistic ("word smarts")

★ Logical/mathematical ("number smarts")

★ Bodily/kinesthetic ("body smarts")

★ Interpersonal ("people smarts")

★ Intrapersonal ("self smarts")

★ Musical/rhythmic ("music smarts")

★ Naturalist ("nature smarts")

Gardner found that everyone has strength in at least one of these intelligence areas, and some have strengths in more than one. If it's true that intelligence itself can take many forms, then it also makes sense that giftedness can come in varying areas. As an audience member observed during one of our presentations, "It's almost as though you have to have valleys in order to also have peaks of high ability."

---

*A ninth intelligence has been tentatively identified by Dr. Gardner. *Existential intelligence* is strong in people who are able to contemplate phenomena or questions beyond sensory data, such as the infinite or infinitesimal.

Until you fully grasp this notion, you may find yourself trapped in the "Bottom of the Top" syndrome. Here's how it works: You know that you're smart. After all, you've been in honors math since seventh grade. But when you look around, you start comparing your performance to that of the other gifted students. Since someone in every class—even a class of gifted students—has to be the *least* smart, you figure that it might as well be you. What you don't know is that at least one-third of your classmates have the same opinion of themselves. They're just as fearful of ending up at the "bottom of the top."

This syndrome affects many gifted students when they start college. They're used to being the high school stars—honor roll, dean's list, advanced classes, valedictorian, National Honor Society, National Merit Scholar, the whole package. Suddenly, especially if they attend a highly selective college, they're surrounded by hundreds of other students whose abilities are equal to or even superior to theirs. Naturally, this shakes their confidence. No longer at the top of the academic heap, they start wondering if they belong at all. But, if Gardner's theory of multiple intelligences is right—and many people believe that it is—then you can stop comparing and start enjoying the entirely unique combination of intelligences that make up who and what you are.

IQ, Tests & Testing

No doubt your school experience is chock-full of numbers—GPAs, test scores, percentiles, class rankings, locker combinations, student IDs, cell phone numbers, and so on. One number you may be pretty curious about as a gifted student (if you don't know it already) is your IQ, or intelligence quotient. What exactly is it, and why is it important?

In Western cultures and some others, two aspects of intelligence that are valued highly are advanced verbal skills and the types of reasoning abilities that are required in subjects like mathematics, science, logic, and philosophy. Indeed, almost any IQ test you take will have a majority of items devoted to these two areas: verbal and analytical functions. Some IQ tests do not contain a verbal component; instead, they require you to look at a sequence of shapes and colors to determine which series of responses best completes the sequence—your reasoning gets you the right answer and a high IQ.

But how high *is* high when it comes to IQ? Since the majority of IQ tests use 100 as an average score—that is, average compared to *other people your age*—if you have an IQ of 130, you will find only 300 in 10,000 people with a score this high. A 150 IQ? Just 9 in 10,000 people are this advanced, and an IQ of 160 puts you in a range where only 1 in 10,000 people can match your mind's acuity.

Some contemporary educators and psychologists dismiss the IQ test as a biased, outmoded, and simplistic way to measure intelligence. While they have some valid points, these tests have been around for more than 100 years and, despite their given limitations, are still valued by many school districts as at least one time-honored way to identify intellectually gifted students. Thus, we predict IQ will be around for some time to come (at least until brain scans replace it, which may be a while; see Chapter 4). Is IQ the entire measure of a person? By no means. But it is a number that our culture—like it or not—deems important.

IQ tests first came into use in the early 1900s, thanks to psychologists Alfred Binet and Theodore Simon. Interestingly, the original IQ tests were developed to identify kids who were "too dull" to be educated in ordinary schools. During the 1920s, Lewis Terman took the Binet-Simon test, revised it as the Stanford-Binet test, used it to identify the "geniuses" for his study, and the era of more widespread IQ testing was born.

Your IQ is calculated by a simple mathematical formula:

$$\frac{\text{mental age}}{\text{life age}} \times 100 = \text{IQ}$$

For example, let's say you are 13. When you take an IQ test, the examiner computes your score by comparing your answers to those given by thousands of other people of various ages. If your responses are both accurate and sophisticated (that is, if you used logic or elaboration), chances are your thinking will be revealed as more like that of a 16-year-old versus a 13-year-old. Thus, your mental age will be higher than your actual age (also called your life age). And here's what happens to the formula:

$$\frac{16 \ (\text{mental age})}{13 \ (\text{life age})} \times 100 = 123 \ \text{IQ}$$

Since the average IQ is 100, a score of 123 puts you above average. Translated into percentiles, it ranks you at about the 92nd percentile, meaning that you scored higher than 92 out of 100 13-year-olds who took the same test.

Some people cite 140 as the cutoff between smart and genius. Very generally speaking, an IQ around 130 indicates the presence of solid intellectual muscle. (Of course, just because it's *there* doesn't mean it's being *exercised.*)

IQ Overview

IQ Score	Classification	Approximate Incidence in Population
160	Very superior	1 in 10,000
150	Very superior	9 in 10,000
140	Very superior	7 in 1,000
130	Very superior	3 in 100
120	Superior	11 in 100
110	Bright	21 in 100

What IQ *Really* Means

Almost everyone believes that IQ bears a one-to-one relationship with being gifted—that someone with an average IQ can't possibly be gifted. But that's simply not true.

IQ scores by themselves mean very little. They don't measure creativity, leadership, character, or communication ability. A high IQ does not guarantee success or high grades. It won't make you president of your class or captain of your track team; it won't win you the lead in the school play; it can't even predict whether you'll pass or fail this year's classes.

What a high IQ does mean is that you have the *potential* to do well at *intellectual pursuits.* Potential unrealized is useless. Some gifted people waste away in prisons or work unfulfilling jobs because they haven't used their abilities in productive ways.

Consider Gerald Darrow. He was one of the Quiz Kids, young people of the 1940s who astonished radio and TV audiences with their brilliance. Darrow died at age 47 after spending most of his final years on welfare and in poor health.

Willie Sidis, another child prodigy, graduated from high school at age 8 and lectured at Harvard at 11. As an adult, he became the target of much resentment by the press. He blamed his father for treating him as an exhibit and grew to reject intellectualism of any sort. He worked by choice at menial tasks and collected streetcar transfers as a hobby. He died at age 46 in a rented room near Boston.

Many more examples are equally compelling. The point is not to alarm you but to put things into perspective. Some people with high IQs experience great successes; others experience failures. On the other hand, countless people with average and below average IQs have done well. Some people have said— and we agree—that *"I Can"* is more important than *IQ*.

Should You Know Your IQ?

Most teachers and parents aren't in favor of sharing IQ scores with students. They worry that you'll use this information inappropriately. There does appear to be an "IQ mystique" that leads people who know their scores to set their expectations accordingly. For example, if you learned that your IQ was a "mere" 117, you might decide that your potential was forever limited to just above average—that you're smart enough to get by, but not to achieve significantly or make a difference in the world. Conversely, if you learned that your IQ was 157, you might conclude that you're so smart you never need to study. Either way, you'd be mistaken.

We're acquainted with several adults who don't want to know their IQ scores. They would rather not get mired in the mystique. As one said, "What if I found out that my IQ was higher than I thought? Would I be disappointed with my life so far? Or what if I learned that it was lower than I hoped? Would I feel as if I had been fooling myself and everyone else?"

On the other hand, some adults do believe kids should know their IQ scores. Often these are people who know their IQs, and they point to themselves as examples of how to behave. And some adults place far too much emphasis on IQ. Some parents of gifted kids (fortunately, not many) spend a lot of time talking about and comparing their children's scores; it's the equivalent of bragging about whose kid walked first, talked first, and brought home the best report card.

In the end, much of the fuss over IQ may signify less than we think. Critics of IQ testing and scores cite plenty of reasons to de-emphasize their importance. The tests are increasingly under fire for being racially and culturally biased; many school systems no longer give them. But if you've taken an IQ test and you really want to know your score, ask your school counselor or parents. If they choose to tell you, store it away under "fascinating facts" in your mental file cabinet and get on with your life. If they won't tell, you have two choices:

★ Wait until you're 18, and if you're still curious, ask to see your school files.

★ Take an adult version IQ test and score yourself. Ask a parent, teacher, or counselor to help you find one.

Either way, don't let *any* test score shape your opinion of yourself, your plans for the future, or your commitment to learn and grow.

Six More Possible Meanings for the Acronym IQ

I Quit

Some people believe that an average IQ predicts a life of menial jobs and dreary relationships. Wrong! IQ is only one way to measure intelligence, and it's by no means the last word. No one should be sentenced by a test score.

Individual Quirks

In one IQ test, you are asked to find the "best, most sensible" word to complete this sentence: "The foundation of all science is _____." Your choices are "observation," "invention," "knowledge," "theory," and "art." Which do you feel fits best? The test developers have a particular word in mind. If your opinion differs, no point for you.

Insufficient Quantity

Some IQ tests last only 20 minutes, which doesn't leave much time for revealing your specific strengths and weaknesses. If you're going to be selected for (or barred from) a gifted program on the basis of your IQ, you deserve more than 20 minutes to show what you know.

Intense Queasiness

Tests have been known to make people anxious. The typical IQ test is administered in a situation that is stressful and constrained by time limits. "Brain drain" isn't uncommon. You may forget everything you've ever learned—only to recall it all five minutes after the test ends.

Impressive Quality

Although IQ tests are criticized, the fact remains that people with high IQs often do very well in life. The tests appear to do an adequate job of locating overall intelligence; a score of 150 usually isn't an accident or a fluke. But do the tests fail to identify some smart people who just don't perform well on tests? The evidence points to yes.

I Question

Even amid all the controversy, many gifted teens we know still question what their IQ is and want access to their scores. Before learning yours, ask yourself this: "If my score is lower than I thought it would be, will I be disappointed and disillusioned? If it's higher than I estimated, will I feel the pressure to live up to the high number?" So . . . can you handle the truth?

When Tests Fail

Intelligence tests, of course, are not the only tests in the lives of gifted students. In this era of content standards and mandated state testing, you are likely inundated with a variety of high-stakes tests and exams, possibly more than any generation before you. However, just because you're required to take a test does not mean that it's a good test. The truth is: *not all tests are created equal.* While many test writers go to great lengths to construct clear, relevant, non-biased test items and assessment measures, they do not always succeed. So whenever you are taking a test—be it an IQ test, an AP exam, or a unit-end quiz—try to keep in mind the following information.

Four Reasons Why Tests Can't Be Trusted

1. Test questions may have more than one correct response, depending on the test-taker's perspective.

"Eliminate the word that doesn't belong in this group: cricket, football, billiards, hockey."

In fact, each one can be eliminated. Cricket is the only one of British origin. Billiards is the only one played indoors. Football is the only one whose object is not to put a ball into a net. And which type of hockey is meant, field or ice?

Thus the *real* answer is "all of the above." But that's not a response option. Which raises an interesting point: Can you be *too* smart and think *too* deeply to score high on some tests?

2. Tests can discriminate against people from poor, minority, or disadvantaged backgrounds.

"Compare and contrast Truman Capote and Norman Mailer for their portrayal of the male figure in the novel."

Many tests, including IQ tests, have a high "verbal load"—that is, they require a good working knowledge of vocabulary, ideas, and situations that are part of life in white, middle-class, advantaged America.

You may know quite a bit about Capote and Mailer. Or you may not, but if anyone asked, you could talk at length about the novels of Gabriel García Márquez, which you've read in the original Spanish.

This raises another interesting point: Would more students perform better on tests if the tests asked more of the right questions?

3. Test scores can be wrong.

Sometimes the score you get doesn't reflect the knowledge you have. A test score that is lower than it should be is called a "false negative." A false negative can have a variety of causes, all unrelated to the subject on which you're being tested. For example, if you're ill on the day of the test or extremely nervous during the test, or if the test itself isn't valid, you could end up with a score that has no relation to what you actually know.

This is not to say that a low test score is always wrong. Sometimes you just don't know the subject matter, or you chose not to study. But if you do know the subject matter and you did study and you still got a lower score, it might be a false negative.

Incidentally, it's almost impossible to get a "false positive." You don't score 140 on an IQ test or 99 percent on a math exam because you faked it or got lucky. You earned it.

4. Tests don't accommodate different learning styles.

Almost every test you will take in school will be either an online or a paper-and-pencil test. You'll fill in blanks, color in or click on circles, write or type answers, compose essays, check true-false boxes, and so on. You may do well

> "Test scores should never 'define' a person, no matter what they may reveal about his or her intellectual or achievement potential. No single test can assess the broad range of traits and abilities that help make a person successful and productive in society, a wonderful person to be around, or even a person of eminence. All tests are imperfect measurers."
>
> ★JEAN SUNDE PETERSON, PROFESSOR OF EDUCATION AT PURDUE UNIVERSITY

on these tests—but maybe you would do even better if the tests were different, or the testing environment was more conducive to your individual learning style.

For example: Say you do your best studying and learning at home while lying on your bed, eating popcorn, and listening to music. On test days, you're forced to sit at a desk (which often has a seat as hard as rocks), you can't even chew gum, and the room is silent, except for the usual pencil-scratching or keyboard tapping, squirming, and coughing noises from your classmates. Clearly these aren't the optimal test conditions for you. You might not be able to do much about this, but it's worth discussing with your teacher, especially if he or she is knowledgeable about learning styles. You may find that the testing environment can be made more flexible in certain circumstances.

Enough Already About Test Scores & IQ . . . What Are Your EQ, SQ & CQ?

With *all* that said about intellectual ability . . . the truth is, it doesn't matter how high your IQ is if you have the emotional awareness, social skills, and creativity of a turnip. In other words, if you have a low EQ (emotional intelligence quotient), SQ (social intelligence quotient), or CQ (creativity quotient).

That's a lot of Qs, but they all serve the same general purpose: to measure and explain the full scope of human intelligence. These are the "smarts" that often truly identify well-adjusted, high-achieving, admired, fulfilled, innovative, and all-around successful people—be they network engineers, business consultants, yoga instructors, lab technicians, novelists, university professors, or turnip farmers. This section will help you apply these smarts to your own life and make the choices that are best for you.

The bottom line: It takes a lot more than a competent intellect to be successful in life.

EQ: Emotional Intelligence Quotient

Every second of your life you experience some kind of emotion[*]—happiness, sadness, frustration, anger, fear, disgust, surprise, contempt, shame—including when you're asleep and dreaming. Obviously, your emotions are not always at the forefront of your consciousness and the strength of them waxes and wanes depending on the situation. For example, if you're in a yelling match with a friend, your emotions are front and center, but if you're solving a calculus problem, they probably take a back seat to a more analytic thought process.

But because you are human and not a computer, you can't think logically and rationally without *also* thinking emotionally. It's in your best interest to get a handle on these slippery, omnipresent things called "feelings," so you're making productive, helpful decisions.

Of course, that's easier said than done. Even for the well-adjusted among us, feelings can sneak out of the backseat and grab the steering wheel at the most inopportune moments (crying during an exam or a job interview, for instance—yes, it happens). And other times when feelings *should* be in the driver's seat, you do not let them (being unable to tell a close friend how much you care about her or him when they're struggling, perhaps).

These instances, unfortunately, will never go away completely, but you can learn how to minimize them so you don't live plagued by unhinged or untapped feelings. In other words, you can develop *emotional intelligence* that will help you now and throughout your life.

What's Your EQ?
How high is your current emotional intelligence? Answer the following questions in a notebook as honestly as you can. Record the first response that pops into your head.

1. Are you usually able to identify and name your feelings?
2. Do you recognize the effect your feelings have on you?
3. Do you listen to your gut intuition when making decisions?
4. How often do your feelings negatively interfere with your performance and success?
5. Do your feelings often get in the way of your relationships?
6. How easily do you adapt to changing circumstances in your life?

---

[*]Although what exactly constitutes "emotion" is still a matter of some controversy among psychologists.

> "Sixty-seven percent of the abilities deemed essential for effective performance are emotional competencies. Compared to IQ and expertise, emotional competence mattered twice as much. This holds true across all categories of jobs, and in all kinds of organizations."
> ★DAVID GOLEMAN, AUTHOR OF *WORKING WITH EMOTIONAL INTELLIGENCE*

Your answers to these questions will help you think about how feelings impact your life. Regardless of your responses, you can always raise your emotional smarts. People with high EQs know what they feel and how their feelings affect them, they handle their feelings in ways that are positive and helpful, and they make decisions about life—what classes to take, what jobs to pursue, what advice to heed, who to befriend or date—with greater assurance and competency than people with low or no emotional smarts. Having people skills makes you more adept at relationships, cooperation, negotiation, leadership, and teamwork. They help you learn more, learn quickly, and be less likely to engage in antisocial, at-risk, or criminal behaviors.

The good news is that, like IQ, EQ is not fixed at birth. We can all learn and strengthen these skills throughout our lives.

How to Boost Your EQ

Here are some suggestions:

Observe and describe. Throughout the day, try this exercise: once an hour, make a list in a journal of the emotions you are experiencing. Don't mistake states of mind, such as boredom or impatience, for emotions. Dig beneath them to locate the feelings (*Hint*: boredom and impatience are usually fueled, in part, by frustration or a feeling of powerlessness). Take care not to judge any of your feelings; simply observe and describe them.

Breathe, count, and wait. Strong emotions are like flames; they do not last long unless they have fuel. When you experience an intense feeling, you can choose not to fuel it. Instead, take several deep breaths, count to ten, take a walk, drink some water, or simply close your eyes and wait for the flame to die down. It will in time. Feelings are never permanent; they come and go frequently. If you need proof of this, sit and watch young kids at a playground for a half hour or so. Observe how many emotions they experience (feelings tend to be obvious on children's faces) and how quickly and fluidly one flows into the next.

Uncover the hidden feeling. When you're having a strong emotion, try to take a moment to examine it—what other feelings may be hiding behind the obvious one? For example, when you're angry, underneath the anger can be other emotions, such as sadness, disappointment, or fear. For some people, anger can dominate most other feelings; for others, sadness or fear can dominate. It depends on which feelings people are most comfortable with. One way to uncover the hidden feelings is to ask yourself, "If I *couldn't* be (mad, sad, afraid, etc.), what emotion might I be feeling instead?"

Seek out others' strategies. Think of people in your life—parents, teachers, friends—that you see as good role models for emotional intelligence. Observe how they react to strong emotions in themselves and in others. Ask them if they have any strategies they use to manage their feelings. If they really are emotionally intelligent, they'll welcome sharing a tip or two with you.

> "Fear is a question. What are you afraid of and why? Our fears are a treasure house of self-knowledge if we explore them."
> ★MARILYN FRENCH,
> FEMINIST AND AUTHOR

Get "triggered" and write. Sometimes the easiest way to get to know your feelings is to seek out art and react to it. Read a poem or novel, watch a film, listen to music, or view a painting exhibit—let your feelings wash over you as you take it in. Then, while your feelings are triggered, write in a journal. You might start off writing about the work of art and eventually start writing about your own experiences and memories and feelings.

Talk to a therapist or counselor. You don't need to have serious mental health issues to seek advice or counseling about how you are feeling. Many people see a counselor simply to maintain or improve their emotional health, just as they exercise and get regular medical checkups. There are many different types of counseling—from in-depth psychoanalysis to cognitive behavioral therapy to basic life skills counseling.

Seek support in your community. Set up a time to talk with a youth leader or spiritual advisor who you trust. Or find out about support groups in your community focused on personal growth and well-being.

SQ: Social Intelligence Quotient

Social intelligence is often grouped together with emotional intelligence. While EQ involves the *intra*personal end of things (self-awareness and self-management), SQ covers the *inter*personal side (social awareness and relationship management). Why do you need it? Well, you don't . . . if you happen to be living in an isolated mountain cabin. In all other instances, you live as a social animal in a world populated by people—*all* types of people—and your ability to relate with these people will ultimately determine whether you achieve your life's goals and dreams.

What's Your SQ?

Ask a close friend or family member to answer the following questions about you in a notebook—as honestly as possible—and then share the answers with you. You can also answer the questions about yourself.

1. How often does she or he smile?

2. Is she or he usually upbeat with a positive attitude?

3. Does she or he have a good sense of humor?

4. Does she or he usually make an effort to be courteous?

5. Does she or he know how to react appropriately in most situations?

6. Is she or he successful in hobbies and activities that involve group interaction?

7. Does she or he usually get along with new people?

8. Is she or he comfortable communicating feelings and ideas verbally?

9. Is she or he usually sensitive to what another person is feeling?

10. Does she or he enjoy listening to people?

11. Is she or he able to inspire and influence others around them?

12. How well does she or he manage conflict?

Are you surprised by the answers the person gave about you or did you mostly agree with his or her observations? Are there areas you could clearly improve upon? If so, the first step is to become an observer of social intelligence—simply watch a group of people interacting. The people who are socially gifted with high SQs are often the ones with infectious smiles, polite manners, sharp senses of humor, genuine facial expressions, and mildly animated gestures. They may be talking to just one or two people at a time, or sharing with a larger group. They appear comfortable in their own skin, put others at ease around them, listen attentively, hold people's attention when they talk, and influence others' opinions.

In short, while they may not be the "life of the party" (sometimes those people do *not* have a high SQ), they are generally well liked by many.

Meanwhile, the people with low SQs may be either standing alone staring at the floor (or at their cell phone screens), talking nonstop to someone who does not appear interested, or loudly cracking jokes but not connecting positively with anyone. These people may be among the brightest minds in the room, yet they often have trouble forming and maintaining mature friendships, communicating well, getting hired and being successful in the workforce, and even gaining admittance to college (for example, social skills are tested for admission to all medical schools in Australia).

Most people fall somewhere in the middle of the pack—with neither a particularly high SQ, nor a low one. And everyone can benefit from having more social intelligence.

How to Boost Your SQ

Smile more often, listen more closely, be more respectful, and help people feel accepted by you. You have total control over whether you greet people warmly or blow them off with a put-down. Interestingly, high SQ behaviors might come easier to you if you're an introvert versus an extrovert. The common belief that chatty extroverts have better social skills and more friends is not proven by research. People with all types of personalities can adjust their communication styles in many different ways to make others feel welcome.

For more ideas on boosting your SQ, read the essay by socially smart and successful television writer Chad Gervich (see page 52).

Tip

When you smile genuinely, the ends of each of your eyebrows should dip down. The *orbicularis oculi* muscles, which control these parts of your brows, cannot consciously be controlled, so when the ends of the brows dip, it means a person's smile is real and not faked. Test this by smiling in a mirror or feeling the ends of your eyebrows when you smile.

Expert Essay

"It's Your Charm That Matters! Advice from the Fart Joke Writer"
by Chad Gervich

I'm a TV writer, which means—let's be honest—I have no business giving advice to anyone, especially kids. I make a living pitching sketches, telling stories, and fine-tuning fart jokes. So what qualifies me to tell anyone how to make it in the world . . . or even survive?

Well . . . *I'm a really nice guy.* I love to laugh. I can talk to just about anyone, about anything. I also love email, and if Facebook came in edible form, I'd eat it for breakfast, lunch, and dinner.

And while all of these seem like ridiculous, meaningless qualities, I'll say this: They're a lot more valuable than those straight A's some of your parents keep pushing for. Or all those honors and magna-cum-whatevers they want you to get. Or that $250,000 college degree you're about to spend four years earning.

That's not to say those *aren't* important, but you'll never get hired because you graduated top of your class, or went through a talented and gifted program, or have a degree from a more prestigious university than your competitors. You will, however, get hired because you made an impression on someone at a party. Or wowed higher-ups at your summer internship. Or sent a congratulatory email to a contact who got promoted.

In other words, when it comes to excelling in the real world, it's not your IQ that matters . . . it's your EQ, your emotional intelligence—your ability to connect, charm, relate to people.

Why? First of all—smart people are a dime a dozen. While you may be the cream of the crop at school, a big fish in a small pond, you become a significantly *smaller* fish in the pond of the "real world," a world full of people who were the cream of the crop at *their* schools.

Secondly, evaluation processes used by schools are different than evaluation processes used by businesses and bosses. There are millions of people who don't test well, or write great essays, or get outstanding grades, but drop them in a laboratory or a design studio or a boardroom . . . and they'll blow their high school's valedictorians out of the water.

More importantly, most jobs involve working on some kind of team, collaborating with others. If you're a basketball player or symphony musician, teamwork is obvious. But lawyers also work in teams. Building a house takes cooperation between architects, contractors, and a construction crew. Ad campaigns are created and produced by firms. Even TV shows are written by staffs that outline, write, and rewrite scripts together. So while knowledge and skills are important, a successful teammate requires other qualities: trust, patience, sense of humor, ability to listen, adaptability, leadership (and knowing when to follow). Unfortunately, these qualities can't be relayed via a résumé, so you need another way to communicate them to colleagues and employers. How do you do that?

You get into the world and meet people. You collect friends and form relationships with people who share your likes, your perspectives, your sensibilities. Think about it: If you're putting together a group—people you trust, enjoy, feel productive with—who do you call? Strangers you've met briefly through résumés and interviews? Or people you know, trust, are comfortable with? The answer, for most of the working world, is the latter.

Of course, making friends and collecting contacts is often easier said than done, and for people who aren't overly social, it can be terrifying. So where do you start? What are effective ways to connect with people and spotlight your sparkling personality?

1. Get involved. In today's diverse world, with the Internet at your fingertips, it's easy to find groups specializing in sports, knitting, fencing, 18th-century taxidermy techniques—whatever you're passionate about! You don't have to be the most outgoing person at the meeting; just show up and observe. Coming out of your shell is easier when you're surrounded by people who share your loves, and if you can't find an existing group, start one!

2. Take people to lunch. Lunches are short, informal, and because they're in the middle of the day, they rarely feel awkward or "date-y." And FYI—you're not going to lunch to blow someone away with your wit, intelligence, or charm; you're going to ask questions, hear their story, learn about them. Focus on *them,* not yourself. (This also helps take uncomfortable pressure off you.)

3. Do small favors. People like knowing you're thinking of them (without being a stalker). So make small gestures that let them know you remember them. This could be a simple "Happy Birthday" note or a congratulations when they've accomplished something special, or an introduction to a new friend or business colleague. These take little time or effort and they require nothing of the receiver; they simply let the person know you've got his or her back.

4. Work for free. Find nearby activities you enjoy—concerts, plays, guest speakers, sports events—and offer to usher, bus tables, hand out programs, or whatever needs being done . . . for *free.* You'll (A) attend fun events without paying, (B) meet interesting people, (C) impress folks with your work ethic, which could eventually land you a job, or at least the respect and admiration of those above you.

5. Facebook. It seems apparent today, but keeping online profiles (Facebook, LinkedIn, Twitter, etc.) is a great way to stay in touch with old and new contacts alike. It also allows you to find interesting local events and acquaintances with shared interests. Of course, online profiles alone aren't powerful enough to form real relationships; you have to back them up with in-person meetings, but they're a wonderful place to start and maintain connections between meetings!

As nebulous—or obvious—as this all may seem, the more you do it, the better you'll get. You'll build a library of jokes and responses, learn to interact with different personalities, master introducing yourself, understand when to talk and when to listen. And eventually, you'll boost your EQ high enough to succeed, or survive, even if—like me—you have virtually no employable skills whatsoever.

***Chad Gervich** has written or produced on such shows as* After Lately, Reality Binge, Malcolm in the Middle, Girls Club, *and* Wipeout, *and is the author of the best-selling* Small Screen, Big Picture: A Writer's Guide to the TV Business. *If you've never seen or read any of them: Congratulations! You have a life. Chad lives in Los Angeles with his wife and one-year-old son, both of whom are much more qualified than he is to advise people on their careers.*

CQ: Creativity Quotient

The last, but certainly not least, measure of a person's overall intelligence is his or her CQ, or creativity quotient. We live in a golden age of ideas—we're more open to creative new ideas than possibly ever before. In fact, we desperately need them; matters of huge national and international importance—from healthcare to global warming—require creative solutions. Creativity is cited by top CEOs as the number one leadership skill of the future. The problem is, just when we need it the most, it appears to be in short supply. Dr. Kyung Hee Kim at the College of William and Mary recently analyzed the scores of over 300,000 people and discovered an alarming fact: the creativity of Americans has plummeted in the past 20 years. We are, some say, in the midst of a creativity crisis.

So we know it's important, but what exactly *is* creativity? Its precise definition is cause for debate, but it's roughly: the ability to produce something original and useful. Moreover, it's usually problem-based, collaborative, and enhanced by constraints and emotion. In other words, you're most likely to hit upon a spark of true creativity when working to solve a particular *problem*, with a *partner or group*, and you have specific *limitations* and are *emotionally engaged*.

Also, contrary to common misconceptions, creativity is not exclusive to the arts; there are equally creative scientists and mathematicians as painters and writers, and the creative process is similar for all. In fact, many highly creative thinkers are talented in several different fields across the arts and sciences.

One famous example of these thinkers at work lies in the history of wireless networking. In the 1940s, a technology called "frequency hopping," which later enabled cell phone communication, was invented by an actress (Hedy Lamarr) and a musician (George Antheil). While this may sound outrageous at first, it really shouldn't come as a surprise, since artists and scientists often share a trait closely linked to creativity: *divergent thinking,* which is the opposite of *convergent thinking.* Here's a way to picture the two:

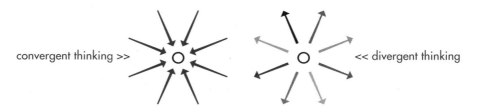

convergent thinking >>   << divergent thinking

In convergent thinking (the kind most often measured by tests), facts "converge" to yield a single answer. While divergent thinking begins with a single fact and generates many ideas from it, often drawing unexpected connections. Divergent thinking occurs when you brainstorm ideas. Both types of thinking are necessary to complete most tasks in life, but, far more than your IQ score, how well you can think divergently determines how creative you are.

In fact, recent studies have shown that a high IQ may even hinder creativity. Why? A low level of a brain chemical known as NAA (*N-acetyl-asparate*) in a region of the brain called the ACG (*anterior cingulated gyrus*) has been correlated with high creativity—specifically, with divergent thinking ability—in people of average intelligence.[*] However, in people with above-average IQs, the *reverse* has been found: a high level of NAA in their ACG. Might this explain why some of the world's most intelligent people sometimes lack originality? Maybe. Of course, this is by no means a sentence for unoriginality if you have a high IQ; but it should prevent you from assuming that because you're highly intelligent, you are, by default, highly creative. The two must be nurtured independently.

Benefits of Being Creative

Research shows that, compared with people who demonstrate a low degree of creativity, creative people are generally:

- ★ better at relationships
- ★ more able to handle stress and overcome obstacles
- ★ less prone to depression and suicide
- ★ engaged, motivated, and open to the world (it's a myth that they're all dark, depressed, anxious, and neurotic; these traits actually *shut down* creativity by making a person less open to experience and novelty)[**]

This doesn't mean that highly creative people are never anxious, depressed, or suicidal. Obviously, they are, as evidenced by suicides among artists, writers, and musicians. Yet overall, possessing creativity is a benefit in life, not a drawback.

"I LIKE TO CRACK JOKES TO KEEP THE MOOD OF THE ROOM POSITIVE BECAUSE POSITIVE ENERGY IS WHAT FUELS MY CREATIVE JUICES."
—*Amari, 16*

"EVERY KID NEEDS THE CHANCE TO BE CREATIVE AND EXPRESS WHAT THEY THINK."
—*Paul, 15*

---

[*]Jung, R. et al. "Biochemical Support for the 'Threshold' Theory of Creativity: A Magnetic Resonance Spectroscopy Study." *The Journal of Neuroscience*, April 22, 2009, 29(16): 5319–5325.

[**]Bronson, Po, and Ashley Merryman. "The Creativity Crisis." *Newsweek*, July 10, 2010. Cited research by Dr. Mark Runco at the University of Georgia.

Test Your CQ

For an article they wrote for *Newsweek*, authors Po Bronson and Ashley Merryman adapted three test items similar to those that might appear on a Torrance Test of Creative Thinking (TTCT).[*] They asked several young people and adults to complete the items and then had a panel of experts assess them. Test items on the TTCT are different from ones you may be familiar with. They often consist of incomplete line drawings and require test takers to turn the drawings into complete pictures. Visit newsweek.com and search for "how creative are you" to see the three sample items, examples of how people completed them, and details on how the experts assessed them.

To score these tasks, experts look not for the best art, but for multiple original, detailed ideas. For instance, you wouldn't score very high if you made the upside-down V in the sample test item into a shark's fin—that's a common idea that many people have, so it's fairly unoriginal. But you may score high if you make it funny, add motion, use unusual perspectives, show emotion, or tell a story with the picture—all traits that relate to divergent thinking and, therefore, to creativity.

Experts look not for the best art, but for multiple original, detailed ideas.

*Ibid.

Ellis Paul Torrance: Creativity Guru

E. Paul Torrance (1915–2003) was an American psychologist and author of more than 2,000 books, articles, tests, and other instructional materials on creativity, including the Torrance Tests of Creative Thinking (TTCT)—the most widely used and trusted measures of creativity in the world. They include a variety of interesting and challenging problems, such as the previously discussed tasks, and responses are evaluated in four ways:

- for *fluency* (the number of responses—the more the better)
- for *flexibility* (the ability to change your mindset)
- for *elaboration* (the amount of detail you include in your answers)
- for *originality* (how unique your answers are when compared with other students' answers to the same questions)

How to Boost Your CQ

What if you have superb intellectual, social, and emotional smarts, yet you can't seem to come up with an original idea to save your life? Regardless of your natural creative ability, you can train your brain to compensate for any lack that may exist. The key is to practice. Alternate intense divergent thinking with intense convergent thinking on a daily basis. Flex those innovation muscles strongly and often. Combine new information with old ideas, and old information with new ideas. Think bilaterally—with both the "random" right side and the "logical" left side of your brain. How? Here are some tips to get you started.

Creativity Tip List

★ **Place constraints** on a seemingly simple project. For example, make a standard three-course meal (appetizer, entrée, and dessert), but use only four ingredients.

★ **Collaborate** with a partner on a short story, with each of you writing alternating paragraphs.

★ **Unplug** from your computer and cell phone at least one day a week. Why? A "plugged-in" brain is in a constant state of focused attention switching rapidly between goals, while creativity requires defocused, more free-form attention.

> "Creative thinking is like a muscle, and it needs to be stretched and flexed, or it will atrophy."
> ★DR. KYUNG HEE KIM, PROFESSOR OF EDUCATION AT THE COLLEGE OF WILLIAM & MARY

★ **Spend time alone.** While collaboration is important, it's also crucial to make quiet space in your life for deep reflection and freedom from all interruptions.

★ **Play a musical instrument.** The chromatic musical scale may have only 12 pitches, but they can be manipulated in unlimited ways.

★ **Mix mediums.** Set a math problem to music, act out a chemical reaction, or paint a philosophical idea.

★ **Create a *paracosm*,** a fantasy involving a complete alternate universe. This universe can be as simple or as complex as you wish. Add at least one new detail to it each day.

★ **Role-play** being a friend, family member, or fictional character while you perform one activity every day.

★ **Act childish.** Make time each day to build something, deconstruct something, explore, and play—and don't forget to let your feelings flow freely, as kids do.

★ **Go see comedy** performances, or better yet, participate in improv comedy yourself. A good joke can create a positive, open, playful state of mind that is conducive to the insight required in creativity.

★ **Make messes.** Being too organized and neat can stifle creativity. Designate one area of your living space where you can freely experiment and be messy.

★ **Use technology.** Technology is built by creative minds and is meant to be used creatively. Cell phone scavenger hunts, anyone? How about virtual spaceships?

"There are two ways to use computers in the classroom. You can have them measure and represent the students and teachers, or you can have the class build a virtual spaceship. Right now the first way is ubiquitous, but the virtual spaceships are being built only by the tenacious oddballs in unusual circumstances. More spaceships, please."

★JARON LANIER, RESEARCHER AT MICROSOFT, AUTHOR OF *YOU ARE NOT A GADGET*

The Survey Says . . .

Q: Describe the most challenging creative activity, project, or assignment you've ever done in school.

"In gifted English in sixth grade, we got to create our own planet. We had to create a name, a government, a system of money, transportation, and much more. It was a great way of expressing our creativity." —*Brooke, 17*

"For AP U.S. History, we did this newscast about colonial America. We had to have three relevant commercials and a whole program about our portion." —*Rachael, 15*

"I had to make a Rube Goldberg machine last year in gifted class. It was difficult but very fun and rewarding." —*Will, 15*

"In my engineering class, we had to make roller coasters for a marble out of card stock and tape. It took many tries to get each loop and turn just right, but it was very fun and engaging." —*Laurel, 16*

"We had to create our own culture/species. We had to know what they looked like, their language (we wrote our own letter and number system), government, adaptations to their environment, food, how they got food, clothing, housing, and everyday life. We explored all areas of their culture, which, even though it was all made up, has helped me understand parts of existing cultures." —*Chelsea, 15*

"I was in what we called a Middle East Peace Conference, and I was representing Israel. We all had to come to try to work out an agreement over the issues going on in the Middle East (i.e., Jerusalem, Palestine vs. Israel, nuclear weapons, etc.)." —*Elena, 13*

"Our world history teacher gave us an assignment to build our own trebuchet and try to make it as accurate and powerful as possible. It was really fun, but hard too, because we had to build a large, three-dimensional object instead of writing an essay or something. It stretched a different part of my brain." —*Saul, 14*

"The most interesting project to date that I've had to do in school was to make something I called a *mythodex*—a catalog of many mythical creatures." —*Kiddest, 17*

chapter 3
Whoa, That's Intense

Based on what you've read so far, being gifted clearly means more than computing square roots at the speed of sound or understanding James Joyce's *Ulysses* on your first reading. You can also be gifted with a high EQ, SQ, and CQ (see pages 46–59). But wait: there's even more to it than that. Throughout our careers, we have discovered that the gifted teens we taught and counseled often came with a package of related attributes that combined to make them very intriguing characters. In fact, we have found that gifted teens, more often than not, are in possession of things labeled *intensities*, which can take a variety of forms.

> "AS YOU GET OLDER, ALTHOUGH THE INTELLECTUAL GAP BETWEEN YOU AND YOUR PEERS LESSENS, THE ESSENCE OF WHAT MAKES YOU GIFTED, THE EXPERIENCE OF BEING GIFTED, REMAINS. THE ABILITIES TO SEE CONNECTIONS, TO LEARN RAPIDLY, TO FEEL PASSIONATELY—THOSE THINGS DON'T LEAVE, AND, IN MANY WAYS, THEY DEFINE WHO WE ARE. THE FEELING OF BEING INEFFABLY DIFFERENT WILL NEVER REALLY LEAVE."
> —*Bianca, 18*

All About Intensities

The idea of intensities originated with Polish psychologist Kazimierz Dabrowski, who devised the theory of "overexcitabilities," sometimes called supersensitivities. The five overexcitabilities Dabrowski identified were physical, emotional, intellectual, sensual, and imaginational. His theory was later elaborated on by Michael Piechowski and Susan Daniels, who began referring to the overexcitabilities as intensities. These traits can create wonderful, creative, rich personalities—and they can also produce behaviors that are not always understood or accepted by others. Researchers discovered that, while all people may exhibit these intensities, brighter people often possess more and stronger intensities than people of average intellectual ability.

Following is an essay by Susan Daniels describing in-depth each of the five intensities and how they relate to your life as a gifted teen.

Expert Essay

"Do You Have to Be So Intense? Are You Always So Sensitive? Can't You Just Settle Down?"

by Susan Daniels

I wonder if you often get asked questions like these. Do you wonder why you are so intense, sensitive, and energetic? Or perhaps you wonder why other people seem to see you as being intense?

Well, being gifted is not just about being unusually smart. Being gifted is also about how you feel and how you experience the world around you. Being gifted may also mean you have more energy, are more aware of your surroundings, question ideas more extensively, and feel emotions more deeply.

Being gifted is not just about being unusually smart. It is also about how you feel and how you experience the world around you.

Why is that? It has to do with things called *intensities*—originally coined as "overexcitabilities" by Kazimierz Dabrowski—which come in five forms and tend to be common among bright people. So what are these five types of intensity and how do they relate to being gifted?

1. **Intellectual intensity** is intense curiosity and keen observation, wanting to understand how things work and why they are the way they are, and contemplating philosophical questions, such as "What is the meaning of life?" Intellectual intensity is different from intellectual ability. It's the mental energy that fuels a person's intellectual passions, the need to know, and the search for truth. Intellectual intensity is about the drive to understand.

2. **Psychomotor intensity** is a surplus of bodily energy, the need to move, the physical expression of emotional tension, rapid speech, internal drive, and a great capacity for being active and energetic. This physical energy (*motor*) interacts with the activity of the mind (*psycho*), too.

3. **Sensual intensity** includes enhanced sensory and aesthetic pleasure; intensified seeing, smelling, tasting, touching, and hearing; delight in beautiful objects, sounds of words, music, form, color, and balance. Sensual intensity might also include a tendency to overeat or overindulge in buying things that are pleasing to the senses, such as clothes, art, or music.

4. **Imaginational intensity** involves a rich imagination; vividness of mental imagery; a great capacity for vivid dreams, fantasies, and invention; poetic and dramatic perception; and a need for novelty and variety. People with intense imaginations may seek expression for their imaginations through creative outlets, including writing, acting, video and game design, dance, music, and more.

5. Emotional intensity is an important part of Dabrowski's work. He said that gifted people often experience intense emotions; a wide range of positive and negative feelings—from great joy to deep despair; complex emotions—sometimes feeling many emotions at one time; and a sensitivity to and awareness of the feelings of others as well. Sometimes these strong emotions bring with them strong physical sensations, such as a tense stomach, sweating palms, blushing, flushing, and a pounding heart.

What unusual things make you tear up?

Michael Piechowski offers these insights on emotional intensity: "Perhaps you feel things so strongly that others tell you to 'chill out.' But you know that is impossible, because you are just made that way. Maybe the singing of birds makes you cry because it is so beautiful. What else brings tears to your eyes?" If you experience this type of intensity, take out your journal and make a list.

Perhaps as you were reading through these descriptions you thought, "Oh, wow, that is so like me," or "Nope, not at all like me." Maybe some of the examples brought to mind situations where you are very intense and others where you're not so much. Maybe you thought, "I need to show this to my English teacher (or your mom or dad or best friend) . . . that will explain a lot!" Maybe you had an "aha" realization about yourself, or about a friend or relative.

Keep in mind that, as a gifted person, you may have experienced several of these intensities, or even all five of them. On the other hand, some gifted people are very gifted but are not so intense. And sometimes a person is intense, but you might not notice it, because the intensity runs deep and is experienced internally.

Perhaps you now might be wondering, "Well, okay, now what?" There are certain advantages to having these intensities . . . as well as certain challenges. And there are ways to positively channel these intensities that might also help mediate the challenges that come with them. Let's look at each type of intensity again with this in mind.

Intellectual intensity can leave you feeling very impatient if you have it and other people around you do not. If you ask a lot of questions in class, your teacher may be delighted or might feel uncomfortably challenged. It can be frustrating when friends, family members, or teachers can't keep up with your train of thought or if they don't find your topics of conversation as fascinating as you do. Often, finding intellectual peers might mean looking for other like-minded learners in different settings, for instance a chess club or a book discussion group, or maybe taking a college class online. Finding a mentor or a tutor for a topic or activity you feel passionate about is one way to make a connection with someone who shares your passion, and likely the intellectual intensity that goes with it.

Where is our Pensieve when we need it?

Intellectual intensity can also be exhausting at times! In *Harry Potter and the Goblet of Fire*, Harry's mentor, Albus Dumbledore, pulls his protégé aside after an especially trying day, offering this solace to his young friend: "I sometimes find, and I am sure you know the feeling, that I simply have too many thoughts and memories crammed into my mind . . . at these times I use the Pensieve. One simply siphons the excess thoughts from one's mind, pours them into the basin, and examines them at one's leisure."* Wouldn't this be glorious—to have a place to store your excess thoughts until you had the time to deal with them? If you were charged with designing and marketing an actual Pensieve, what might it look like? Draw an illustration and write a product description in your journal.

Harry Potter and the Goblet of Fire by J. K. Rowling (Arthur A. Levine Books, 2000).

Psychomotor intensity may mean that you get your best ideas while doing something physical, and that sitting still is stressful for you and you feel like you might burst if you don't get up and move—especially when your mind is full of ideas. This can be tricky in some classrooms. Yet, if you talk with your teacher, you might be able to negotiate an agreement that you can pace at the back of the room if need be, or have a desk at the back and at least stand while you read or work on assignments.

Sensual intensity, while providing heightened appreciation of sensory details, can also cause some experiences of taste, touch, smell, sound, and sight to feel unusually awful. So, being mindful of sensory needs may be helpful in school. Of course you can't control all aspects of your sensory environment, but sometimes just slight adaptations can make a big difference. Wear comfortable clothes, ask to sit near the window for natural light, or keep a favorite calming or happy photo in your notebook or cell phone.

Imaginational intensity is a key to creativity. Imagination paves the path to new and different places and perspectives. Having a great imagination enriches our inner life, and it can be a great asset in terms of hobbies and careers in science or in technology or in the arts. I teach a class at the university on creativity, and I often talk about the work of J. K. Rowling and Leonardo da Vinci. It's common to think of imagination and creativity in terms of art and creative writing. Certainly, great leaps of imagination—and sustained effort—were needed to create the creative worlds of the Harry Potter series. It is less common that people think of imagination in terms of the sciences. That is unfortunate.

Albert Einstein himself said, "Imagination is more important than knowledge." And Leonardo da Vinci, while a great artist, also kept copious notebooks and journals with detailed drawings of dozens, if not hundreds, of inventions, including a helicopter, a submarine, a tank, and more. And that's the one suggestion that I believe is really important for nurturing imaginational intensity: Keep a journal. Write, draw, doodle, cut out and paste pictures from magazines that inspire you, make diagrams and to-do lists. Imagination expands the way we see the world and experience life, and you never know when one of your ideas may spark something more!

Emotional intensity can be seen as both a blessing and a curse. You don't just feel more emotions, the quality of your emotions is different. Joy, despair, and every nuanced feeling in between can seem to permeate your entire being. This can be elating, and it can be overwhelming. Just knowing that this is part of how you are hardwired and the insight that it provides may be helpful in itself. If you are emotionally intense, it is important to be aware of your feelings and to give them your attention, so you can address them and manage them.

Deep emotions can be essential to forming close and deep friendships and relationships. Difficult emotions can make it hard to get through the day or even a class period. Some strategies I've found helpful with the teens I work with include deep breathing, getting focused, and naming the emotion and writing about it, your feelings, and your responses. Another good reason to keep a journal. This can help with clarity, it can provide an outlet for expression when there may not be a friend to talk with just then or when you are in class. Try putting your emotions down in writing, and then putting them away for a bit. This may feel odd at first, especially if you are very emotionally intense, but having a "safe space" for your emotions where you can get back to them in a different time or space and with a different perspective can be a very useful approach for exploring and managing deep feelings.

See pages 47–49 on emotional intelligence for more ways to identify and manage intense emotions.

I wish you great travels and adventures exploring your own intensity and all the depth of experiencing that living with intensity brings with it.

Susan Daniels was a gifted teen and is an intense adult. She is a professor of educational psychology and counseling at California State University in San Bernardino, an author and speaker, a mixed media artist, and the educational director of the Summit Center in Walnut Creek, California.

The Survey Says . . .

52% of respondents want to know more about how to deal with intense feelings of sadness, depression, anger, frustration, and anxiety.

A Few Additional Intensities

Along with the five intensities Susan Daniels describes in her essay, we've observed three more during our years of working with and getting to know gifted kids on deeper levels.

Intensity of Purpose

If you are the type of person who is driven to see something through to its conclusion—mastering a musical instrument, beating your school's 400 meter backstroke time, getting a local candidate who shares your politics elected to an important office—then you probably have an intensity of purpose. You persevere in situations where others throw in the towel, and your satisfaction is not complete until you have wrung every ounce of learning or joy out of your experience. You are selectively obsessed—and you get things done.

Some people move from idea to idea, task to task, interest to interest, without lingering for very long in any one place. And then there is you. Once you put your mind to learning a new skill—basketball, guitar, calculus—or to finishing an important something that you started—a marathon, a novel you began writing in sixth grade—you do not give up. Despite setbacks and calls from others to "broaden your horizons," you hunker down in your favorite niches and stay there until your goals are realized. "Give it up!" others say, "Move on!" they shout. But that's just not who you are. You prefer depth to mere coverage. While others travel wide, you dig deep.

A good example of someone who has an intense sense of purpose is a girl we know named Makenzie. Makenzie was seven when she met two foster kids who told her that they had to place their toys and clothes into a garbage bag to carry with them when a social worker came to take them from their foster home. Makenzie felt this was wrong and just added more pain to an already painful situation. That weekend, she and her parents purchased used suitcases at local yard sales and gave them to social services agencies. By age 14, Makenzie's efforts went viral, and her nonprofit organization Children to Children now has a chapter in every state. Makenzie has raised over $1 million in needed supplies for kids in foster care. She continues to devote her life to what began as a simple mission. Visit her website at childrentochildren.org.

Intensity of Spirit

Did your parents forbid you (do they still?) from watching the TV news, because they knew how upset you'd get whenever you saw how cruel people can be to others, themselves, animals, or our planet? When you were in elementary school and a new student enrolled in your class, did your teacher always sit that person next to you, knowing you would share your supplies and watch the new kid's back? Are you always the person trying to convince classmates that they have to get off the sidelines and take action in their school or local community? Do you bring home stray animals? If so, you may have an intensity of spirit. You see the world from a realistic, vivid vantage point and want to work to make it better.

A first grader we know named Matt came home one day with a picture he had drawn in class. It was a house, two trees, and a few stick-figure people playing a game. The entire picture was drawn in black. His parents panicked, thinking that dark thoughts lurked in their young son's mind. But it was something else, something the boy was fearful to share, thinking he would get in trouble if the truth came out.

"A new boy came into our class," Matt explained, "and he didn't have any crayons. I let him have all of mine except one black one." Matt looked to his parents, hoping not to get punished. "He said he'd never had so many beautiful crayons before," Matt said, smiling tentatively.

Yes, that's a person with an intense spirit, one who has no idea what it means to be selfish. If you share Matt's intensity, you often put other people's needs before yours—gladly, not grudgingly. And when you walk by the television when the news is on, you get angry, sad, or moved by both the beauty and the ugliness that engulf our world. You take up causes that are important to you, and you support the underdog—be it a person, an animal, or the environment—who is getting ridiculed, bullied, or ignored.

Your heart goes out to just about everyone around you, and, if your crayon box is empty, it's because others are enjoying the colors.

Intensity of Soul

Imagine you're seven years old and watching *The Wizard of Oz* for the first time. As each character collects the attribute he or she wants most—a brain, a heart, a home—one big question comes to your mind: "If the Cowardly Lion gets the courage he seeks, what's to stop him from eating Dorothy and Toto?!" And maybe when you were four, you wondered, "Do people feel the same way right before they are born and right after they die?" or "What does it really mean to be alive?" or "If God made the world, then who made God?" These are the kinds of questions asked by people with intensity of soul. Their logical leaps and deep ponderings often cause others to ask, "How on earth did you ever come up with *that* idea?"

If you identify with this intensity, you've likely been seeking to understand the meaning of life since you were very young, perhaps while you were also learning how to tie your shoes. Your "Why?" questions are constant, and even if the answers are elusive, you still find the questions worth asking. People may observe that you have "an old soul in a young body," which you take as a supreme compliment—because it is so. You might find yourself hanging out with older teens and adults who take your questions as seriously as you do, and reading books that deal with philosophy, ethics, religion, and other esoteric topics. You have a state of mind and being where nothing is definite and every theory has an equally plausible opposite one. You live in the land of limbo—forever questioning, questioning, questioning...

Intensities Are Totally Normal for *You*

A few disclaimers about intensities: they are *not* a prerequisite to being gifted, even though most gifted people we know have one or more of them. Likewise, people who have not been identified as gifted also may have any number of these intensities. We present them here as separate entities, yet in the real world, they often overlap. If you experience one or more of these intensities, it will be in varying degrees and at different times of your life. Some may hibernate for a while, depending on your life's circumstance, but they will eventually wake up. You can't simply discard them. Finally, as inconvenient as these intensities may sometimes be, they are, in the end, a huge part of the person you are.

True, at times intensities can be unwelcome or embarrassing. For example, if you and some friends are watching a movie and a particularly touching scene leaves you bawling like a baby, you might wish you could be touched a little less. Or, if you are in your social studies class and begin preaching on the need for deficit reduction and economic austerity, the kid next to you might poke you and say, "Dude ... *Nobody. Else. Cares.*" At times like these, you may begin to wish you could just be "normal."

"SOMETIMES I WONDER IF 'GIFTED' IS CODE FOR BEING SOCIALLY WEIRD."
—*Cameron, 15*

Well, guess what: you *are* normal. Having intensities does not mean you are abnormal. If you think, feel, hurt, or enjoy life in a higher key than most, that is who you are. Respect your own individual normality. Statistically, you may be in the minority—gifted kids, by definition, already are—which makes you atypical from others your age. However, there is a huge difference between the words *abnormal* (which few people aspire to be) and *atypical* (which means being unique or distinctive). If you can accept the fact that intensities are often a part of growing up gifted, you are more likely to see them as benefits versus burdens.

Let Your Freak Flag Fly

In 1970, Crosby, Stills, Nash and Young released a song titled "Almost Cut My Hair." The band members, of course, chose not to cut their hair, as society would've liked them to, and instead, to quote a lyric from the song, to "let their freak flag fly" and celebrate rebellion and individuality. Twenty years later, in 1990, that lovable, flatulent green ogre Shrek let *his* freak flag fly in movies and a Broadway musical—which featured the song "Almost Cut My Hair"—showing countless millions of viewers that although differences are not always convenient, they make each of us the person that we are.

With intensities, you can follow Shrek's lead and embrace your uniqueness. How to do this? Here are some suggestions:

Surround Yourself with Other People Who Have Intensities

When gifted kids talk about why they enjoyed their gifted programs in school, they seldom mention the cool projects or advanced lessons they were taught. Instead, they mention finally finding connections with other kids who "got it"—meaning other kids their age who understood their humor, who also had passions for particular subjects, and who were easily frustrated when others didn't see the bigger picture of a situation.

Eric, a gifted eighth grader, said: "Before attending this gifted program, I always felt isolated knowing that many people didn't understand what I was thinking or saying. But these barriers were stripped away as I found other people in my gifted class who spoke and thought as I did. I no longer had to think my ideas through before I spoke for fear of being misunderstood. I could speak freely . . . I found a refuge."

Whatever you call it—your refuge, haven, sanctuary, safe place—you need to find others who share your passions and intensities. Some of these supersensitive peers might exist in your school, in higher-level classes or clubs and organizations that cater to intellectual or artistic pursuits. Or, they may not be formally identified as gifted students but clearly share your interests with fervor. Some may not be in school at all, but are homeschooled instead, while others may be found in summer programs specifically for gifted kids. Still more will be hanging around college campuses, which is a great incentive to take some university coursework while you are still in high school. And if your world includes online conversations, you might look into blogs or chat rooms whose participants are eager to fly their freak flags at full mast. (See page 253 for social networking suggestions.)

Locate an Adult Who Reminds You of You

Intensities don't appear and disappear in random fashion. If you have them as a kid, you'll have them as an adult. So take a look around: which grownups in your life, whether you know them through school, family members,

Scouts, community classes, or sports, really seem to enjoy being passionate individuals in their pursuits? Which of these adults, in talking with you, works to break down the barriers that can exist between adults and teens, and they actually talk to you as the intelligent person that you are? Which of these adults interacts with you not because it is his or her role to do so, but because the person actually seems to *enjoy* your conversations? If you have such an adult in your life, connect with him or her and mention how and why you appreciate interacting with someone who treats you with respect.

Do Something Positive

Intensities are most frustrating when they are not being expressed in a positive way. For example, if you are disturbed about the lack of concern in your community about recycling, who can you approach to make a positive change? City council? Your neighbors? Even if you make just a small dent in the amount of trash tossed away, it is a bigger impact than if you had done nothing at all. *Proactive* beats *reactive*, any day.

Maybe you've never tried out for a school play, although the Drama Club's next production of *David and Lisa* has a lead character that fits you perfectly. Now's the time to audition. You can't get a role you didn't try out for in the first place.

Are your school's Advanced Placement options limited, or its honors courses available in only one or two subjects? Meet with the National Honor Society faculty advisor to see what it takes to move forward in getting more substantial courses offered for students, like you, who are ready to take them.

The bottom line is: your intensities are at their best when they are being explored, not ignored. As risky as it might be to show your differences and thus stand out from the crowd, isn't it worse to deny those parts of you that make you . . . *you?*

Educate Yourself

Intensities are a well-researched, vibrant area of inquiry that psychologists, educators, and psychiatrists have explored for generations—but is only now getting its full exposure. See page 250 for some resources you can check out to learn more.

Gifted People SPEAK OUT "Harnessing Your Passions"

by Zach Ricci-Braum

I see things differently, and I know I do. That's the great gift, as well as the trouble with being gifted. There are so many instances where I love having such a complex and deep view of life's situations, and others where I wish that I could see things simply.

Just think of the eye of a hurricane: a small area of calm in the midst of a tumultuous storm. It's the same with my emotions. There is such a high level of intensity, but inside of all of it, I can find a tiny place where I feel completely comfortable. All this emotion is useful in that I find it easy to be sympathetic to my friends' problems, and also to give pretty good advice. In most cases, I like being able to help them, but other times, it becomes burdensome. Whatever the case may be, they are my friends and I want to be there for them. I need to be there for myself, too. It might sound silly, but I really can't begin to help others if I am unwilling to look at myself and my own emotional problems. Well not so much *problems* . . . maybe more like challenges.

One of my biggest challenges is that I pick up on emotional subtleties that others—whether my peers or adults—miss. This can really put me in an awkward place, especially if the adult (or friend, for that matter) is trying to hide what is going on. I know there is more than the person is letting on, and I feel that they need someone to talk to about it. I've been met with thankfulness as well as anger. A girl, I'll call her Sara, was acting a bit off from her usual happy self. She still greeted me with a smile, but behind her expression was angst. I asked Sara what was wrong and she became defensive, responding, "Nothing. I'm fine." I knew inside that something wasn't right and that she was lying to me. She eventually decided to share what was causing her anguish. It turned out that her parents were considering a divorce, something that I am familiar with. All she needed was someone to vent to, but she didn't want to seem weak by asking for help. She was so relieved after she talked to me.

Unfortunately, some people do not find this kind of attention to their emotional state helpful. A much younger me, around age 12, picked up (by observation) that an adult in my life was lonely. She didn't act like it or pine publicly, but I saw in her kind face that she had something missing. While talking to her, I mentioned that a cousin of mine was living alone, and that she said it was lonely. I asked her if she was lonely. She became upset with me, and told me that it was rude to say things like that. I know now why she became upset. A 12-year-old told her what she was trying to ignore herself. She *was* lonely. But I never brought the issue up again.

If this ever happens to you, don't be afraid to act on your emotions, but do so in a manner that's just as subtle as the emotional signals you are picking up. Instead of doing something bold and public for the person, ask quietly and privately if there is anything you can do to help. Then, respect his or her answer. This is always the hardest part for me; I want to help so badly. You'll find that some people do want help, so be selfless and help them. You'll benefit greatly if you don't act in your own self-interest. I have.

It's all about harnessing the intense passion of your emotions and using it for good. I've found that I can locate that "eye of the hurricane" I mentioned before by taking in a situation that confuses me and thinking about it, talking about it, and becoming the master of my own thoughts. Of course this doesn't work all of the time, but when it does, I feel much better.

Life is a series of important emotional events and revelations. I know that I have come upon a great deal of these early in my life. Sometimes I think I'd be better off without the depth of understanding I have, but I always come around to knowing that it is my capacity to understand and see what others don't that makes me the person I am. And I would never trade that for anything.

Zach Ricci-Braum is currently attending West Virginia University for a degree in mechanical engineering on full Air Force ROTC scholarship. He is looking to earn his master's degree in four years. An Ohio native, Zach will always have a warm spot in his heart for his home state.

You've Got Personality

In addition to intensities, other character markers of gifted people show up in the category of "personality types." You might have heard of the Myers-Briggs assessment, which is the most famous model of personality type theory and is frequently used in workplaces, therapist's offices, career counseling centers, colleges, and schools. According to this theory, 16 types of personality account for most individual differences. You are born with your type and it remains your natural preference throughout your life, although it can shift somewhat if you work at it. Your MBTI (Myers-Briggs Type Indicator) is divided among four main "preferences":

Extrovert **(E)** or Introvert **(I)** *How are you energized?*	Sensor **(S)** or Intuiter **(N)** *How do you take in information?*
Thinker **(T)** or Feeler **(F)** *How do you make decisions?*	Judger **(J)** or Perceiver **(P)** *How do you orient to the outer world?*

For example, a person's type might be an ENTP or an IFSJ. Gifted people are represented in each of the 16 types. However, studies have shown some interesting findings among gifted individuals[*]:

★ They are most likely an **N** and a **P**, which alone puts them in a unique group, as the majority of the U.S. population is S and J.

★ They have a higher chance of being an **I** than do members of the general population, especially if they are gifted males.

★ They have a greater tendency toward **T** than do members of the general population—especially if they are gifted females. There are more "thinking" females among gifted people than in the larger populace.

★ If they are gifted males, they have a higher likelihood of being an **F** than do males in the general population. There are more "feeling" males among gifted people than in the larger populace.

What Are the Benefits of Knowing Your Type?

If you'd like to find out your Myers-Briggs type, you'll need to complete the assessment, which consists of a series of questions about all of your likes, dislikes, habits, tendencies, skills, and difficulties. It can provide you with many benefits, such as these:

Gain self-acceptance. Understanding your strengths and your "stretches" (those qualities outside of your natural preferences that you may need to stretch for to attain) can help you combat perfectionism and accept yourself for who you are.

[*]Sak, Ugur. "A Synthesis of Research on Psychological Types of Gifted Adolescents." *The Journal of Secondary Gifted Education.* 2004 15(2) 70–79.

Increase achievement. By training yourself in your non-preferred "stretch" areas (these are often **S** and **J** activities for gifted people), you can meet and even exceed expectations in school and life that may be difficult for you.

Improve your emotional and social intelligence (EQ and SQ). When you know your natural personality preferences, you may better understand feelings of isolation or frustration and be more able to communicate them to others. You may also develop more empathy and respect for other people.

Have fun! As we've said, you might be surprised how much fun learning about your personality type is. Afterward, discuss your results with a parent, teacher, counselor, or a trusted friend or two. They may already know their own types or be interested in learning them. Then, you might choose to check out some resources on MBTI together and marvel at your interesting differences in personality and your compatibility with other types.

Remember: Your type reflects your *preferences* only; your behavior is always a choice. Personality type is never an excuse for bad behavior. Also, keep in mind that personality type theory is just that: a *theory*, with its proponents and detractors. And it's not meant to be used to "boil you down" into a mere four-letter acronym. No psychological theory is that powerful, thankfully!

Once an Ogre . . .

Following up on our Shrek analogy . . . if you've watched *Shrek 2*, you may recall that in the midst of a spat, Fiona tells Shrek he is acting like an ogre. Shrek's reply is: "Well, whether your parents like it or not, I *am* an ogre. And guess what, Princess, that's not about to change." A leopard can't change its spots, an ogre can't change his greenness, and a gifted teen cannot change the fact that he or she may be sensitive, probing, inquisitive, or passionate, and may have preferences toward introversion, perceptiveness, or intuitiveness. So you might as well get used to these things. They are as much a part of you as are your height and eye color. Freak flag? It's time to *fly!*

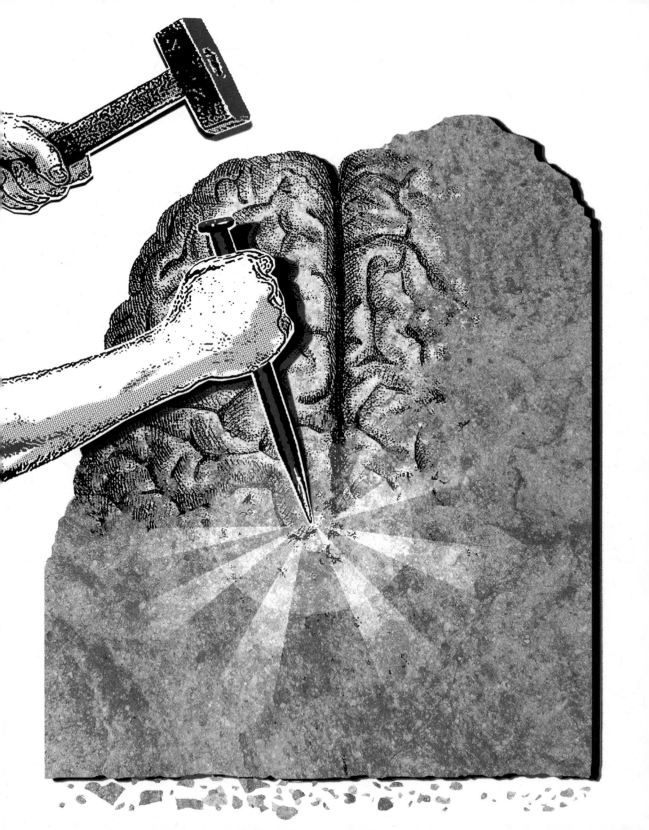

chapter 4
How to Shape a Gifted Brain

Now that you know a bit about how your mind, heart, and soul work, it's time to slip behind the scenes to take a look at the source of it all, the "wizard behind the curtain"—your brain. What? You think it can't be looked at while it's inside your head? You're in for a surprise. New technology called fMRI (functional magnetic resonance imaging) now enables researchers to study brains in detail *as they're developing*—including the brains of gifted young people. As you might suspect, giftedness is not just a label; it's a neurological trait.

Brains on Fire

If you were to see an fMRI of your brain, the first thing you would notice is bright red blazes bursting across the image. These red patches represent millions of tiny combustion events, or "fires," in which glucose is being metabolized into fuel for your brain. Basically, it would look like your brain is on fire, for gifted brains are extremely active metabolizers.[*]

The next thing you might notice, if you placed your fMRI alongside the brain fMRI of a teen of average intelligence, is that your *prefrontal cortex*—the front area of your brain where your forehead is—is slightly thicker. This does not mean your brain is any better or worse than the other teen's brain; it simply goes through a different development process.

Here's the deal: People used to think that the brain went through only one huge growth spurt from birth to age 18 months and then underwent a lengthy

> **The Survey Says . . .**
> **70%** of respondents want to know more about brain development and how the brain works.

---

[*]Eide, Brock, and Fernette Eide. "Brains on Fire: The Multimodality of Gifted Thinkers." *New Horizons for Learning*, Johns Hopkins University School of Education, December 2004.

Your Brain by the Numbers

100 billion = estimated number of neurons in the average adult brain

1.8 million = estimated number of neural connections an infant creates *per second*

10^{81} = estimated number of possible connections just 60 neurons are capable of making

10^{80} = estimated number of particles in the observable universe*

pruning process, keeping some circuits and letting go of others. Thanks to new studies using fMRI scans, we now know there is a *second* wave of growth, which mainly involves a thickening of your prefrontal cortex. This wave begins around age seven and, in most kids, reaches its peak around age eight or nine, before it starts its pruning process. But as a gifted kid, you had a prefrontal cortex that started out thinner than other kids', and then it kept growing until its peak at around age 12. This extended period of growth likely helped your brain develop more complex circuits for high-level thinking. Once it reaches its peak, your brain's pruning process is remarkably swift and efficient.

Ultimately, all people's cortexes finish developing around age 30 and end up about the same thickness. In short, being gifted doesn't have as much to do with the size of your brain as with how your cortex matures. In fact, it's possible that in the future, a person's intelligence will not be measured by IQ tests or standardized exams, but by simple scans of her or his brain at certain ages. How cool is that?

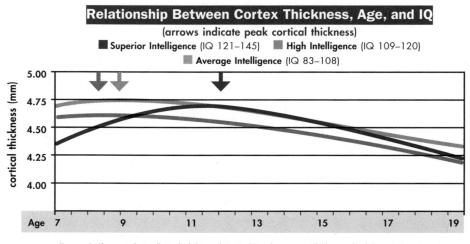

Relationship Between Cortex Thickness, Age, and IQ
(arrows indicate peak cortical thickness)
■ Superior Intelligence (IQ 121–145) ■ High Intelligence (IQ 109–120)
■ Average Intelligence (IQ 83–108)

Source: P. Shaw, et al. "Intellectual Ability and Cortical Development in Children and Adolescents," *Nature, 44* (March 30, 2006), pp. 676–679. Based on a longitudinal MRI brain study of 307 kids, ages 5–19.

*The numbers 10^{81} and 10^{80} are written in exponential form. For example, 10^{80} equals 10 x 10 x 10 x 10 . . . . [repeat 80 times]. In other words: it's a big number.

What This Means for You

On the simplest level, it means that lots of things are happening in your brain right now—if you're under 12, as a highly intelligent kid you're probably still in the midst of your second brain growth spurt; if you're over 12, you've likely embarked on a massive molting process that will last for the next 10 to 15 years. Several key areas of your brain are not even built yet, and you may be far more able to shape these parts of your brain than we ever thought possible.

If you're thinking: So what? Consider this: *Everything* you do as a teen has a direct impact on your brain, not just for the next school day or week or year . . . but for the *rest of your life*. You are literally molding your brain as you read this. And however you choose to use your brain as a teen will determine how it permanently develops. The cells you actively use will stay and the ones you don't will die off. Use it or lose it.

So if you spend your time making music, reading, playing a sport, studying, solving problems, and otherwise being actively engaged, then the brain cells and neural connections that support these activities will become hardwired. And if you spend your time lying on the couch playing *Resident Evil*, then the cells and circuits you're using for that activity are the ones that will survive. (*Note:* While this could serve you well in the face of a zombie apocalypse, in most other scenarios, your zombie fighting skills may not be very useful.)

We encourage you to take full advantage of this time! Ride the extended wave of neural development you are in. Think of yourself as the chief executive officer, or CEO, of your brain (after all, the prefrontal cortex controls your "executive" functions, such as organizing, strategizing, prioritizing, and managing outcomes) and get to work. It's time to streamline your operations, maximize your profits, focus on your goals, and broaden your horizons. Which departments (a.k.a. neural circuits) do you want to develop? Human Resources (a.k.a. social skills)? Data Analysis (a.k.a. math and science skills)? Research and Development (a.k.a. creative skills)? Pour your capital into those areas and let some other areas take a backseat. Get lean, mean, and agile, ready to bend with challenges that come your way.

If business isn't your thing, think of this pruning process as an art project—perhaps a sculpture. The recent explosion of new circuitry in your brain is like an unformed lump of clay that you can mold into any shape you wish. Just carve out the angles, shapes, curves, and lines where you want them. Move some clay (a.k.a. your energy and attention) away from one area of life or study and build it up in another, as you constantly refine your own unique sculpture.

Brain Pruning Tips

★ Make a list of your priorities and a list of your current strengths. Compare the lists—do they match up? If not, how can you make them match better? (*Note:* Just because you're good at something now doesn't mean you have to keep getting better at it. You probably developed many strengths when you were young, and some of them might not interest you much now. That's okay. You can let go of things.)

★ Sample as many ideas and activities as you can now, so you can begin building neural pathways to master them should you choose to. You likely have multiple potential talents and passions that you haven't even discovered yet.

★ At the same time, don't try to be an expert at everything. It's not possible and it's not the best use of your brain. It can be good to be a well-rounded person, but it's better to focus on being very good at a few things than being only adequate at a lot of things. Also, you may have a tendency toward mental overload and fatigue, so be aware of your limits and stay healthy.

★ Surround yourself with people who value learning and who can offer you support and guidance in whatever areas you choose to hone in on.

"I'M INTERESTED IN THE COGNITIVE WEAKNESSES THAT ARE FREQUENTLY LINKED WITH GIFTEDNESS, SUCH AS TROUBLE WITH MANAGING EMOTIONS OR ORGANIZATIONAL DIFFICULTIES." —*Shane, 16*

Where Is Your Mind?

Here you are smack in the middle of a neural revolution, and meanwhile life goes on. And you still don't have a fully formed brain. Sure you may have stellar grades, excellent study habits, impeccable social skills, creativity to spare, and a future scholarship to a prestigious school with your name on it, but do you sometimes *still* . . .

1. Lose your house key, get lost in the mall, or send not-so-smart text messages to your friends?

2. Stop in the middle of the sidewalk to pet a cute dog even though it means missing your bus?

3. Forget things left and right, like how to play a song on the piano that you used to know by heart?

4. Feel like everyone in the world is mad at you?

5. Feel so angry sometimes you want to punch a wall? Or so humiliated that you want to lock yourself up in your bedroom for the next 10 years?

6. Doze off daily in your morning classes at school?

Odds are that you answered yes to at least a few of these, and that you probably are assuming that it's all just because of hormones like everyone's been telling you for years. But they're wrong. It's also due in large part to your brain development. Here's a list of the *real* reasons you might experience things similar to those just listed and what you can do about it:

1. As we've already said, your prefrontal cortex is still forming, which aids things like organizing, strategizing, and controlling impulses. In addition, as a gifted person, you may be prone to emotional intensity, personal disorganization, and delayed processing (or "getting lost in thought"). Hence, why you might seem to be a little scatterbrained or impulsive sometimes.

SOLUTION: Keep to-do lists so you don't forget things. And ask others to play backup for you, especially adults and older friends and siblings whose brains may be a little more reliable in these types of situations. Ask for their company on errands, give them spare keys, and get their advice *before* hitting the "send" button.

2. At your age, dopamine levels in your brain are still not at optimum levels. *Dopamine* is a chemical that helps you prioritize where your attention should be directed. Also, as a gifted teen, you might be prone to distractibility.

SOLUTION: Try to recognize when you're feeling especially impulsive or distractible (this can happen when experiencing intense emotions—both positive and negative) and don't put yourself in dangerous situations, such as driving, walking, or biking in a busy area during those times.

3. Because your brain is in major molting mode, those skills you're not using regularly will begin fading away during this time, even given your perhaps better-than-average memory.

SOLUTION: Make a point to regularly practice those skills you want to retain.

4. Your teenage brain is less able than an adult brain to accurately interpret other people's facial expressions and vocal inflections. Moreover, your gifted brain may be hypersensitive to and intensely analytic of the emotions of people around you, even if you misjudge those emotions.

SOLUTION: Instead of constantly guessing what people are feeling, simply ask them. Then, marvel at the number of times you are way off base! Meanwhile, if you want to get a head start on correctly reading emotions, check out a fascinating methodology called the Facial Action Coding System (FACS). Visit face-and-emotion.com.

5. As a teen, you use a different area of your brain to process feelings than adults do. While adults rely mainly on the prefrontal cortex, you rely more on the *amygdala,* a region tied to memories of past emotions. For this reason, you may tend to be moodier, more impulsive, and less apt to consider the ramifications of your actions. For example, if your brother says something that makes you mad, your brain may instantly dredge up past memories of being mad at him, which only serves to make you madder. Plus, your intensities (if you have them) can sometimes contribute to a "feelings overload."

SOLUTION: Stop, breathe, think. Whatever the feeling is that is telling you to punch something or hide under your bed, it can be dealt with far more effectively in other ways. See pages 249–250 for ideas.

6. Teen brains require about an hour more of sleep per night than adult brains—roughly nine hours vs. eight. Also, your circadian rhythms are shifting so that melatonin (a hormone that regulates your sleep cycles) rises later in your brain than it did when you were younger; hence your brain is actually programmed to stay up later and sleep later. On top of this, as a gifted teen you may have a tendency to overload your schedule and barely leave enough time to sleep.

SOLUTION: Get more sleep, however you can. Aim for nine and a half hours a night, get nine on average, and settle for eight and a half on occasion. Keep in mind that just 40 minutes less than that may cause difficulties in school, including falling asleep in classes, and the effects can multiply over time. You might even campaign to get your school to start an hour later, as many schools have done recently. The benefits are well confirmed by research, so you won't have trouble proving your case with a little help from Google.

Gifted People SPEAK OUT "My Sleep Experiment"

by Anonymous

I'm highly gifted. For a long time, I had trouble relating to much of anyone because of this. I had very few social skills and no friends. Eventually, I realized that if I only slept four hours a night, it effectively gave me a partial lobotomy. Although my brain function decreased, I was still pretty smart. So I kept myself sleep deprived for a year and a half. In that time, I was able to form friendships. I paid attention to how different people reacted to different things. I learned to take someone who was hostile toward me and turn him into my best friend. In short, I became a social genius.

About four months ago, I was with a group of people comparable in intelligence to me. I got along with them great, as I could make a friend out of just about anyone I chose to. Unfortunately, I did not take full advantage of this opportunity. Being sleep deprived, I wasn't able to follow the truly complex conversations. I was still able to relate, but it could have been so much more. About a week later, I realized what I was missing out on. That night, I got a full night's sleep, and have almost every night since. Since then, I've actually been more social. Now, I can really pay attention, as opposed to dedicating half my mental energy to trying to stay awake. (As a sidelight, getting only four hours of sleep at night doesn't do much for one's physical appearance—and physical attraction, like it or not, does have something to do with social attraction. Getting enough sleep means I no longer look like a raccoon.)[*]

Gifted male, age 17

Important

Just because your teen brain is not fully formed and may cause you to experience certain difficulties, this does *not* excuse poor choices and irresponsible behavior. The same is true of having a gifted brain, which doesn't give you permission to get away with things others can't, or act in ways that are arrogant or insensitive. Learning about your unique gifted teen brain is simply a way for you to become more aware of your potential as well as your limitations, and to accept and celebrate them in equal measure.

[*]Adapted from *More Than a Test Score* by Robert A. Schultz, Ph.D., and James R. Delisle, Ph.D. (Free Spirit Publishing, 2007).

chapter 5
Taking Charge of Your Life

Although you can't control many things in your life—such as how thick your prefrontal cortex is, where you live, who your parents are, the legal driving age, the weather, and your math teacher's questionable taste in clothes—you *can* control or at least influence certain things, such as how you deal with expectations, success, failure, mistakes, schedules, habits, stress, and more. This chapter suggests ways for you to take charge of these elements in your life—by deciding what you want and need, being yourself, and building life skills.

> "PEOPLE EXPECT ME TO BE AN ORGANIZED, WELL-BEHAVED, WELL-DRESSED, PARTICIPATING PERSON WHO ACTS JUST THE WAY GIFTED PEOPLE ARE 'SUPPOSED TO,' NOT LETTING ANY PART OF MY INDIVIDUAL PERSONALITY COME OUT. BUT THAT'S JUST UNREASONABLE."
> —*Haleigh, 16*

The Survey Says . . .

51% of respondents want to know how to deal with people who think, "If you're so gifted, why don't you get straight A's?"

45% want to know more about the difference between perfectionism and striving for excellence.

46% want to know more about how to give themselves permission to fail sometimes and be easier on themselves.

54% want to know more about how to make better use of their time.

Great Expectations

Try as you may, you can't escape from the planners, plotters, prodders, predictors, strategists, and dreamers in your life. Parents, teachers, friends, neighbors, siblings, and strangers will try to tell you what to do (and not to do) with all that potential you have.

Potential. It's a word to love . . . and loathe. It implies that you have something to offer, so in that sense it's positive. But it can also be a burden, a drag, a voice urging you to try harder, work smarter, do better, go farther, and achieve more. As in:

You	The Voice
"I want to be an actor."	"You have the brains to be an astronaut."
"My grade point average is 3.6."	"It could be 4.0 if you applied yourself."
"I joined the student council."	"You should have run for class president."
"I got an A in my AP class."	"You could be going to college a year early instead."

The voice that diminishes your goals and achievements is seldom the voice of experience. It's the voice of *expectation*. Sometimes it comes from other people—teachers, parents, grandparents, aunts, uncles, siblings, or friends; but often it comes from within your own mind. If you listen too closely, you can end up making decisions and choosing paths that aren't right for you.

Expectations aren't all bad. They can provide us with goals to strive for, aims to achieve. But if you're a gifted teenager, they can also create demands that are difficult or impossible for you to meet. To make things worse, it's often the case that the harder you try to please adults, the more you alienate your friends. You've heard the names kids call each other: "brainiac," "brown-noser," and "miss (or mister) perfect." What's the solution? Should you defer to adults who insist on planning your future and determining your direction? Should you resist? Should you start doing less than you're capable of so the adults in your life will lower their expectations and your peers will accept you more readily?

It's not just the adults you know personally—your parents, other family members, and teachers—who put on the pressure. Our world is full of messages that exhort us to be number one. You've seen them on T-shirts and in advertisements: "If you can't win, don't play." "Second place is for the first loser." The athlete who earns Olympic gold is literally put on a higher pedestal than the silver and bronze medalists. At high school graduations, the valedictorian gives the commencement address instead of the salutatorian, whose GPA might be within .003 of a point of the valedictorian's. Awards, honors, salaries, promotions, and success seem to depend on being the smartest, fastest, strongest, most beautiful, most popular, etc. Although nothing is wrong with extolling the accomplishments of winners, there is something unhealthy with believing that first place is the only place worth being.

How can you deal with this attitude when it's thrust upon you by others? Here are three suggestions:

> "I don't know the key to success, but the key to failure is trying to please everybody."
> ★ BILL COSBY,
> ACTOR AND COMEDIAN

Listen Selectively

There are probably people in your life who feel that they, and they *alone*, know what's best for you, now and in the future. They'll warn you that "colleges are getting more choosy," so you must earn straight A's in everything but lunch. They'll insist that the career you want to pursue may not be challenging enough for "someone with your talents," so you'd be better off with cardiology or corporate law. They'll pay you $20 for each A on your report card but only $1 for Bs. In countless other direct and subtle ways, they'll try to convince you to strive for their standards of success. Fortunately, nature has given you two ears. What goes in one can escape out the other.

Are we proposing that you ignore these people? Yes . . . and no. If you truly respect their knowledge, experiences, and opinions, then by all means listen. If you don't, nod enthusiastically (the better to dislodge their words from your brain and ease their exit), then excuse yourself as soon as you can.

Speak Up

Even people whose opinions you value can sometimes go too far. Out of deference to their age or position, you may remain as mute as a ventriloquist's dummy. Or, since you're no blockhead, you may decide to speak up.

For example:

> **Dad says:** "Your grades are good this time, but I noticed you dropped down a grade in Spanish."
>
> **You say:** "The final was a killer."
>
> **Dad says:** "Maybe if you studied more . . . "
>
> **You say:** "I did study. I did the best I could."
>
> **Dad says:** "I believe you, but I'm concerned that these lower grades will become a pattern."
>
> **You say:** "Dad, can I be honest with you? When you say you're worried that my grades will keep dropping, it sounds like you think I'm just fooling around and not being responsible."
>
> **Dad says:** "That's not what I mean . . ."
>
> **You say:** "But that's how I feel. Believe me, I want to do well in school, too. But there will be times when I'll do better . . . and times when I'll do worse. Just trust that I'm still the responsible kid you thought I was last quarter."
>
> **Dad says:** "And if you need help . . . ?"
>
> **You say:** "I'll ask you for help—except in Spanish, since you're clueless in that department. *¿Comprende?*"
>
> **Dad and you:** [Laughter.] (Hopefully!)

In this scenario, Dad learns that the message he means to send ("I'm concerned about you") can easily be interpreted as "Why aren't you working up to your potential?" or "You're not good enough." Your willingness to talk things over shows maturity and affirms that you and he aren't adversaries after all.

Find Allies

When you're being assailed by others' expectations, you need someone who will be on your side. Find a sympathetic friend, a supportive teacher, an understanding neighbor or family member—anyone who will listen and encourage your efforts without trying to direct them. What if you can't find allies? Try developing imaginary ones. *Seriously.* Think of historical or present-day figures you find inspiring, or admirable characters from fiction, then mentally enlist them as your advocates. Imagine them praising you and cheering you on. In time, relying on these imaginary allies can help you learn how to obtain the help you need from real people.

Gifted People SPEAK OUT

"Off-Center & Smudged"

by Amanda Rose Martin

Of all the things I've ever done, I've never been terrible at any of them. The few things that managed to go over my head were polished off with a bit of extra study and work. Almost everything else that I had attempted in my life came easily. Reading, writing, history, science, foreign languages—most subjects were so simple to me that I could do them in my sleep. Surprisingly enough, the first class that I was terrible at was photography; that was where I realized for the first time that I wasn't perfect. And I panicked.

An elective taken in your senior year shouldn't be your hardest class, but for me it was. Walking into the darkroom for the first time was overwhelming. All of the machines were foreign to me and the enclosed space smelled overpoweringly of chemicals. I made my way over to an enlarger and prodded it until another girl took pity on me and helped me locate the button that turned the light on. That day, I ruined about 10 sheets of photo paper—not a cheap thing to waste. I kept exposing the papers to light, which then turned black in the developer. All of these failed attempts I threw into the trashcan, disgusted with the outcome and with my incompetent self.

Somehow, one photograph managed to turn out right. I tossed the paper into the developer and slowly shifted the plastic bin from side to side. It took about 20 seconds, but a picture started to appear. I held my breath as the picture continued to develop. One minute in the chemicals and I picked it up. It was a waterfall scene I had taken the week before. The picture was sharp and in focus. Elated, I completed the development process and showed the finished product to my teacher.

"Now *that's* a job well done!" he said.

When my teacher smiled at me and handed me back my photograph, I realized something. Not many things in my life had meant as much to me as that picture *because I had to work for it*. For the first time in my life, I had been clueless and confused. For the first time in my life, I had to fight for my grade and for my own mastery of a subject. And, for the first time in my life, something else happened . . .

As I admired my photograph, I realized that its borders weren't even. There were white dust specks that had made their home on my lovingly developed negative. There was a small smudge in the corner where I had dropped the photo paper into a small spot of water. Yet I realized that in spite of all this imperfection, I cherished my photo. I was proud of my accomplishment, even with its flaws.

Those first few weeks of photography class were extremely difficult for me, but in the end, I discovered something that would be more important to me than my grade. Before this experience, I felt everything I did had to be perfect; in fact, *being* perfect was a necessity to me, as essential to life as breathing. I found, though, that I was wrong with this assumption. I found that *imperfection* gives something character, a personality and a story. The defects in my photograph added to, not subtracted from, my accomplishment.

Prior to this, I often wondered how my parents could love me in spite of my flaws—my bluntness, my love affair with books, and my too-trusting nature. Now I understand that their pride in me has nothing to do with perfection; rather, it has to do with the hard work and challenges that it took to get where I am today.

> I often wondered how my parents could love me in spite of my flaws—my bluntness, my love affair with books, and my too-trusting nature.

My photograph (it now has a place on the wall above my bed) is in focus and its subject is sharp. Yes, it may be a bit off center. Sure, there may be a few dust spots on it. And, of course, that small smudge in the corner will always be there. But after all that, this photograph is still something to show the world.

I am that photograph, off-center and smudged, but all-the-better for it.

Amanda Rose Martin graduated from Case Western Reserve University with degrees in English and psychology and is currently pursuing a law degree. Over the years, she has learned to embrace her own imperfections as well as the auto-focus on her digital camera.

The Perfectionism Plight

If there are two surefire truths in life, they are: nobody's perfect, and everyone fails sometimes. But if you're similar to many gifted teens, you might need help learning how to let yourself fail, not to be so hard on yourself, and not to set your own expectations so high. As demanding of you as other people are, you may be even harder on yourself. You might even be a perfectionist.

 QUIZ Are You a Perfectionist?

Answer the following yes or no questions in a notebook. Don't think about the questions too much; answer with the first thing that pops into your head, because that's most likely to be the truth for you.

1. Do you set unreasonable, impossible goals for yourself?

2. Are you often not satisfied with even a great result?

3. Do you have difficulty enjoying the present moment because you're preoccupied with overcoming the next hurdle?

4. Do you avoid taking risks (academically and/or socially) because you fear "failing," "not being the best," or "not doing it well enough"?

5. Do you take an all-or-nothing view: "If I can't do it perfectly, there's no point in doing it at all"?

6. Are you highly self-critical and preoccupied with expectations (your own and others')?

7. Are you often critical of others?

8. Are you highly competitive and constantly comparing yourself to others?

9. Do you experience a lot of stress and anxiety?

10. Are you often afraid of making mistakes?

11. Are you often afraid of revealing your weaknesses or imperfections?

12. Do you procrastinate because of your need to do something perfectly?

13. Are you prone to depression?

14. Do you have difficulty in relationships because you expect too much of yourself and others?

15. Do you feel that your self-worth depends on performance?

16. Are you highly sensitive to criticism?

17. Do you have difficulty accepting that love can be unconditional?

18. Are you a compulsive planner?

19. Do you have difficulty seeing situations, performances, and projects in terms other than "good" or "bad"?

20. Are you dissatisfied with situations and relationships that are not "ideal"?

If you answered "yes" to many or most of these, you likely deal with some level of perfectionism in your life.

Perfectionism affects many people, not only gifted individuals, and psychologists and educators have long argued about how and where it begins. Is it self-inflicted or other-inflicted? (Do people choose to be perfectionists, or are perfectionists "made" by their parents, teachers, etc.?) Whatever its source, perfectionism can block your way to success and threaten your peace of mind.

> "I EXPECT PERFECTION FROM MYSELF, WITH THE NORMAL AMOUNT OF EFFORT. I'M TRYING TO STOP THINKING THIS, BUT I CAN'T."
> —Micah, 14

If you never can settle for anything less than first place, you're in for a lot of disappointment. Perfection simply isn't possible. And even when you do reach the top, you may find that holding on isn't worth the effort. Fortunately, there's help for perfectionists. What it takes is the will and ability to put things into perspective. Here are some examples:

EXAMPLE 1: You see yourself as an A student—until the day you get your first B+. You're shocked, stunned, and furious with yourself. *But wait:* What did you get that B+ in? Rotation Biology II? Advanced Placement Medieval Literature? A course in which all of the material was new to you or especially challenging? It makes a difference. Alternately, some gifted students report that the *less* challenging classes are sometimes more difficult for them to earn top grades in, because they are less motivated to put forth the required effort.

EXAMPLE 2: For years, everyone has been telling you what a terrific athlete you are. You start high school expecting to letter in every sport you participate in, from football to jujitsu. *But wait:* Do you know any athletes who are good at everything? Even Olympic athletes tend to specialize in one sport. Have you ever heard of an ice skater who was also a sumo wrestler? Or a championship swimmer who went from the pool to the soccer field with equal ease?

EXAMPLE 3: You're nominated for student council president—and you lose the election. You feel dejected, rejected, and embarrassed. *But wait:* Out of the dozens or even hundreds of students in your class, you were among the two or three whose names appeared on the ballot. That's something to be proud of. There's a big difference between "I lost" and "I came in second (or third)."

A healthy alternative to perfectionism is the pursuit of excellence. Here are three important ways in which the two differ:

1. Perfectionism means thinking less of yourself because you earned a B+ instead of an A. **The Pursuit of Excellence** means thinking more of yourself for trying something new.

2. Perfectionism means being hard on yourself because you aren't equally talented in all sports. **The Pursuit of Excellence** means choosing some things you know you'll be good at—and others you know will be good for you or just plain fun.

3. Perfectionism means chastising yourself because you lost the student council election. **The Pursuit of Excellence** means congratulating yourself because you were nominated and deciding to run again next year—if that's what you want.

> "Striving for excellence motivates you; striving for perfection is demoralizing."
> ★HARRIET BRAIKER, CLINICAL PSYCHOLOGIST AND AUTHOR

How can you become a pursuer of excellence versus a prisoner of perfectionism? By:

★ determining the sources of your perfectionism

★ reassessing your feelings about failure and success

★ standing your ground against people who pressure you to be perfect

★ learning ways to be easier on yourself so you're free to take risks and try new things

Fear of Failure, Shy of Success

Much of what fuels perfectionism is fear—both the fear of failure and the fear of success. The two go hand in hand. Sometimes when you think you're avoiding something because you simply don't want to do it or don't have time to successfully complete it . . . deep down you may be afraid that if you try it, you'll fail. And other times when you say you're terrified to be imperfect and fail at something, in truth, you might be even more afraid to actually . . . succeed.

> "I WANT TO EMPHASIZE THE IMPORTANCE OF THE ABILITY TO FAIL. I ALWAYS PRESSURED MYSELF TO BE PERFECT AND IT WASN'T HEALTHY." —*Melissa, 17*

How Do You Feel About Failure?

Gifted people are often driven to perform and excel. To them, *fail* is a four-letter word. Taken to the extreme, the fear of failure can halt your forward motion and trap you in unchallenging classes and tasks. After all, if your teacher gives you a choice of homework assignments, why take a risk on the most difficult one when you're guaranteed an A on the basic one? It's safer to stick with the sure thing, right? Sure it is. But it's also the surest way to turn off your brain and bore yourself silly . . . and never know what you might truly be capable of.

The most successful people are those who have figured out how to *face* failure—to live with it, take it in stride, and learn from it. They realize that the road to achievement is paved with mistakes. They trip over them, pick themselves up, and move on.

Ask yourself: How do you feel when your performance is less than flawless? What can you tell yourself the next time you don't do as well as you hoped you would? How can you develop a healthier, more positive attitude toward the possibility—and the reality—of imperfection?

> "We don't make mistakes. We just have learnings."
> ★ANNE WILSON SCHAEF, PSYCHOTHERAPIST AND AUTHOR

The Value of Mistakes

Question: What do these six things have in common?

cheese	chocolate chip cookies
Coca-Cola	penicillin
Post-it Notes	Silly Putty

Answer: All six were discovered or invented by mistake.[*] According to Mark Twain, accident is the greatest inventor who ever lived. In *Mistakes That Worked*, author Charlotte F. Jones points out that accident (not necessity) is the mother of invention.

Here are more reasons why mistakes are great:

★ **Mistakes are universal.** Everybody makes them, from preschoolers to presidents. They give you something in common with the rest of the people on our planet.

Failures or . . . ?

Thomas Edison tried 1,500 different filaments for the lightbulb before finding the right one. After the final experiment, an assistant asked, "Mr. Edison, how do you feel about having 1,500 failures to your credit?" Edison replied, "They weren't failures. We now know 1,500 lightbulb filaments that don't work."

[*]Google each one to find the story behind its invention. You may be surprised!

★ **Mistakes show that you're learning.** Whether you incorrectly apply a geometry theorem or say something foolish in front of someone you're trying to impress, a mistake is a point of information that inspires you to do better the next time you're in a similar situation.

★ **Mistakes show that you're trying something new or different.** It's rare that you (or anyone else) will accomplish something perfectly on your first attempt. If you had spent your whole life doing only those things you could master on the first try, you never would have learned to walk, read, or ride a bicycle.

★ **Mistakes allow you to see your own improvements.** If you had filmed your first attempt at the backstroke, then filmed yourself after three months of swimming lessons, you'd notice a significant change for the better.

★ **Mistakes allow you to learn from others.** Often, gifted students are reluctant to seek help from others, believing that asking for help is tantamount to admitting failure. That belief is mistaken.

The Five Stages of Making a Mistake

Stage 1: The deed. You goof, err, blow it, slip up, screw up, stumble, bumble, or otherwise make a mistake.

Stage 2: Embarrassment. You blush, cry, cover your face with your hands, withdraw, or run away. You are absolutely convinced that people will remember your mistake for the rest of your life.

Stage 3: Denial or downplay. You refuse to acknowledge your mistake ("I could have gotten 100 percent on that math test; I just didn't want to set the curve too high for the rest of the class"), or you blame your mistake on some convenient other (your sister, your teacher, your dog), or you proclaim your indifference to the fact that you flubbed ("So what? I'm only human"). But deep down inside, where no one else can see, you hold onto the self-appointed title of "World Champion Dolt."

Stage 4: Laughter. This usually occurs anywhere from one minute to one year following your mistake. It all depends on the mistake. You can overcome minor infractions (a lower-than-usual test grade, a stupid remark made at a party) within a week. For bigger blunders (destroying someone's confidence, getting caught doing something expressly forbidden by your parents or teachers), it can take many months before you're able to crack a smile. Even then, the laughter doesn't minimize the seriousness of your mistake; it's just a step in the healing process.

Stage 5: Acceptance. Again you proclaim, "I'm only human," only this time you really mean it. You know that you messed up in a minor or major way, you apologized for an error in judgment if it was appropriate, but you also know that mistakes are a part of life . . . thank goodness.

How Do You Feel About Success?

"Our deepest fear is not that we are inadequate. Our deepest fear is that we are powerful beyond measure. It is our light, not our darkness that most frightens us. We ask ourselves, 'Who am I to be brilliant, gorgeous, talented, fabulous?' Actually, who are you not *to be? . . . Your playing small does not serve the world. There is nothing enlightened about shrinking so that other people won't feel insecure around you. We are all meant to shine. . . . And as we let our own light shine, we unconsciously give other people permission to do the same. As we are liberated from our own fear, our presence automatically liberates others."* —**Marianne Williamson, from** *A Return to Love*

This passage by author Marianne Williamson was famously quoted by Nelson Mandela in his 1994 presidential inauguration speech in South Africa after he fought heroically to end apartheid in his country. Mandela had spent most of his adult life in prison because of his belief in freedom and equality and fought against the evils of racism and bigotry. Do you think he feared his success? Do you think he had moments during his struggles for justice when he feared what might actually happen if he was victorious? Of course he did. Because with victory comes expectations and pressures and responsibilities to fulfill your promises. Once you succeed at something, people will expect you to *keep* succeeding . . . and what if you don't? You may think that the higher you climb, the farther you have to fall.

On a scale closer to home, imagine this scenario: Your history teacher asks you to direct a class play on the apartheid movement to be performed at the celebration of Black History Month in two months. You're thrilled to be asked—you enjoy bossing people around, which is what directors do—so you say yes. You're enthusiastic, you work hard, and the play is a hit.

And that's when the trouble begins. The drama teacher approaches you and invites you to join the drama club. They need a good director, and you've proven that you can more than handle the job . . . or so she says. You, on the other hand, are not so sure. Maybe the class play was a fluke. Maybe you got lucky. Maybe your success was due to the fact that you knew a lot about apartheid from the start. Maybe the crowd at the celebration event was easy to please, but the drama club is uncharted territory. Deciding that it's better to quit while you're ahead, you decline the invitation.

QUIZ Do You Fear Success?

Find out by taking this quiz. In your notebook, for each statement give yourself three points if you *strongly agree*, two points if you *somewhat agree*, and one point if you *disagree*. Don't think about the questions too much; answer with the first thing that pops into your head, because that's most likely to be the truth for you.

1. Other people enjoy my successes more than I do.

2. People expect too much of me.

3. Other people are generally more satisfied with my work than I am.

4. I'm worried that my successes are due to luck, and someday my luck will run out.

5. I'm not really as smart as people think I am.

6. Success can be a burden.

7. I seldom reach a level of performance that makes me happy.

8. I'd rather do something I know how to do than try something new.

Interpreting Your Score:

19–24 points: Whose life is it, anyway? Are you more interested in making other people happy than you are in pleasing yourself? Once those "other people" are no longer involved in your daily life, you'll still have to live with yourself and your choices. It's time to start making your own decisions—ones that are right for you.

14–18 points: It seems as if you're still struggling with the question of which goal should be your top priority—pleasing others or pleasing yourself. That's okay, as long as you maintain a balance between the two.

8–13 points: Some people would call you "self-assured," while others might label you "arrogant." Still, it does appear that you are your own person, and you're relishing your successes. Congratulations!

> "I was thought to be 'stuck up.' I wasn't. I was just sure of myself. This is and always has been an unforgivable quality to the unsure."
> ★BETTE DAVIS, ACTRESS

What to Say to Those Who Pressure You to Be Perfect

At times, brains can be a burden. Such as when people tell you how smart you are—and how smart they know you could be and should be. They mean well, but that's no excuse. You'd like to tell them to _____ (fill in the blank). Actually, it's okay to tell them how you feel, but it's best to do it diplomatically, politely, and succinctly. Here are some examples:

> "The principal mark of genius is not perfection but originality, the opening of new frontiers."
> ★ARTHUR KOESTLER, AUTHOR AND ACTIVIST

To your parents:

★ "I know you like it when I get A's, but I need you to understand that I worked just as hard for that C in Chinese as I did for my A's in other classes—maybe harder."

★ "I probably could have gotten an A in regular biology, but we all agreed that I should try the advanced course. I think I'm learning a lot, and I want to stay in it even though my grades aren't as high. I need your support."

To your teachers:

★ "I wish you wouldn't always call on me and expect me to know the answers. I feel pressured to perform all the time."

★ "Your pre-calculus course is a lot tougher than I thought it would be. I know it's worth the effort, but I feel like you always expect me to be the star student."

To your friends:

★ "Just because I'm a good student doesn't mean I spend every weekend with my nose in a book or my eyes glued to a computer screen."

★ "You're right, my grades were pretty good this period. Let's go shoot some hoops."

Be assertive, not aggressive; honest, not arrogant. Most of the people who are pressuring you may not be aware of how you feel.

10 Tips for Combating Perfectionism

1. Be average for a day. Allow yourself to be messy, late, incomplete . . . imperfect. Then celebrate your success.

2. Get involved in activities that are not graded or judged—activities that focus on process, not product.

3. Take a risk. Sign up for a course with a reputation for being challenging. Start a conversation with someone you don't know. Do an assignment or study for a test without overdoing it. Alter your morning routine. Start a day without a plan.

4. Give yourself permission to make at least three mistakes a day.

5. Stop using the word "should" in your self-talk. Remove "I have to" from your conversation and change the self-talk to "I choose to . . ."

6. Share a weakness or limitation with a friend. Recognize that he or she doesn't think any less of you as a result.

7. Acknowledge that your expectations of yourself might be too high, even unrealistic.

8. Savor your past accomplishments. Write about how good they made you feel.

9. Ask your friends to help you "cure" your perfectionism. Perhaps they can give you a sign or a word when they notice you are being a perfectionist.

10. Join the human race. It's less lonely when we accept our own and others' imperfections and feel part of life.

If you need more help combating your perfectionism, talk with your teacher, school counselor, psychologist, or social worker. Explain your situation and ask for suggestions.

The Matter of Your Mindset

One thing that often happens to gifted kids when they are young is that adults tell them constantly how smart they are. When you brought home your piles of papers in elementary school with stars or top grades on them, well-meaning parents or grandparents would extol the extent of your brain. They'd say things like, "How did you get to be so smart?" or they'd squeeze your cheek and predict that "your fine mind will take you far in life!" Little did they know that these constant compliments to your mind's prowess could actually serve to *inspire* perfectionism and undercut your future confidence and success.

Stanford University professor Carol Dweck has studied this phenomenon of what she calls *mindset* and here is what she finds . . . again and again: Kids who are told that they are smart tend to shy away from difficult subjects or tasks for fear they will not succeed, while those students who are rewarded for "trying hard" willingly accept complex assignments and activities, knowing that mistakes are a natural and expected part of learning.

This all comes back to a person's perspective on intelligence. If you believe that your high intellect was provided to you at birth—what Dweck calls a *fixed mindset*—you will do whatever you can to preserve the aura of being smart, including shying away from sports, academics, or social relationships that may challenge you and show you to be lacking in some way. However, if your view of intelligence is that you believe struggle and effort can actually *make* you smarter—what Dweck calls a *growth mindset*—then you are more willing to take on tasks where initial success is not guaranteed.

> "I THINK I WILL REMAIN AT THIS LEVEL OF INTELLIGENCE MY ENTIRE LIFE." —*Isabelle, 11*
>
> "PART OF BEING GIFTED IS THE ABILITY TO NEVER QUIT LEARNING." —*Karl, 17*

QUIZ
Are You a *Born-Smart* or a *Try-Hard?*

Read each statement and decide whether you mostly agree with it or disagree with it.

1. Your intelligence is something very basic that's hardwired at birth and basically stays the same throughout your life. *Agree or disagree?*

2. You can learn new things, but you can't really change how intelligent you are. *Agree or disagree?*

3. No matter how much intelligence you have, you can always do things to alter it. *Agree or disagree?*

4. You can substantially change how intelligent you are. *Agree or disagree?*

Do you agree more with questions 1 and 2? If so, you likely have more of a *fixed* or "born-smart" mindset. Do you agree more with questions 3 and 4? Then you may have a stronger *growth* or "try-hard" mindset. You can be a mixture, but most people lean toward one or the other.

An experiment: To test the effects of mindset, Dr. Dweck gave students a simple, nonverbal task where success was pretty much assured. One group of her students was praised for "being so smart" in completing the task well (in other words, using a fixed mindset), while the other group was rewarded for "trying hard" to get the job done (using a growth mindset). When these same groups were then asked which of two new problems they would like to complete—a hard one or an easy one—that's where things got interesting. The so-called born-smart students chose the easy assignment over the hard one, while the try-hard group dared to attempt the more difficult activity.

What in the world's going on here? Here is the distinction between the two groups: the born-smarts see failure as a *person*, while the try-hards perceive failure as an *event*. The born-smarts stop trying at the first hint of defeat, for if you never even complete a difficult task, no one will question whether you could have succeeded; therefore, your "smart" image is maintained. The try-hards are the more resilient of the two groups, living by the mantra of "If at first you don't succeed, try, try again." To the try-hards, it is both natural and acceptable to mess up on your path to learning something new and complex.

> **The born-smarts see failure as a *person*, while the try-hards perceive failure as an *event*.**

Failure deflates the ego of the born-smarts, while it just bounces off the self-images of the try-hards.

What This Means for You

Carol Dweck's theory of mindset has profound implications for gifted teens. Consider these scenarios:

SCENARIO 1: You have the option of taking an honors science course at school, where an A is not guaranteed, or enrolling in a relatively easy course of the same subject, where the content is less complex and you'll need little effort to get an A.

Q: *Which course do you take?*

SCENARIO 2: Ever since you can remember, you've received praise for your intellect and academic accomplishments, but when it comes time to consider colleges, you question whether you even want to apply to the most competitive ones. After all, what if you don't get accepted?

Q: *Which colleges do you apply to: the most competitive, where your admission is iffy, or a less-arduous school, where admission is guaranteed?*

If you find yourself opting for the easy A or the less competitive school, think about what you may be missing out on by just getting by with your intelligence instead of challenging it. Sure, you may get those top grades and score a spot at a good school, but what if you could've learned even more, gained richer experiences, and succeeded beyond *all* expectations? How will you know the true limits of your abilities if you never push them?

"I WILL NEVER STOP TRYING OR WASTE MY GIFTEDNESS BY BEING LAZY. [BEING GIFTED] WILL ULTIMATELY PUSH ME HARDER IN COLLEGE, WORK, AND EVERYDAY LIFE."
—*Brianna, 17*

Although Dweck's work did not focus much on how mindsets apply to other aspects of life, logic would predict the same results in other circumstances of risk taking. For example, why try out for a varsity sport where getting cut is common, when a junior varsity no-cut team is an option? Or, why stay in a friendship or relationship that is not very satisfying, but at least it gives you someone to be with on a Friday night? Branching out to other people is a risk, as they might not accept you, but is it a risk worth taking to discover new friends and allies?

Risk Taking vs. Risk Making

People often talk about risk taking, when what they should really be talking about is risk *making*. When you take a risk, the word *take* implies it was given to you by someone else—a teacher, coach, or parent who believes in you and wants you to do something that is important to *them*. In risk making, the person most interested in pursuing something new is *you*. Your "why not?" attitude allows you to challenge yourself to do something for your own benefit, whether or not others approve.

Perhaps this risk taking versus risk making distinction gets to the root of Dweck's ideas about why we do what we do when presented with challenges. So, consider the benefits and drawbacks of playing it safe and relying on a born-smart mindset versus taking the try-hard approach and exposing yourself to possible defeat. In the end, maybe being smart has less to do with accumulated knowledge and more to do with the willingness to forego perfection.

Gifted People SPEAK OUT "Escaping the Perfectionist Trap"

by Sarah Boon

Since you've picked up this book, you likely identify with being gifted. People may have high expectations of you and may pressure you to meet them. But if you're like me, that just doesn't fit the bill. It's like your mom giving you an iPod full of her music—she thinks you'll like it, but it's not really what suits you. This is where my problems started. To meet these high expectations, I fell into the perfectionist trap of trying to control situations and outcomes, people's expectations, and my ability to meet them. I felt compelled to avoid failure because it would disappoint people, and they might think I wasn't actually gifted after all!

This need for control can cause problems in other aspects of life, too—even the process of learning. I see many students who are aiming for an A+ and don't care how they get it. They come to my office and argue that—even though their answer is clearly wrong—they should still get full marks because it's actually correct based on their (incorrect) interpretation of the question. Or they argue it's my fault: the question uses different wording than what they heard in lecture or read in the textbook. But since most other students are doing fine, this clearly isn't the problem. These students are trying to control the situation: lectures, exams, assignments, and even me. All to get an A+ that will support their gifted label.

Yes, you're gifted. That's great! But don't let that be all you are.

What are these students really learning? How gifted are you if you've abandoned creativity and lateral thinking in order to focus exclusively on high grades? How does this single-minded perfectionism affect the other facets of your personality—the ones that make you a unique person? In my case it made me afraid to try new things because I might not excel—in fact I might even fail. I became afraid to express myself outside the narrow confines of my gifted personality because that's what people expected, and I didn't want to rock the boat.

Think about your own life. Maybe you want to play guitar in a garage band, but you don't because you figure you're probably not any good anyway, and plus everyone will think you've gone off the deep end because it's just "not like you." That's how perfectionism can kill the very giftedness it intends to perfect.

So how can you avoid—or extract yourself from—this trap? Speaking from experience, it isn't easy. But you can begin by taking some pressure off your gifted label, and instead thinking of your giftedness as just *one* facet of your personality that makes you a unique person, like having brown hair and blue eyes, or being a comedian versus a philosopher. What's your favorite ice cream, the book you hate the most? How do you learn best—doing, reading, or visualizing? What do you love doing that never feels like a chore? Mowing the lawn, helping cook a family dinner, working on cars . . . ?

In my junior high we were divided into three categories: gifted, average, or slow—nothing in between. But each of us can be *any* of these things—depending on the day, the subject, the teacher, or even what we had for breakfast. I've learned that being gifted isn't about being in a category. It's about how we deal with the challenges of everyday life: with enthusiasm, curiosity, and creativity. While we may not achieve perfection, what we learn from *not* doing well—adaptability, perseverance, humility—is what makes us human. It gets us farther in life than perfectionism and straight A's ever will, and teaches us something that many gifted kids forget—everything's *not* all about us.

Yes, you're gifted. That's great! But don't let that be all you are. You're a multifaceted, wonderful person with likes, dislikes, strengths, and shortcomings who just happens to encompass this word *gifted*. So get out there and enjoy yourself, find out who you are and what's important to you—outside of that gifted box—and run with it.

Sarah Boon, Ph.D., *is an assistant professor in the Department of Geography at the University of Lethbridge in Alberta, Canada.*

Managing Your Time Online & Off

Michel de Montaigne (quoted on the right) lived from 1533 to 1592, which only goes to show that time management is a timeless topic. However, because time management usually isn't taught in school, you'll probably need to learn and practice this important skill on your own. Fortunately, whole books and websites are devoted to this subject. Scan through some resources on time management to see which ones appeal to you. You might also benefit from asking people around you—people you view as productive and efficient—how they accomplish so much. It's likely they have developed a series of habits and attitudes about time use, and they may have helpful suggestions for you.

"It is possible that for persons who use their time well, knowledge and experience increase throughout life."
★MICHEL DE MONTAIGNE, French ESSAYIST

Certain trusted tactics (setting goals, handling papers and reading emails only once, making and prioritizing to-do lists, not procrastinating, etc.) are worth trying even if they don't seem very exciting. But the degree to which you improve your own use of time will largely be determined by your internal beliefs, not by mechanical steps or routines. These internal beliefs or values are what give you the power to do what needs to be done. Remember that what works for someone else might not work for you, keep trying various techniques you read about or hear about, and stay focused on your values until you find one or more methods that are a good fit with your learning style, personality, energy level, intellect, and needs.

- If we all have the same number of hours in a day, why do some people accomplish so much more than others?

- How do you define *accomplishment*? What does "effective time management" or "good time management" mean to you personally?

- What are some of the things that "steal" time from you? (Think about external and internal influences, interruptions, and distractions.) What can you do to keep your time from being stolen?

- Describe a day in which you managed your time exceptionally well. What specific actions made it possible for you to achieve your goals for that day?

Gauging Your Gadgetism

In today's world, it's impossible to talk about time management without considering the hours of time people spend online and attached to their electronic gadgets. You are probably sick to death by now of hearing about the trials and tribulations of living in the Information Age and the pitfalls of growing up as a "digital native." According to this familiar diatribe, you presumably spend every free second of your time wired into a smartphone, laptop, netbook, gaming console, tablet, or desktop computer. You cannot have a thought that's not texted, IM'd, or posted on Facebook, YouTube, or Twitter. And you lack the ability to form letters with a pen or spell out the phrase "talk to you later."

Of course, this is a stereotype. In reality, you probably do not spend quite as much time online as adults think you do. But by all accounts, you spend *far* more time than any generation before you.

Yet the fact of the matter is: you *need* technological skills to succeed in the modern world. Cell phones and the Internet have obvious advantages: convenient communication and access to the world's largest library of information. And through social networking, you're learning how to interact with others with various degrees of formality, how to manage a public identity, and how to present yourself and your interests and abilities. You're also improving your writing skills and visual composition skills (photography, graphic design, etc.). In addition, social networking sites may provide more freedom and autonomy than you receive at school, at home, or anywhere else. Most teens respect each other's authority online and are often more motivated to learn from peers than from adults.

All that said, the jury is still out as to how all this screen time and "gadgetism" is actually affecting your brain and your life.

Caution: Wide Cognitive Load

What research tells us is this: constantly having your attention interrupted by incoming texts, emails, Facebook comments, hyperlinks, RSS feeds, streaming ads, and other information bits prevents you from thinking on deeper levels. Instead, it keeps you trapped at a shallower, more reactive mode of thought. Why? Because each time you respond to an impulse to refresh your profile page or read an incoming text, you are activating a reward mechanism in your brain that dates back to your cave-dwelling days. Your reward is a tiny squirt of dopamine or adrenaline (the "feel good" chemicals) into the part of your brain that experiences pleasure—in this case, the pleasure of receiving attention or information from another person. And with each squirt, you want more . . . and more. This often leads to *multitasking,* which is just a fancy word for doing many different things at once—texting, surfing the Web, playing a game, composing a document, watching a video, listening to a podcast, etc.—jumping from reward to reward, often at a rapid rate. Meanwhile, your brain is absorbing an ever-increasing amount of information, which is called your *cognitive load.*

Constantly having your attention interrupted by incoming texts, emails, Facebook comments, and other information bits prevents you from thinking on deeper levels.

This would be all fine and good if your brain had an unlimited memory capacity. But it doesn't, no matter how intelligent you are. Your brain's computer can only hold so many bits of information in its memory at a time, and when your cognitive load exceeds this limit, your intellectual ability takes a hit. When you're multitasking and responding to chemical rewards, information begins flying in and out of your brain so quickly you never get the chance to get a good mental grip on it and turn it into actual knowledge. Hence, you retain less knowledge, grow more distracted, make more mistakes, and are less able to think critically. What's worse is that soon enough, when you're away from your phone or computer and unable to obtain the chemical squirts from multitasking, you may go into withdrawal and feel bored.

What Can You Do?

You know when you're multitasking too much—you might start getting a little dizzy from the quick vision shifts and you may find yourself getting distracted more frequently during every task you are trying to do, to the point of getting distracted from one task, only to get distracted from the distraction, and so on.

You also know when you hit a saturation point with any single activity (call it *monotasking*)—be it cruising your friends' Facebook pages for hours on end until your eyes start to bug out, or sitting and playing *Halo* for so long that you lose all feeling in your lower extremities. Your body and your brain will tell you when enough is enough, if you stay aware of the signals.

Keep in mind that *your* brain, in particular, which belongs to a gifted teen with possible intensities along with an immature prefrontal cortex (see page 77), may need *extra* awareness and coaxing to moderate and avoid impulsive behavior. Most of the time, you can combat cognitive overload by simply using common sense and taking breaks. Shut off and unplug your computer, put your phone in a drawer, go out for a walk or a bike ride, eat a snack, invite a friend over to play a board game—whatever you do, take your eyes and your brain away from the screen.

When You Really Need to Draw the Line Online . . .

★ During times that you desperately need to study or finish a project, hand over your electronic devices (yes, *all* of them) to a parent, sibling, or friend while you study, and tell them not to let you have them back until you've met a specified goal.

★ You might also ask a friend to change your password on a website you'd like to avoid. Be sure to also ask him or her to change your contact email address at the site, so you can't simply click the "I forgot my password" option and have it mailed to you. When you're ready to have access again, ask your friend for the password. Two students we know do this for one another on a weekly basis during exam time, so they can only spend time on Facebook on the weekends.

★ Another option is to install blocking software such as BlockSite, StopDistractions, and SelfControl on your computer to prevent yourself from visiting certain websites while you're trying to study for a test or finish a project. Of course, once you block a site like Facebook or

YouTube, you can always unblock it if you happen to lose your resolve . . . however, to do so, you usually need to restart your computer, which places at least one obstacle in the way of your distraction—and one obstacle is sometimes all you need to avoid temptation. You might also choose to let someone else (a parent, sibling, or friend) set the password for a blocking app so that you need to go through that person in order to disable it.

★ Take a social networking vacation, posting an away message on your Facebook page or Twitter feed indicating people can text or call you if they need to reach you. Another option is to go off one or more social networking sites altogether. If you choose to do this, be sure to let your friends and contacts know ahead of time and have a strategy in place for staying in communication with important people in your life.

★ Finally, ask for help from an adult who has better impulse control and can help you keep your online habits in check. Also, discuss with him or her any underlying reasons *why* you may be spending so much time online. For example, are you avoiding other issues in your life by hiding in cyberspace? Are you feeling unmotivated, lonely, or depressed? Do you suspect you might be experiencing Internet or gaming addiction? See the resources on page 251.

While these options may seem drastic or difficult at first, you'll thank yourself in the long run once you've finished that mammoth paper, aced that test, completed your novella, or mastered that cello suite!

Gaming for the Gifted

More than any other time spent with technology, gaming gets a bad rap. You know the stereotype: gamers are lazy, addicted, antisocial, and certainly not *gifted*. Right? Wrong. Most video games require players to constantly make decisions, think about patterns, set goals, consider resources, and then adjust their decisions based on feedback from the game. These strategizing skills are crucial in today's competitive world.

Even violent and offensive games challenge players to find the right strategies to use in a given situation and then to learn from their decisions. Other games mentioned by respondents in our survey teach elements of history, like *Assassin's Creed* set in

> "The importance of video games in the lives of anyone growing up in the 1990s and beyond is changing the way coming generations will work and manage data."
> ★ JOHN BECK AND MITCHELL WADE, AUTHORS OF *GOT GAME: HOW THE GAMER GENERATION IS RESHAPING BUSINESS FOREVER*

Renaissance Italy, while games such as *Portal* involve physics, and ones like *Fallout 3* let you create your own characters and narrative.

Aside from warranted concerns about their ethics, many popular video games have real educational merit and could probably even meet some national content standards. Moreover, many of them may serve to challenge gifted learners in ways that perhaps they aren't being challenged in school, while also preparing them for life beyond the classroom.

What to Say to Those Who Question Your Gaming Habit

Them: "Are you playing *Modern Warfare* again?"
You: "Umm . . . maybe. But just as a warm-up before I do my civics homework."

Them: "There are so many other more productive things you could be doing with your gifted brain, so why play video games?"
You: "My fluency in gaming is going to give me a distinct advantage over others in my future education, career, and social life."

(*Note:* You may wish to recite a short poem at this point, such as the one below—providing it does not interrupt your current gaming activity.)

Video games

that take me places away from harsh reality,

that allow me to be the kind of person I want to be,

that test my abilities,

that raise my awareness level,

that teach me strategy,

that improve my hand-eye coordination,

that teach me math skills,

that teach me history,

that teach me a foreign language,

that are mostly made of RPGs, FPSs, and RTSs,[*]

made me who I am today.

—Gifted gamer, 14

[*]RPG = Role-playing game, FPS = First-person shooter, RTS = Real-time strategy

The Flip Side

As discussed in Chapter 2, whenever you sit down to play a video game—no matter how educational or strategy-rich it may be—the fact remains that you are not taking part in a creative activity. Instead, you are participating in *someone else's* creative activity; namely, the programmer or game designer. Although there may be an enormous number of possible responses or actions in a given game, as a player you are limited to the playing field and therefore have a limited number of opportunities for creative problem solving or pro-active response.

That said, here is an alternate response you might give in the previous dialogue:

You: "Okay, how about I limit my gaming time and instead see if I can alter the game's software? Or better yet: I'll design my *own* game."

Instead of spending your time mastering a video game programmed by another (possibly gifted) person—and thus lowering your creative thinking potential by merely learning how to *operate* versus *innovate*—why not initiate your own game? Then, others can argue with *their* parents about time spent playing *your* creation!

Revolutionize Your Study Habits

Regardless of how difficult or easy certain classes are for you as a gifted student, part of managing your life means, yes, *studying*. And even if you couldn't care less about the grade, chances are you'd like to retain at least some of the heaps of information imparted in class—even if only the juiciest bits—otherwise, what's the point of learning it in the first place?

The problem is: much of the studying you currently do could simply be a waste of time. Cognitive scientists say it's time to rethink the way you study. Many long-held beliefs about effective studying may well be flat-out wrong. So tune your ears to these suggestions, which explain why some of your current practices may need a fresh take.

Much of the studying you currently do could simply be a waste of time.

Six Study Habits That Will Change the Way You Learn

1. **Change up your environment.** Common wisdom used to advise students to find one quiet area without distraction to use as their study space. But experiments, such as one by Robert A. Bjork at the University of California, Los Angeles, have shown that students actually retain more information if they alternate the settings in which they revisit material. For example, one night you might read about the Monroe Doctrine in your bedroom with red walls and halogen light, while the next time you study it might be on a Saturday afternoon on a blanket in a park, surrounded by bright sun and a green canopy of trees. When you vary the context like this, the material you're reading is enriched, which means you'll remember it better.

★ If possible, set up at least three areas in your home (or outside your home: a friend's house, public library, park, coffee shop, etc.) where you can alternate studying.

★ If there's a concept or narrative that is crucial for you to remember or if you're having trouble comprehending it, try reviewing it several times in very different environments.

★ If your circumstances prevent you from varying your study space, try to alter your existing space regularly—use different lighting, sit in a different spot in the room, rearrange the furniture, hang alternating colors on the walls—so that your brain isn't making the same sensory connections every time you study there. (*Note:* Don't go overboard! Rearranging the furniture and wall art in your bedroom every night could give your family real grounds for doubting your sanity.)

2. Study mixed content in each sitting. In addition to varying the setting you study in, also vary the type of material you study during each session, according to researchers at the University of South Florida and Williams College. Keep the skills and concepts *related but distinct*. For example, if you're studying Spanish, instead of drilling yourself on verb conjugation for a solid hour, focus on vocabulary flashcards for 20 minutes, reading fluency for 20 minutes, and speaking practice for 20 minutes, while taking short breaks in between. For math, practice sets of mixed problem types, versus repeated examples of the same problem. For literature, read poems or stories by assorted authors grouped together, instead of immersing yourself in all the works by one author at a time.

When studying in this way, you teach your brain how to constantly approach material in a fresh way based on when it comes up in rotation. You're also able to detect deeper patterns in the content by making comparisons between what came before and after it in your study.

3. Space out your study sessions. This one is probably not new to you: *Don't cram*. Now new research confirms it. While cramming your brain full of facts the night before the test may indeed lead to a high grade, it's akin to jamming an entire six-course meal into your mouth in the first five minutes of dinner. Sure, you might keep it down for a while and even absorb a few nutrients, but soon everything will . . . er . . . "come up" the way it went in—virtually undigested. When you consume your content gradually and chew it carefully, you are able to retain and use the nutrients far longer. Studying a topic for an hour tonight, another hour on the weekend, and another hour next week will improve your long-term recall of it. Why? Because each time you revisit the content—especially after a few days have passed—your brain has to essentially relearn it, and each time it learns it a little more effectively.

4. Do more and harder practice tests. Studies by researchers at Washington University in St. Louis, Missouri, show that giving yourself periodic practice tests while learning new material improves your retention of the material. Why? Because testing forces your brain to retrieve an idea on-demand and then to "re-shelve" it back in your mental library, typically in a format that makes it easier to retrieve in the future. Also, the *harder* it is for you to initially retrieve the information (i.e., the more difficult the practice test), the *easier* it will be to retrieve next time.

5. Don't limit your learning modes. You may have heard of a theory that has gained a lot of popularity in past years called *learning styles theory*. It says that every student has a preferred learning style: either visual, kinetic, auditory, or verbal/linguistic. However, current research suggests that this theory still needs more evidence.[*] It's true that, as a student, you probably have a preference in how you like information presented to you. It's also true that you likely have higher abilities for certain types of thinking. But it has not been proven that you actually learn better when you're always taught in your favorite style. So even if you strongly prefer, for example, visual representations of information, don't overload yourself with graphs and drawings. Rather, expose yourself to *all* the different styles—listen to recordings of lectures (auditory), act out concepts (kinetic), and compose journal entries (linguistic). Better to be prepared for whatever form or style that content may take in the world around you, than to be an expert only in your preferred style.

6. Find your passion for (or against) the material. Not surprisingly, you'll remember stuff a lot better if you're interested in it. If you're a Shakespeare fanatic, for instance, it's probably not going to be too difficult for you to memorize the plot of *Macbeth*. However, for those topics that you're not so keen on, it can be a lot harder. One trick is to find your unique connections to the topic. Are you bored to tears with ancient civilizations and would you rather be studying biology all day? Find a connection between the two. For instance, learning how people in Mesopotamia used hand tools and written language might shed an interesting light on aspects of human evolution. Once you have a "hook" like this into the material, your interest will be piqued, which increases your chances of knowledge retention.

> "LEARNING IS NOT ABOUT SIMPLY ACQUIRING KNOWLEDGE, OR FORMULAS, OR DATES, OR AUTHORS' NAMES. IT'S ABOUT TAKING THIS KNOWLEDGE AND REACTING TO IT. THINKING ABOUT THE 'WHY' AND 'HOW' OF IDEAS YOU'RE PRESENTED WITH, RATHER THAN JUST ACCEPTING THE KNOWLEDGE, WILL HELP YOU LEARN BETTER—AND LEARN MORE."[**] —*Benet Reynolds, junior at Goucher College, Maryland*

---

[*]Pashler, Harold, et al. "Learning Styles: Concepts and Evidence," *Psychological Science in the Public Interest,* December 2008, vol. 9 no. 3, pp. 105–119.

[**]Excerpted from "The Class I Used to Hate," *Imagine,* Johns Hopkins Center for Talented Youth, Vol. 17, No. 4, Mar/Apr 2010, p. 40.

Another option is to find your passion *against* a topic you're not so keen on. Investigate why you are having such a strong reaction to it. What do you find boring about the topic? Do you disagree with the way it's being presented? How would you present it differently to make it more interesting? The truth is: your reaction to the material you're studying is just as important as the material itself.

Handling Stress

As a gifted teen facing high expectations, academic pressure, performance anxiety, perfectionism, boredom, teasing, too many choices, over-involvement, competition, and intensities, among other things—you are probably well acquainted with stress. So what causes it and how best can you deal with it?

Stress often occurs when you have too much, or too little, of something. Things like this would fall in the "too much" category: too much homework, too much pressure to excel in everything, too many tests, too much work at home. Culprits in the "too little" category are: too little time to complete everything you need to do, too little chance to socialize and relax, too little opportunity to pursue your passions because of everything else you are expected to accomplish.

"The process of living is the process of reacting to stress."
★STANLEY J. SARNOFF, MEDICAL RESEARCHER AND AUTHOR

The causes of stress and anxiety are many and, of course, they are not limited to gifted teens. People of every age and intellect encounter stress. And as luck would have it, most of the solutions to conquering stress are tried-and-true strategies that involve both the body and the mind, two aspects of humanity that everyone shares. See the resources on page 251 for ideas.

"I'M INTERESTED IN ANXIETY AND ITS PREVALENCE AMONG GIFTED KIDS . . . AND FORMS OF YOGA AND HEALING TO COMBAT STRESS EXPERIENCED BY GIFTED TEENS."
—Stephanie, 14

But before you can tackle stress head-on, you have to get to its source— and that source is frequently inside you.

For example, have you ever noticed that when two people are placed in the same conditions—say, both have multiple tests on a particular Friday—one person gets anxious and jittery and fears that failure is just around the corner, while the other person simply shrugs off the pressure and says "I'm as ready as I'll ever be, so let's get these tests over with and get the weekend started"? Part of the reason for such different attitudes toward stress has to do with personality—some people are just naturally laid-back while others are not—but another reason for the distinction is something more controllable than your personality: your preparedness to confront the sources of your stress.

When you are anxious about something, take a few steps back and use the H.A.L.T. strategy: Are you **H**ungry? **A**ngry? **L**onely? or **T**ired? If you can pinpoint that one of the reasons you are stressed is that you've been surviving on a diet of caffeinated drinks and snack cakes for the past week, or that the sum total of sleep you've gotten in the last seven days is less than the length of the movie *Avatar*, then your solution is apparent: eat something healthy or doze for a while on the couch.

The H.A.L.T. strategy: Are you Hungry? Angry? Lonely? or Tired?

If you are angry, try to pinpoint its source: Are you ticked off at your teachers, who pile on work without regard for what *other* teachers have assigned? Are you agitated because your parents are demanding that you study when you'd rather be out with friends? Are you angry at yourself for waiting until the last minute to complete a report assigned three weeks prior? Once you've homed in on the source(s) of your anger, ask yourself which ones you can control. Your teachers? Nah . . . teachers have *always* scheduled tests when they feel like it. Your parents? Perhaps, if you can convince them that letting you socialize for a while will let you return to your studies with a fresh attitude. Yourself? Bingo! Just kick (or gently nudge) yourself in the butt for procrastinating and move on to the task at hand. Anger is best handled when you arrive at a solution to diminish it. When it festers inside you, it's like a blister ready to burst—and the results are just as messy.

If you suspect your anger is more than just a passing instance of feeling mad at yourself, someone else, or a situation—if it feels bigger and deeper than that, it's time to talk about it with someone you trust. Pervasive, deep-seated anger is not something to take lightly, and, if left unaddressed, can lead to more serious problems such as depression and violent behavior.

When it comes to the L-word—lonely—that one may or may not be easy to tackle. If you have friends you haven't spent time with recently, it'd be worth it to connect with them sooner instead of later. Give yourself a certain amount of time, stick to it, and return to your work with a refreshed sense of being. If the loneliness is caused by being rebuffed by others when you try to join in their fun, or by feeling isolated even in a crowd because no one seems to "get you," that's a lingering stress that has no quick solution. At this point, you'll need to reach out to a caring adult and ask for help. That in itself may be stress-inducing, but the end result is bound to leave you in a better place than you are in right now.

As you've read in this chapter, you wield considerable control over many areas of your life. You have countless opportunities for managing expectations, communicating your needs to others, taking (and making) risks, wildly succeeding and constructively failing, maximizing your time and energy, and, most importantly, learning about yourself and the skills you need to flourish. It's up to you to embrace life and take charge!

I have a right to an education that fits my unique learning needs.

I have a right to learn at my (own) speed.

I have a right to opt out of work I already know and understand.

I have a right to be educated by teachers who are specially qualified to teach me.

I have a right to work with peers who share my interests and abilities.

I have a right to study things that interest me and go beyond the basics.

chapter 6
Making School Rule

Most students want school to be a positive experience— challenging, meaningful, interesting, and enjoyable. And many schools do a decent job of providing this experience for students with average abilities. One reason for the emphasis on "average" is the need for cost-effectiveness. Schools have to get the most for their money because they simply don't have the funds to do everything. Except for those relatively few private schools with large endowments and wealthy supporters, public schools never have and never will. As a result, there isn't much room for creativity or so-called "extras." Often lost in the shuffle are students who need special assistance—a category that includes students with disabilities or learning differences as well as gifted kids. Laws such as NCLB (No Child Left Behind) and IDEA (Individuals with Disabilities Education Act) have improved this situation for the former group, but not for the latter.

"HOW DO I COMBAT THE FORCES OF BOREDOM AT SCHOOL?" —*Ross, 17*

It doesn't help that gifted kids are sometimes assumed to "have it all" and not need individualized attention. The overworked teacher faced with a fourth grader who can't yet read at the first-grade level and another who already reads at the eighth-grade level will concentrate (understandably) on the slow reader. Apply this scenario to math, science, history, etc., and it's no wonder so many gifted students claim that school is boring, irrelevant, and unchallenging.

By the time you reach your senior year, you will have spent over 12,000 hours in school. You don't have to be a math whiz to figure out that this can translate into endless weeks, months, even years of daydreaming, thumb-twiddling, fingernail-biting, hair-twisting, toe-tapping, napping, texting, and other coping strategies.

What you want is an education that fits the way your mind works. Nothing militant, nothing extraordinary; you just want to:

★ learn at your own speed

★ opt out of work you already know and understand

★ study things that interest you and go beyond the basics

★ work with abstract concepts that require more than simple thinking

★ work with peers who share your interests and abilities

★ participate in options that connect your learning to the "real world"

The Survey Says . . .

50% of respondents want to know how to get teachers to be more flexible (for example, letting students test out of material they already know, skip some repetitive assignments, and/ or pursue alternatives to traditional assignments).

49% want to know more about how to earn college credit while still in high school.

46% want to know more about the legal rights of gifted kids.

If students don't have opportunities to stretch their minds in at least some of these ways, they get bored. And when they get bored, they may act out, underachieve, or drop out—either by quitting school before graduation (for example, to work at a job that seems more meaningful to them) or by mentally withdrawing into themselves and giving up on school.

In fact, this withdrawal actually happens chemically inside the brain. Researchers have found that, if a curriculum is redundant for the child—beneath that student's level of readiness—the brain is not inclined to engage or respond and, consequently, does not release the levels of dopamine, noradrenalin, serotonin, and other neurochemicals needed for optimal learning. The result is apathy.[*]

Content Standards: Why Should You Care?

Put simply: the advent of content standards, and the tests that measure them, has *a lot* to do with this boredom you might be experiencing. A quick history lesson . . .

---

[*]Schultz, W., et al. "A Neural Substrate of Prediction and Reward." *Science,* 275 (1997): 1593–1599.

Nothing in the U.S. Constitution requires that children be educated. Instead, since the birth of the United States, the responsibility for educating children has fallen to each state. For generations, this has resulted in a hodge-podge of laws and uneven achievement expectations across the country. With the passage of the No Child Left Behind law, each state was required to test every child annually in language arts and math, in hopes of raising achievement for all students in all states. This effort was met with some success; however, each state's standards and assessments were still not uniform. To address this, the federal government recently stepped in and introduced a new set of standards, called the Common Core State Standards, which have now been adopted by most states. In short, uniformity, while never a sure thing when it comes to curriculum, looks a lot closer now than it did 10 years ago. But at what cost?

Some critics of content standards worry that the *only* topics that will be addressed in school will be those that the subsequent tests will measure—that teachers will have no choice but to "teach to the test." They ask: Will this national homogeneity result in less rigor and creativity in classrooms? Will current events and topics of personal student interest be discouraged because those are not being measured at year's end? Will subjects not standardized, such as the visual arts, be neglected?

Proponents of content standards claim the standards are not so specific that they will force a teacher to give up all innovative practices. Also, even though language arts and math are the main focus of state and national standards, it does not dismiss the importance of other subjects, because the skills learned through these two core subjects are necessary to comprehend history, archeology, physics, forensics, and countless other fields of study.

It's too early to tell if this rise of content standards will rock the world of education or not. But this much is clear: if you are a gifted student who picks up content readily and rapidly, you may satisfy these learning benchmarks far earlier than other students—leaving you at risk of apathy, underachievement, or total withdrawal as you wait for the class to catch up. In this case, you will have to take matters into your own hands and advocate for your right to an education that caters to your advanced abilities. You will need to create your *own* standards.

Gifted People SPEAK OUT   "I Was a Teenage Underachiever"

by Elizabeth Chapman*

My name is Elizabeth and I am a recovering underachiever.

As a child, when someone asked me, "What do you want to be when you grow up?" I never gave a standard answer; instead, I would say that I hoped to become a chemist or a teacher, perhaps an astronaut or a doctor or a spy, or, if I wanted to give my parents a bit of a jolt, a freelance artist. But the real answer, the secret answer that I never shared with anyone, was this: I wanted to be *great!*

Heracles, Julius Caesar, Leonardo da Vinci, Queen Elizabeth I, Madame Curie, Neil Armstrong, Georgia O'Keeffe—they haunted me from an early age. "Human beings can do incredible things!" my childhood ghosts would cry out from the storybook illustrations I held in my lap. If only I could wait patiently, make it through my teen years, I, too, would be able to shape the world in extraordinary ways.

Fast-forward about a decade. I'm standing in the middle of a parking lot with a hideous, cheap plastic graduation robe tossed over my shoulder. In my arms, I'm grasping a stack full of certificates acknowledging my tenure as class president and involvement in virtually all of our school's extracurricular activities. Clenched between my lips I have a few ribbons for academic merit. And in the pit of my stomach, I have a deep sense of unaccomplishment. Despite the armful of awards that seem to shout "model student," I know the truth—I had never written a paper any earlier than the night before it was due, and "studying" for me consisted of cracking open the textbook for only the second or third time in that semester. The glowing sense of victory I had always expected to show up at high school graduation had stood me up.

"But honestly," I say to myself as I stuff my robe, papers, medals, and diploma unceremoniously into the trunk of my car, "what else could I have done? It's not *my* fault that everything was always so easy." And as I zoom forward on the freeway, my mind floats backward lazily to those first awkward years of high school . . .

*Adapted from *More Than a Test Score* by Robert A. Schultz, Ph.D., and James R. Delisle, Ph.D. (Free Spirit Publishing, 2007).

My social studies teacher walked into the room, clapping his hands brusquely. "Okay, class, we have three weeks until the end of the school year and 10 chapters to cover. Turn to the section on the Korean War."

We opened our books.

"All right, now raise your right hand and place it palm down over the first page."

We looked around at each other, confused, but followed his instructions. "Now, we've *covered* it," said the teacher, his chins jiggling as he chuckled at the pun. "Let's move on."

"We're not going to learn about the Korean War?" protested one student.

"You don't need to know about the Korean War unless you're Korean."

A hand shot up in the back of the room. "I'm Korean."

"Oh . . . well, you can read the chapter on your own."

Unfortunately, this was the norm rather than the exception for a great chunk of my time in school.

Almost a year after my depressingly anticlimactic high school graduation, I'm sitting at an enormous round table in an honors history seminar, delivering a presentation on the Korean War's implications for the Vietnam War—which I put a grueling half-hour into preparing. "As I'm sure you know," I say, looking up nervously from my notes, "Korea is quite close to China, so it's no surprise that the Chinese leadership was interested in preventing an American presence in the regions of Korea closest to their country."

"You mean the part of Korea that *borders* China?" asks a student.

(Korea borders China? That was certainly news to me!)

"Heh, heh. Yes, that's exactly what I meant: the part of Korea that *borders* China." The entire class stares back at me as though they suspect I've never seen a map of Asia. I feel tiny pin pricks on my face as the blood rushes to my cheeks.

Half an hour later, as I'm packing my books, papers, pens, and shame into my bag, it occurs to me that despite the acute probability that my high school history teacher was perhaps negligent in his instruction, *he* was not the one turning bright pink from embarrassment at this moment.

So while I did go home and pull up a map of the eastern hemisphere online, the big lesson I learned was that being "great" is about more than attaining that perfect GPA, or getting into your dream college, or building a résumé that takes half a ream of paper to print. It's about tackling every challenge head-on—giving it your all, so to speak. Along the way, people may give you papers stating that you are wonderful, or small glass sculptures with your name on the bottom, or even money to go to college. These will all be nice, but they are not the point of all your efforts. I'm sure Shakespeare never said to himself, "Oh, one hit play is good enough for me. The public already adores me. I think I'll retire now."

Despite the acute probability that my high school history teacher was perhaps negligent in his instruction, *he* was not the one turning bright pink from embarrassment at this moment.

The heroes of my childhood did not achieve immortality by measuring themselves against society's standards and expectations; they did it by exceeding their own.

Postscript by Elizabeth, 15 years later[*]:

As fortune would have it, I eventually became a teacher . . . of gifted students. Now I am a gifted program administrator. I'm at the point in my life now where my friends are finishing with law and medical school and going into business, where they make two to three times my salary, eat at lavish restaurants on corporate expense accounts, and travel across the country and around the world for meetings. Yet I don't envy them for a second, because I have a job where I have been able to work with hundreds of bright, sensitive, creative young people, and any teacher worth her or his salt would tell you the same thing. You may not realize it, but you are the reason why someone is getting up in the morning to go to work, and is looking forward to it.

When I last wrote, I was reflecting on what my experiences as a student had taught me about giftedness and achievement. Here is what I've learned as a teacher:

The achievement standards that you set for *yourself* are going to be the most meaningful challenges you face. We live in an era of standardized testing, and there is little to indicate that that is going away. You may very well spend 12 years in a classroom almost wholly devoted to test preparation,

---

[*]This section begins a new essay written by Elizabeth specifically for this book.

where the measures of your achievement will be both arbitrary and low. Be careful! Do not be lulled into a false sense of accomplishment. Your teachers and principals and even your fellow students may make a very big deal of The Test, but the truth of the matter is that in the real world there are no multiple-choice questions, nor is there a limit to how high you can score.

Don't wait for your parents or teachers to fix a situation. *Take charge yourself.* By reading this book, you are already going in the right direction. Continue to advocate for yourself by getting online and finding out about the communities for gifted children that are there to support you, as well as the learning opportunities that you can pursue from almost anywhere in the country. Find out what you want to do with yourself, and ask the adults in your life to help.

Elizabeth Chapman is currently an administrator at the Texas Academy of Leadership in the Humanities, a gifted honors program for teenagers in Texas. She spent the past four years as a teacher at the Webster Academy for Visions in Education, the same program that she attended as a student and the school where she first read an earlier edition of this book.

The Survey Says . . .

Q. What do you think schools could be doing differently to help gifted kids get the most out of their education?

"Allow gifted students more flexibility in their curriculum. In my experience, schools are extremely reluctant to allow gifted students to advance if they already know the material. A system needs to be put in place to allow them to prove their knowledge and move on." —*Camille, 18*

"Every teacher needs to get trained on how to identify and teach a gifted child in the regular classroom. It should be a state and federal mandate." —*Erik, 13*

"Technology should be used to provide online courses in the classroom." —*Anna, 13*

"Classes should focus more on the ideas of the student than on the ideas of experts. Rather than make students analyze poetry, literature classes should encourage students to write poetry of their own and analyze it instead." —*Graham, 16*

"Assign gifted kids to a teacher, similar to a mentoring program. The teacher would be there to talk to the student about life and the student would be able to pick the teacher's brain." —*Stori, 17*

"I feel that once you hit high school, the GT program kind of dies off. You don't have many regular meetings and projects. Keeping the GT program going could help gifted students." —*Kathryn, 17*

"Offer more opportunities for trips, or different styles of learning, or more out-of-the-box things to really get us thinking." —*Logan, 15*

"Encourage the development of more unorthodox talents. I think math and science are both very well covered, but we need to look at all the other types of gifts people have and help nourish them." —*Sacha, 15*

"School should have more outdoor education opportunities. I live in a town close to the wilderness and have an understanding of how important the outdoors are." —*Liam, 14*

"Put an emphasis on independent study plans. Because the range of giftedness is so vast, schools cannot lump all gifted students together. The focus should be on honing independent critical thinking skills." —*Mario, 17*

"We watch videos in class and write essays and do research at home, when it should be reversed. I believe we should do all the rigorous stuff during daylight hours when we are fresh." —*Jenna, 17*

"Test us. Pit our wits against the impossible. The biggest problem with my gifted program was that I could still do so much more! Leave doors open for dual-enrollment, and let children skip grades as needed." —*Grace, 13*

Asserting Your Rights: Four Steps Toward Change

Before you can begin creating standards for yourself and advocating for change, it might be helpful to realize that, as a gifted student, you have legal rights (granted by your state) to a challenging and appropriate education. Will your rights always be recognized and respected? Unfortunately, no. But understanding your rights is the first step to getting them met.

When trying to effect changes in your educational program, you might follow these four steps:

1. Be informed. Know your rights.
2. Identify your needs, interests, and ideas.
3. Prioritize your needs and interests. Choose the top two or three and plan your strategy around them.
4. Communicate your strategy with a positive attitude.

Step 1: Be Informed, Know Your Rights

If you have a supportive teacher or guidance counselor, start by asking what he or she knows about students' rights in your school. Find out if anything on this topic has been formalized in writing, and if it has, request a copy.

States, school districts, and some individual schools have formulated philosophy, mission, or policy statements that describe their goals and objectives for education. Some are specific to the needs of gifted and talented students. Locate your state's policies online at davidsongifted.org.

Here are two examples of policy statements that focus on gifted students:

From the California Education Code:
The Gifted and Talented Education (GATE) program, authorized by Education Code (EC) sections 52200-52212, provides funding for local educational agencies (LEAs) to develop unique education opportunities for high-achieving and underachieving pupils in California public elementary and secondary schools who have been identified as gifted and talented. Special efforts are made to ensure that pupils from economically disadvantaged and varying cultural backgrounds are provided with full participation in these unique opportunities.

LEAs may establish programs for gifted and talented pupils consisting of special day classes, part-time groupings, and cluster groupings. GATE curricular components are required to be planned and organized as integrated differentiated learning experiences within the regular school day and may be augmented or supplemented with other differentiated activities related to the core curriculum, including independent study, acceleration, postsecondary education, and enrichment. For all programs for gifted and talented pupils, including those programs for pupils with high creative capability and talents in the performing and visual arts, each participating LEA shall concentrate part of its curriculum on providing GATE pupils with an academic component and, where appropriate, with instruction in basic skills.[*]

From the Minnesota Statutes:
Minnesota Statutes, section 120B.15 GIFTED and TALENTED STUDENTS PROGRAM sections (a) and (b) permit school districts and charter schools to identify students who are gifted and talented, develop and evaluate programs to serve them locally and provide staff development to ensure that they have access to challenging educational programs. The legislation also provides guidance for districts to adopt procedures for assessing and identifying students.

Section (c) directs school districts and charter schools to adopt procedures for the academic acceleration of gifted and talented students that include an assessment of students' readiness and motivation for acceleration and a match between the curriculum and the students' academic needs. (Districts may wish to implement policies that reflect gifted and talented best practices, consistent with Minnesota Statutes, section 120B.15.)

Gifted and talented revenue (Minnesota Statutes, section 126C.10 Subd. 2 (b)) provides school districts and charter schools with 12 times a district's adjusted marginal cost pupil units (AMCPU). Uses of this revenue:

1. Identify gifted and talented students.

2. Provide education programs for gifted and talented students.

3. Provide staff development to prepare teachers to best meet the unique needs of gifted and talented students.[**]

When you learn the goals and objectives that pertain to your school, chances are you'll discover that your rights are already represented in whole or in part. Your school district probably recognizes your right to an education that meets your needs—at least on paper. The Big Question is: What, if anything, is being done in real life?

As you read your school's goal statements, highlight the catch phrases. You can use them later to substantiate your case for alternative education proposals. Here are some sample phrases pulled from several school districts' goal statements: *academic recognition . . . challenged to reach highest*

[*]Education Code (EC) sections 52200-52212, California Department of Education.
[**]Minnesota Statutes, section 120B.15, Minnesota Department of Education.

intellectual potential . . . changing society . . . commensurate with potential/ability . . . creative development . . . differentiated learning experiences . . . enrichment . . . equal opportunity . . . expanded opportunities . . . individual independence . . . meeting student needs and interests . . . prevention strategies . . . relevant curriculum . . . scholastic pursuits . . . social pursuits . . . standards for excellence . . . student exploration . . . superior ability . . . underserved populations.

Once you're informed about the situation in your school—once you know what's already in place for you to work with—you're ready to move on.

Step 2: Identify Your Needs, Interests, and Ideas

The following questions are meant to help you plan and articulate the questions you'll ask your teachers and administrators. Think about which individuals you'll need to approach.

Tip: Choose the people who have the power to make changes—for example, an influential teacher, your principal, the curriculum coordinator, or the superintendent.

1. In what ways are your educational needs already being met? (Whenever you're trying to implement changes that require enlisting the cooperation of others, it's smart to start with the positives. School usually isn't *all* bad.)

2. In what ways are your educational needs not being met? (Be specific.) What changes do you think need to be made for school to be more meaningful, relevant, exciting, engaging, and challenging for you? (Again, be specific. *Example:* If you're tired of having to "learn" material you already know, you might suggest that you take a test to prove what you know, then use class time for a project or activity of your choosing.)

Step 3: Prioritize Your Needs and Interests

Choose the top one or two specific issues that you want to start addressing in school, and *put it in writing.* Some students find a proposal format helpful. A proposal shows teachers that you're serious, you've spent time and effort formulating your plan, and you aren't expecting them to do all of the work.

Make your proposal as clear, concise, and comprehensive as you can. Not only will this impress your teachers, it will also give you room to negotiate. You might use the following outline to start organizing and formalizing your thoughts.

Proposal

    I. Goal (what you want to change about school)

    II. Steps (what you plan to do to reach your goal)

    III. Resources (the people and things you need to reach your goal)

    IV. Roadblocks (the people and things that might get in your way and impede your progress toward your goal)

    V. Rewards (what you expect to get out of reaching your goal)

Step 4: Communicate Your Strategy with a Positive Attitude

To become an effective change agent for your own education, there's another important tool you'll want to use: a good attitude. Teachers and administrators aren't going to bend over backward to accommodate you if you act like Genghis Khan.

First and foremost, you want to communicate an attitude of cooperation, not condescension. Present yourself as an ally, not an aggressor. Most teachers want to help their students; that's one reason they've chosen the teaching profession. Acknowledge that, respect it, make it easier for them to work with you, and the rewards will be substantial. There's nothing better than having your teachers on your side, and it's not that difficult to enlist their aid. All it takes is a little diplomacy and the willingness to recognize that teachers are people, too.

As a condescending aggressor, you create a situation in which someone will win and someone will lose. The battle lines are drawn and there's no going back. As a cooperative ally, you invite the other person to work with you to recognize, understand, and solve a problem. Rather than attacking or accusing, you state very clearly and directly, "Here's what's going on, here's how I feel about it, and this is what I suggest as an alternative. I'd like to know what you think, too."

A teacher we know once observed: "Teaching school can get boring, and sometimes I feel as though I have to be a superstar to get my students turned on. If a student approaches me in a nonthreatening and helpful way, I appreciate hearing ideas about how things can be made more interesting. It takes some of the burden off me. I'm human. I don't react very well to a verbal attack about how boring school is—especially when the person hasn't got any ideas of his own."

Granted, you won't always achieve your objective, no matter what approach you choose. Unfortunately, some teachers believe that they're the boss of their students. But you're much more likely to be heard if you put aside the verbal boxing gloves and come out smiling.

Know Thy Teacher

When presenting your ideas for change, it helps to understand a bit about the person you're talking to. So what makes teachers tick? And how do they feel about gifted students?

"I'M INTERESTED IN LEARNING HOW TO HANDLE BEING IN A REGULAR CLASS OR BEING TAUGHT BY A TEACHER WHO DOESN'T ACCOMMODATE FOR GT NEEDS." —*Mary, 16*

Knowing how to teach gifted students takes something that not every teacher is willing to reveal: vulnerability. Successful teachers of gifted kids can accept being corrected (occasionally) by their students; they can face the fact that some kids have knowledge they don't have; they can listen to different points of view with an open mind. But it isn't easy. One question teachers often have is: "What am I supposed to do with students who already know much of what I'm about to teach?"

Some teachers respond by being intimidated or threatened by intelligent students like you. This often has more to do with the teachers' lack of self-confidence and self-esteem than it does with your intellectual abilities. Certain teachers simply can't accept the fact that some students may be smarter in some areas than they, the teachers, are. (Notice that we say "some areas," not "all." You may be the world's greatest genius, but your teachers will always have something you don't: life experience, maybe even wisdom.) What can you do if you end up in one of their classrooms? Be courteous; be respectful; be willing to learn. If there's a specific problem you need to address, see our "10 Tips for Talking to Teachers" on page 133).

But then there are the teachers who, as Elizabeth mentioned in her essay (page 122), see you—and all their students—as the reason to get up in the morning to go to work. They are honored to educate you and, in turn, be educated *by* you. You might take a moment to think back on those great teachers who have welcomed you, encouraged you, and changed your life for the better—the ones who have treated you with respect and kindness, understanding, and even appreciation. And you may wish to thank them, either in person or by writing a letter. We can honestly (and modestly) admit that we've received a few of those letters in our lifetime, and they mean a lot to us. Go ahead; make someone's day!

The Survey Says . . .

Q. What makes the difference between a good teacher and a great teacher?

"A good teacher is fun, and keeps class interesting. A great teacher does all of the above, while providing learning opportunities for those students that excel above the rest. They stick with them and make sure all of their students succeed." —*Ethan, 13*

"Great teachers are always coming up with ideas that make doing schoolwork fun and creative. They also make sure every student understands, instead of telling them to read the textbook." —*Matthew, 12*

"Teaching is all about relationships. Great teachers will go out of their way to truly get to know all of their students personally." —*Simone, 17*

"Great teachers are the ones who not only make you love the subject they teach, but explore that subject more. A great teacher should 'light my fire.'" —*Kennedy, 12*

"A great teacher understands that just because someone isn't great in one area, it doesn't mean that they can't still be gifted." —*Asad, 11*

"Being personal. A great teacher needs to have the ability to make the classroom a little smaller. They should have the time to talk with you and help you out when you need it, but they should also be able to let you do things yourself." —*Heidi, 16*

"Flexibility and kindness. A caring, yet stern teacher who can adjust their strategies to deal with gifted or disabled students would be my perfect teacher." —*Joshua, 11*

"A great teacher recognizes students as they are, and is able to utilize their judgment in order to maximize the education of every person involved—including the teacher's!" —*Bo, 18*

10 Tips for Talking to Teachers

Many students have told us that they don't know how to go about talking to their teachers or administrators. The following suggestions are meant to make it easier for everyone involved.

1. **Make an appointment to meet and talk.** This shows the teacher that you're serious and you have some understanding of his or her busy schedule. Tell the teacher about how much time you'll need, be flexible, and don't be late.

2. **If you know other students who feel the way you do, consider approaching the teacher together.** There's strength in numbers. If a teacher hears the same thing from four or five people, he or she is more likely to do something about it.

3. **Think through what you want to say before you go into your meeting with the teacher.** Write down your questions or concerns. Make a list of the items you want to cover. You may even want to copy your list for the teacher so both of you can consult it during your meeting. (Or consider giving it to the teacher ahead of time.)

4. **Choose your words carefully.** *Example:* Instead of saying, "I hate doing reports; they're boring and a waste of time," try, "Is there some other way I could satisfy this requirement? Could I do a video instead?" Strike the word *boring* from your vocabulary. It's a negative and meaningless buzzword for teachers.

5. **Don't expect the teacher to do all of the work or propose all of the answers.** Be prepared to make suggestions, offer solutions, even recommend resources. The teacher will appreciate that you took the initiative.

6. **Be diplomatic, tactful, and respectful.** Teachers have feelings, too. And they're more likely to be responsive if you remember that the purpose of your meeting is conversation, not confrontation.

7. **Focus on what you need, not on what you think the teacher is doing wrong.** The more the teacher learns about you, the more he or she will be able to help. The more defensive the teacher feels, the less he or she will want to help.

8. **Don't forget to listen.** Strange but true, many students need practice in this essential skill. The purpose of your meeting isn't just to hear yourself talk.

9. **Bring your sense of humor.** Not necessarily the joke-telling sense of humor, but the one that lets you laugh at yourself and your own misunderstandings and mistakes.

10. **If your meeting isn't successful, get help from another adult.** "Successful" doesn't necessarily mean that you emerged victorious. Even if the teacher denies your request, your meeting can still be judged successful. If you had a real conversation—if you communicated openly, listened carefully, and respected each other's point of view—then congratulate yourself on a great meeting. If the air crackled with tension, the meeting fell apart, and you felt disrespected (or acted disrespectful), then it's time to bring in another adult. *Suggestions:* a guidance counselor, the gifted program coordinator, or another teacher you know and trust who seems likely to support you and advocate for you. Once you've found help, approach your teacher and try again.

What to Say When Teachers Say No

You know your rights, you've come up with a proposal that seems reasonable to you, and you've talked to your teacher clearly and politely . . . to no avail. Sometimes the best-laid plans go awry in the face of that formidable opponent known as The Implacable Teacher. Don't give up just yet! Depending on what your teacher says (and your own energy level), you can attempt a few more rebuttals to the following "standard refusals."

If your teacher says . . .	You might respond . . .
"I can't make an exception for you."	"That's okay with me, since I think there are a number of students who might benefit from being allowed to [fill in here with whatever it is you're suggesting]."
"It's always been done this way."	"I know. And I'm sure there are probably some very good reasons for that. But how about letting me try this one time, and if it doesn't work, I'll agree to go back to the way it's been done in the past?"
"It would cause chaos in my classroom."	"I'd be willing to help see that chaos doesn't prevail. I could form a small committee of students who really care and who would help set some guidelines that would keep order in the classroom. We'd agree that if things got out of control, we'd lose this opportunity."
"You're a straight-A student. Why not be satisfied with that? After all, what more could you ask for?"	"I know I get straight A's, but the thing is, I feel I could be learning so much more. If it were possible to get a higher grade than an A, just think of the possibilities! You know the old cliché—'The sky's the limit.' I'd like to aim higher, and I really need your help and support."

What if nothing works? If every response you make falls flat? Then it's time to stop trying, to accept that there are some things you simply can't change. Throughout your life, you'll encounter people who have "role power" over you—meaning the power to tell you what to do *just because* they're in charge. It's not reasonable, it's not fair, but sometimes that's the way it is. Take a deep breath, thank the teacher for his or her time, and be glad that this situation is only temporary. It may seem as if the school year will last forever, but it won't.

> "SO MANY TIMES EDUCATION IS FORCED UPON US, AND NOT SOMETHING WE ARE ALLOWED TO PARTICIPATE IN. BUT I HAVE FOUND THE MORE I AM ASKED TO PARTICIPATE AND AM TAKEN SERIOUSLY, THE MORE I WANT TO LEARN." —*Erin, 15*

Let the following essay by teacher Paul Andersen inspire you to "disrupt" your class (in a positive way) and be an agent for change.

Expert Essay
"Be Disruptive"
by Paul Andersen

Hours of my youth were spent creating mix tapes on my dual cassette tape recorder. It was an extremely time-intensive process but I was always happy with the results. The invention of the portable CD player and then the iPod eliminated the need for mixing tapes. The creation of playlists now takes only minutes. The iPod not only replaced the cassette player, it shifted the entire playing field.

Author Clayton M. Christensen calls these new forms of technology "disruptive." They push technology forward by switching tracks and are only negative for those who are left behind. Education has been stuck on the same track for some time. Real change must come from the parents, teachers, and students directly involved in learning. One group that has been underrepresented in educational reform has been the *students*. Disruptive students could push us forward by changing the tone of the discussion.

Many teachers fear disruptive students because they can ruin a classroom. These students have behavior issues and they are not the students I refer to in the following section. I have had a number of gifted students over the last 17 years of teaching. However, only a small percentage of these students will dramatically change the world. What separates these few students from the rest could be best described as their ability to *disrupt*.

The Seven Characteristics of DISRUPTive Students

D is for Desirous
Intellectual giftedness does not necessarily produce academic success. If I had to choose between a classroom of talented

students and a classroom of passionate learners I would choose the latter. In order to be successful in the academic realm you must be willing to put in the required amount of work. According to studies conducted by psychologist Anders Ericsson it takes thousands of hours of practice to become an expert in a specific field. This rule applies to music, sports, and academics.

This "10,000-Hour Rule" was highlighted in Malcolm Gladwell's book *Outliers*. Talent can only take you so far and a lack of desire will stop you short of the required amount of practice. The first step is to become a passionate learner. This trait will carry you through all future classes regardless of your interest in the subject material. Students should set aside a block of time each day for focused study. The investment is small but the rewards will last a lifetime.

I is for Independent

The simple secret to being a successful student is staying ahead of the instructor. You should never come into a lecture with little or no knowledge of the material. You will be unable to ask intelligent questions when you are seeing the material for the first time. I didn't learn this important fact until I was in college, so I now try to pass it on to all my students.

Technology is transforming the way we learn. I have been posting lectures on YouTube for the last four years. I continue to be amazed by the responses I get from learners around the world. I will lecture as much in one day on YouTube as I will in five years in my regular class. As long as you have access to the Internet you have access to the sum of human knowledge. Do not miss out on this opportunity. Learn how to learn early

and you will be rewarded with a lifetime of academic success.

S is for Sincere

Stop reading this article if you aren't genuinely interested in making the school a better place. Schools were designed for you, the learner. If you are bored in school, it may not be entirely your teacher's fault. You can improve any class by becoming an active participant in the process. Ask interesting questions in class to stimulate conversation. Bring in additional information to supplement the classroom discussion. Volunteer to help students in the class who are struggling.

I am a good judge of student character and I am much more likely to invest time in a student who truly cares about my class. If you enjoy a class let the teacher know. If you don't enjoy the class, work to make it better.

R is for Relational

Most teachers enter the profession because they genuinely like children. Many teachers claim (and I agree) that their students keep them young. I am able to see the material new each year through the eyes of my students. Forming positive relationships with your teachers is not difficult. Don't send them a friend request on Facebook; this is not appropriate. Simply talk to them before or after school. Let them know that you are interested in the class and that you are willing to help. I can't think of anything more rewarding than having a student come up after class to say, "Thanks, that was really helpful."

U is for Useful

Teachers who are truly concerned with improving education will never have enough time in the day. I spend as much

Stop reading this article if you aren't genuinely interested in making your school a better place.

time preparing for my classes each day as I do teaching. Students can lessen this load by helping out. The help that my students provide varies greatly. It can be as simple as cleaning beakers or organizing papers. It can also evolve into assistant teaching.

I use a learning management system in my class called Moodle. I have given several students in my class teacher privileges, and they have done some amazing things. Students have added notes, podcasts, wikis, and practice quizzes to my class. They receive no points for the hours they spend improving class. They do it because they are fascinated by the material and they want to make learning easier for other students. I am constantly impressed by the level of their work.

P is for Professional

A professional is a person who has received specialized training in a specific field. This definition doesn't preclude a student from being considered a professional. By the time students have reached my class, they should be professional students. Professional students take their jobs seriously. They are always prepared for class and they are intrinsically motivated. They adhere to a higher standard of behavior and ethics than typical students. I am willing to invest more time and energy in professional students, because I know that they will not let me down.

T is for Teacherly

Although I have a degree in the subject, I never *truly* understood the concepts of molecular biology until I started teaching AP biology. In order to explain a difficult concept to a student who is struggling, you must have a firm grasp of the material yourself. You must be able to explain the concepts in various ways. You must be patient, reactive, and understanding. Teaching is the highest level of the learning cycle. Tutoring students who are struggling in your class will not only solidify your own understanding, it will make the world a better place. If you are doing well in class, talk to your teacher about becoming a tutor.

I was identified as a gifted student when I was in elementary school and spent time each week with four other students receiving enrichment activities. I remember enjoying these activities, but I also remember being teased mercilessly by my friends about my "giftedness." Truthfully, I probably could have received all of the benefits of a gifted program in my regular classes if I would have taken on some of the responsibility myself.

Gifted students today should be positive agents for educational change. Any other position is an analog message in a digital world.

Paul Andersen *teaches science and AP Biology at Bozeman High School in Bozeman, Montana. He was the 2010 Montana State Teacher of the Year and a finalist for the 2011 National Teacher of the Year. He was also named by The National School Boards Association as one of its "20 to Watch" technology leaders. Visit his website at bozemanscience.com.*

Exploring Your Options

Although schools weren't (and aren't) designed specifically for gifted students, there are many provisions *within* schools that can benefit the most intelligent students.

In elementary school years, you might have participated in a "pull-out" (also called a "send-out") program, where you got together weekly with other gifted students for projects and lessons that were targeted toward your advanced abilities or creative energies. Of course, you are gifted more than one day each week, yet these pull-out programs were often enjoyed and remembered fondly by those who participated in them—being "gifted on Tuesdays" was better than never being gifted at all, right?

Middle schools seldom have pull-out programs, and once high school hits, any semblance of a specific gifted program is as rare as a snowflake in Key West. Yet oddly enough, secondary school may be your best chance yet to get an appropriate education. The options offered, both inside and outside the school walls, are numerous and varied. Let's explore a few of them.

"I have never let my schooling interfere with my education."
★MARK TWAIN, AUTHOR

"You have to get everything you can from whatever environment you're thrown into."
★TONI MORRISON, AUTHOR

Acceleration

Just as a car's accelerator allows you to move faster, the many provisions under the umbrella term of *acceleration* do the same thing. The most potent method of acceleration is *grade skipping*, a practice frowned upon by many educators and some parents, even though virtually all evidence points to the positive impact of such a jump. Looking back on your youth, if you entered kindergarten at age four, you were, essentially, grade skipped. Or, if you went from a fifth-grade elementary classroom directly into a seventh-grade middle school placement, you grade skipped.

Other forms of acceleration are a bit more subtle and may include the following:

★ subject-matter acceleration (for example, you take a senior-level class as a sophomore)

★ curriculum "telescoping" (you take a placement test at the beginning of the school year that allows you to skip Algebra II and get into geometry); also called compacting

★ credit by exam (instead of sitting through a course of material you already know, you test out of it and get high school graduation credit for it)

Enrichment Programs

School enrichment programs (sometimes called honors programs or gifted programs) are designed to replace or extend the regular school curriculum. The goal of enrichment should be to help you work on higher-level skills, such as divergent and evaluative thinking, problem solving, and creativity. Some of the ways these skills can be taught are through debates and discussions, research, or simulations.

Back-to-Back Classes

How many times have you started an exciting new project only to be interrupted by the bell? Pairing classes—scheduling them one right after another—is an inventive way to create an extra-long class period. It gives teachers and students more opportunities to do things that require more time and effort than a 50-minute class can provide. Back-to-back classes (sometimes called double-block scheduling) also make it easier for teachers to use a variety of learning and teaching styles like independent study, debate, drama, field trips, or extended discussions, or to combine one content area with another (for example, language arts and social studies) for more in-depth learning.

Honors Courses

Many middle and high schools serve gifted students by offering honors sections of basic classes. While these classes may or may not offer anything especially new, their intent is to provide you greater challenge and a faster pace of instruction. Like any class, honors courses are only as good as the collective enthusiasm of the teacher and students participating. In some schools, they may be one of your *only* options for advanced learning.

Advanced Placement (AP)

Perhaps the most common form of high school programming taken advantage of by gifted students is AP courses. Enrollment in AP classes is not limited to identified gifted students, and some gifted students don't like AP classes at all. Why not? Even though they offer rigorous content and a chance to earn college credits by taking a course-end test, they can be, simultaneously, strenuous and stifling.

The strenuous part is easy to understand: Essentially, you are learning content at a college level, so the curriculum is rigorous and the requirements for doing well are more extensive than most other high school classes. The stifling aspect (to some students) of AP courses is due to the nature of the evaluation. In May, you will take a national test on your subject—for example, AP World History—and it will be graded on a five-point scale by a bunch of teachers who teach this subject in their own high schools. In order for you to get a score of four or five—which most colleges want you to score before they award credit—your teacher will stick very closely—*very* closely—to the prescribed curriculum. Frequently, this means that your course will cover many topics but may *not* go into great depth on any of them. In effect, you sacrifice depth for breadth—a sacrifice that some gifted students, who often love discussion and deviating from the topic at hand—are not willing to make.

The best way to find out if AP is for you is to take a course or two as a high school sophomore. If the style and intensity of AP instruction fits your personality and learning style, then you'll be prepared to take even more AP courses in your junior and senior years. If AP is not for you, you'll have to scratch beneath the surface of your high school course catalog to find other options that respect your intellect and creativity.

Two more caveats about AP: some colleges and universities don't allow you to use AP credits toward graduation. They will permit you to take a higher-level course in the AP subject where you excelled, but college credit is not given. This policy doesn't show much respect for you as an intelligent student, and it doesn't save you a penny of college tuition (one of the major benefits of AP). So, before applying to the colleges of your choice, be sure to check out their AP policy. Also, if you happen to go to a small high school, there may be only a handful of AP courses offered. If this is the case, don't get discouraged; you may, in fact, still be able to take the AP exams for subjects in which you are especially proficient.

Weighted Grades

Many students are given the option of taking high school courses at the honors level. Although these aren't AP courses, their content and requirements may be just as demanding. Since you'll be asked to expend more effort in these classes, you ought to get more out of them, such as extra credit—literally.

When you take harder courses, you risk earning lower grades than if you take courses from the regular curriculum, so it's not unreasonable to expect something in return.

Ask your principal or guidance counselor what rewards exist for students who take honors-level courses. Often an honors grade will be weighted—that is, a B or B+ in Honors English will be noted on your transcript as being equivalent to an A in the non-honors track. At the very least, a notation should be made on your transcript indicating which courses you took at the honors level.

International Baccalaureate Program (IB)

Started in Europe in 1968, the IB option is one that has gained ground fast, and continues to do so. It began as a program for students from 16 to 19 years old, but it has extended downward to now include children as young as 3. The high school component (called the Diploma Programme) is now available in more than 2,100 schools in 130+ nations. More than 880,000 students are enrolled in one of the IB options.

Unlike AP, IB is not simply a singular course that you take in order to get college credit. Rather, it is a comprehensive, multiyear program of study that offers a framework for complex learning. A look at IB's mission statement says it all:

> *"The International Baccalaureate aims to develop inquiring, knowledgeable and caring young people who help to create a better and more peaceful world through intercultural understanding and respect."*

The desire to create a better world through education is the main thrust of this global network of schools. Not every school that wants to become an IB school is allowed to do so. A commitment of time, money, and resources for teaching teachers some new ways to instruct their students is required. However, the rewards of participating in an IB program are many and varied.

The Diploma Programme is, generally, a two-year course of study. Classes are taken in five required content areas: languages (yours and another one), social studies, experimental sciences, and math. A sixth area of study is the arts, although students may opt to take another course in one of the other five areas, if they wish. Some of the cornerstones of the IB experience include:

★ The extended essay: basically, a thesis that is conducted independently in an area of your interest

★ Theory of Knowledge: a year-long course designed to encourage reflection by examining different *ways of knowing* (perception, emotion, languages, reason) and different *kinds of knowledge* (scientific, artistic, mathematical, historical)

★ Creativity, Action, and Service: an outside-of-school project that exposes students to the real-world application of the skills they are learning in school

Exams are given, of course, and if enough points are earned, the IB diploma is awarded—which is a huge accomplishment. Generally considered to be your "passport to higher education," the IB diploma opens doors to the world's greatest universities.

As you might suspect, the IB option is one that attracts many gifted teens, because it provides a level of instruction that is rigorous, a depth of knowledge that intelligent people savor, and a chance to see your education from a global perspective.

Independent Study

Independent study enables you to work at your own pace in a program designed to accommodate and address your special interest. A mentor or teacher serves as your guide, but mostly you're on your own. Independent study programs usually require you to:

★ develop a plan stating the object of your study

★ list your goals and objectives

★ plan activities to achieve your goals

★ complete a final project

In one high school independent study program called the Autonomous Learning Project (ALP), students contract for projects throughout the school year and meet regularly in small groups. In the words of two ALP students:

CHARLES, 17: "The main thing this program has taught me is how to kick myself in the rear. In a normal classroom, the teacher hangs over you ready to cut your head off if you don't do the assignments. In ALP, you get a project and it's up to you to get it done. I think it's important to learn to be responsible for yourself."

Greg, 15: "For me, the best part of this program is being able to do your own thing. I do about three major studies each year—all things I wouldn't have the opportunity to study in regular classes. It really challenges you to accomplish more."

Early College Entrance

Early college entrance is a time-tested strategy that's available to many gifted high school students. It usually works in one of two ways:

1. Early admission. You do well enough in your freshman through junior years to apply early to a college of your choice. If you show strong promise (high grades and ACT/SAT scores), many colleges will consider accepting you as a full-time student at the end of your junior year. Check with the colleges you're interested in to see if they allow for the early admission option.

2. Dual enrollment. This option allows you to take college courses at a local university while you're attending high school. It works best when you live near a college campus and transportation between the two schools isn't a problem. Even if the nearest college is 100 miles away, you may be able to take summer courses to augment your academic credentials.

Akash attended college while still in high school, and here's what he says about his experience:

"When I told people that I was planning on taking a few college classes in my senior year of high school, the most common questions they asked me were, 'Won't you miss all of your friends?' and 'Do you think you can handle it?' Many people share these misconceptions about high school students taking college courses. In fact, I think it has been one of the most enriching and beneficial experiences of my life. I didn't lose any of my old friends; instead, I made several new ones. Not only were the college courses more challenging, they were also fun. I learned more than I ever could have at high school, and I received college credit at the same time. I highly recommend that any motivated student give college a try while in high school."

Which option is right for you? If you asked your parents, teachers, and counselors, they would probably vote for dual enrollment over early admission. Many adults believe that it's important for high school students to participate in high school social events—proms, pep rallies, yearbook committees, clubs,

Get a Running Start!

A dual-enrollment program called Running Start provides an opportunity for academically qualified high school juniors and seniors to enroll in college classes as part of their high school coursework. Running Start provides up to two years paid tuition at any state-run community college or four-year university that participates in the Running Start program. Check to see if your state offers this unique program.

and the like—and they have a point. It's easier to make up for lost time in academics than it is to go back and form friendships you wish you would've had time for. On the other hand, some high school students couldn't care less about football, dances, and homecoming floats. We feel that each decision about early college entrance should be made on an individual basis. When it comes to planning academic futures, there's no such thing as "one size fits all."

Mentorships

In a mentorship, a student is paired with an adult (or sometimes another student) who is an expert in a particular study or profession the student would like to pursue. Mentors can come from the academic, artistic, or business communities. Usually students and mentors agree to work together closely for a set period of time; meetings are arranged during or after school hours, as determined by the participants. Accelerated and enriched learning are the natural consequences of mentorships—which also provide good career exploration opportunities.

Summer School

Summer school programs vary greatly from school to school and district to district. When budgets are tight, some schools eliminate summer school altogether. But when schools can, they may offer a variety of classes designed to challenge and motivate gifted and talented students—especially on summer mornings!

Virtual Learning

What if you're dissatisfied with the course options offered at your school and yet you don't live near a college campus? You might supplement—or altogether substitute—your school experience with some combination of full-credit courses at virtual secondary schools, virtual gifted programs, free virtual (noncredit) university courses, and free video and audio lectures. If you're an ambitious student, the Web is your oyster!

In 2000, approximately 50,000 K–12 students enrolled in at least one online course in the United States. By 2009, 5.6 million enrolled.*

Virtual Secondary Schools & Programs

East High (*High School Musical*) and William McKinley (*Glee*) aren't the only onscreen high schools out there; there are hundreds of others—and they're completely nonfictional, fully accredited, and even meet national content standards. These virtual high schools and middle schools conduct classes wholly via the Internet by using tools like Web-conferencing programs, interactive whiteboards, text chats, and video and audio podcasts. They offer a dizzying array of course options not often found in brick-and-mortar schools. Here's just a small sampling of full-credit courses offered by secondary schools in cyberspace (in addition to *loads* of AP courses):

Game Design, Young Adult Literature, Arabic, Ancient Mythology, Screenwriting, Astronomy, Criminal Justice, Zoology, Conspiracy Codes, Ocean Ecosystems, Foreign Policy, Entrepreneurship, Peace Studies, The Holocaust, James Joyce, Fractals, Sports Training, Advanced Music Composition, Digital Photography, Flash Animation, and Python and Ruby Programming . . . are you drooling yet?

As if that's not enough, many also offer summer school, IB programs, honors credit, gifted student services, career counseling, and dual enrollment. Some virtual schools even grant actual diplomas, while some merely provide curriculum designed to supplement your existing school experience. The best things about taking virtual courses are that you meet people online from all around the world—including other gifted teens—and you can study and participate anytime from anywhere.

So what's the catch? Online courses require serious self-discipline and offer no face-to-face contact with an instructor or other students. You must work independently to complete all assignments on time. But for some, this mode of learning can be ideal, especially if you tend to be more comfortable expressing yourself in writing versus speaking. Just be sure that the course is of high quality. A good online course is far more than simply reading text onscreen. Read the course description or ask the teacher to find out if it

---

*Class Differences: Online Education in the United States, 2010, The Sloan Consortium.

includes a combination of presentations, audio, video, animations, and discussions. Communication between teachers and students is done through online discussion groups, email, text, or phone. Also, before enrolling in any online course, first check with a teacher or school counselor to confirm that you'll receive high school credit for completing it.

The other catch to online learning is cost. Some virtual schools and courses are very affordable, such as $10 AP courses or the K[12] Online School, which is around $72 per month (plus materials) for a course load of five classes. But many are pricier, ranging from $10,000 to $15,000 a year for places like The Laureate School or Stanford's EPGY High. However, you don't have to enroll full-time in most of these schools and can instead take one or two classes at a time to make it more affordable (a single AP course at Stanford will run you around $300). Also, scholarship options are available at some schools; check their websites for details.

Here are 10 of the top virtual schools and academic programs that cater to gifted students:

1. **Virtual High School** (grades 9–12, plus gifted students in grades 6–8) offers over 400 courses, including dual credit, summer school, AP and IB courses, and special high school courses specifically designed for middle school gifted students. (govhs.org)

2. **K[12] Online School** (grades K–12) is fully accredited, diploma-granting, and currently available via charter schools in 20 states, many of which include gifted student services. (k12.com)

3. **George Washington University Online High School** (**GWUOHS**) (grades 9–12) is an online private prep school operated in partnership between K[12] Online School and George Washington University. Admission to the program is highly selective. (gwuohs.com)

4. **National Connections Academy** (grades K–12) is a virtual private school available in over 20 states that specifically addresses gifted and talented students. It even offers a unique "dual diploma program" where you can earn a high school diploma *and* an associate degree in four years. (nationalconnectionsacademy.com)

5. **The Laureate School** (grades K–12), a division of the Laurel Springs School, offers online curriculum individualized for gifted students. (laureateschool.org)

6. **The Education Program for Gifted Youth (EPGY) Online High School** (grades 10–12) is an independent high school run virtually through Stanford University. Unlike many other online schools, EPGY is primarily synchronous, which means students and teachers meet online in real time. (epgy.stanford.edu/ohs)

7. **Duke University's Talent Identification Program (TIP)** (grades 8–12) is a virtual place for you to connect with other gifted students and with a TIP instructor as you pursue advanced high school and college-level online coursework. (tip.duke.edu/e-studies)

8. **The Center for Talented Youth (CTY) Online** is a program of Johns Hopkins University that provides challenging courses online all year long for eligible gifted students. (cty.jhu.edu/ctyonline)

9. **Gifted LearningLinks (GLL)** (grades K–12) is a program run by Northwestern University's Center for Talent Development that combines gifted education expertise with advanced technology. (ctd.northwestern.edu/gll)

10. **The Institute for Mathematics and Computer Science (IMACS)** (grades 1–12) offers distance-learning AP and university-level courses in mathematics and computer science for gifted students. (eimacs.com)

University Online Courseware

Following MIT's lead in the late 1990s, the world's most distinguished universities have been in a race to upload their course content to the Web for free public use. Sure, you won't get actual credit or teacher attention, but you *will* get incredibly valuable course materials that often include in-depth reading lists, video lectures, tests and quizzes, multimedia presentations, and audio recordings. Here are the current main sources:

★ **OpenCourseWare Consortium (OCW)** is a free and open digital publication of high-quality university-level educational materials from institutions around the world using a shared model. Participants include MIT, Tufts, Johns Hopkins, and Notre Dame, as well as universities in England, Spain, France, South Africa, Latin America, Korea, Israel, Japan, and many others. (ocwconsortium.org)

★ **Individual Universities** like Yale, Harvard, Stanford, University of California-Berkeley, and Carnegie Mellon all have their own open courseware programs. Check their websites for details.

Attend Harvard Medical School for Free from Your Bedroom

That's right. You can now download the open courseware materials for all the required classes for a four-year degree at Harvard Medical School. You can read the books and articles and notes, watch the lectures, view the slideshow presentations, and take all the quizzes and tests. You can even grade yourself. But, alas, you *can't* get a medical degree from Harvard. (mycourses.med.harvard.edu/public)

iTunes U

If you're simply searching for brilliant brain candy online, look no further than iTunes U. Download free audio and video podcasts of lectures from the world's leading academics at more than 800 universities across the world, including Stanford, Yale, MIT, Berkeley, and Oxford, as well as no-campus learning from places like The Museum of Modern Art (MoMA), the New York Public Library, and Public Radio International. Get iTunes U for free here: apple.com/education/itunes-u.

Special Interest Programs

Are you eager to get outside school walls to explore your passions and talents in the real world? All kinds of opportunities are available to become more involved and gain hands-on experience in your areas of interest at the local, city, state, national, and international level. Here are just a few examples:

★ **Poetry Out Loud** Got a gift for verse, spoken word, theater, or hip hop? Poetry Out Loud's mission is to celebrate poetry as an energetic oral art form. The program is a poem recitation contest for students in grades 9–12, administered by the National Endowment for the Arts. Contests begin at the classroom level, but winners progress through to the city, state, and national competitions. (poetryoutloud.org)

★ **Medical Explorers** Dreaming of med school? Medical Explorers is a free program offered in many areas to teens interested in learning about careers in medicine. Groups meet regularly during the school year at a local hospital where they explore departments and are given unique opportunities to shadow medical professionals, participate in hospital drills, and even view live surgeries. Check with your school and local hospitals or visit exploring.learningforlife.org and click on the "Health Exploring" badge for details.

★ **Model UN** Ever wonder what it's like to be an international ambassador? In Model UN, you'll get a chance to step into the shoes of ambassadors from UN member states to debate current issues on the organization's agenda—from maternal health to landmines to literacy. You'll make speeches, prepare draft resolutions, and negotiate with allies and adversaries to solve the world's problems. United Nations Secretary-General Ban Ki-moon, U.S. Supreme Court Justice Stephen Breyer, and Chelsea Clinton are just a few alumni of the program. (unausa.org/modelun)

Gifted People SPEAK OUT "Say It Out Loud"

by Morgan Brown

My junior year was a year of self-discovery. Cheesy, I know, but bear with me. All throughout high school, I had always been enrolled in Advanced Placement classes and had always known that I wanted to attend a top-notch college, but I had no idea what would come after that. I did not know my strengths, my passions, or my desires . . . until I discovered Poetry Out Loud: a national program designed to encourage teens to memorize and recite poetry and learn about the English language in the process.

When people ask me why I decided to participate in Poetry Out Loud, they usually expect me to prattle on about my love of poetry and how I wanted to make a difference in the world. The real answer? I did it for extra credit. As a high school junior, my prototype of poetry was "*Roses are red/ Violets are blue/ Sugar is sweet/ And so are you.*" I was under the impression that all poetry had to rhyme. With the help of my mentor and English teacher Mr. Haggquist, I have since learned that poetry does not *have* to be anything; poetry is an expression.

Poetry Out Loud has taught me the power a poet holds in the moment before beginning and upon ending a recitation. "The Mother" by Gwendolyn Brooks powerfully elucidates the regrettable consequences of a mother aborting her children. Yes, abortion is an uncomfortable topic. Yes, "The Mother" is an uncomfortable poem. Both of these truths required me to accompany my audience on an emotional roller coaster, starting at discomfort, but coming to a stop nestled between compassion and understanding.

I wanted my audience to see and hear the mother, not Morgan Brown. Given the power to step outside of myself and into the shoes of Gwendolyn Brooks, I desired for the audience to feel her pain, her regret, her suffering, and her loss. Becoming the speaker of the poem remains what I have learned to love most about recitation. The poet does not simply recite the words. The poet becomes the poem.

Becoming the poem in a physical form revealed a talent I was not cognizant of possessing. Much of what drove me to succeed in this competition stemmed from my excitement at discovering something I was genuinely good at. I was passionate about the effect that my recitations had on others and drawn to the effect that my recitations had on me. Subsequently, this new-found confidence transitioned into my joining the Young Writers Club where I learned to love writing my own poetry. The swing in my front yard has since become my poetic sanctuary, as well as the perch of my biggest critic—me. I have written innumerable pieces that I've tossed out and forgotten, never to see the light of day. Fortunately, some poems did survive my biggest critic and were published in the *Cedar Street Times*. What an honor to open to page three and see "Winding Solitude" by Morgan Brown!

The road to becoming the California Poetry Out Loud State Champion, paved by awareness and self-discovery, led me to experience a quiet strengthening of character. However, the most fulfilling moment came a few months after the competition during my shift as a volunteer at the U.S. Open. A darling old woman marched right up to me and asked, "Are you the high school poet who won the state finals?" I replied that I was and a slow smile crept across her face. She hugged me, told me how proud she was, and thanked me. Before I could so much as utter a humble thank you, she turned back the way she had come. It was not Tiger Woods, Graeme McDowell, or Gregory Havret who impressed her; it was me, because I had touched her personally, just as poetry had touched me.

Morgan Brown is a first-year student at Amherst College studying psychology, journalism, and theater. As an 18-year-old recent high school graduate, she is tremendously eager to begin a new chapter in her life. Her goal is to be genuinely happy in the career she chooses to pursue, whatever it may be.

Say Hello to Homeschooling

With such an awesome supply of learning opportunities available online and in the community, you might ask: who even needs to attend school? The answer is: many choose not to. Homeschooling is a rapidly growing trend, approaching 3 million students in the United States alone. The practice is gaining momentum especially among gifted kids, as studies show that homeschooled students test higher than students in public schools and are often more readily accepted into prestigious colleges. In the past, homeschooling parents often have been stereotyped as hippies or religious fanatics, but most of them are just average parents who have decided to take charge of their children's education. At home, you can progress at your own speed, and customize and enrich your learning experiences as much as you want as you work toward graduation, while also earning AP credit or even an IB diploma. With state and national standards all published online, it's now easier than ever to make sure you're hitting all your marks . . . without ever stepping foot inside a school.

> "HOMESCHOOLING IS AN IMPORTANT THING TO DISCUSS, SEEING AS A NUMBER OF GIFTED TEENS ARE HOMESCHOOLED (INCLUDING ME) AND FIND IT A MUCH MORE PLEASING ALTERNATIVE TO REGULAR SCHOOL."
> —*Maddox, 16*

If homeschooling appeals to you, how can you and your parents jump on this trend? Here are some of the most common ways to be schooled at home:

Attend your public school online. If it's available in your school district, simply sign up with an online version of your public school for free. You're counted as a public school student and required to have regular contact with teachers, submit homework, and take tests.

Enroll in an independent online school. Purchase materials from and enroll with an online school that is not part of your school district. In this model, you're pretty much on your own—you don't submit work or tests to anyone in your district and you progress through the prescribed material at your own pace. See the list of virtual secondary schools on pages 146–147 for examples.

Create your own curriculum. Make up your own courses of study based on your personal criteria. You can assign yourself tests and homework, but you don't have to. Some states want you to keep a portfolio of material to prove you're actually doing the work at home, and other states want you to submit

- From 1999 to 2007, the number of homeschooled children in the United States increased by 74%.

- 75% of homeschooled adults ages 18–24 have taken college-level courses, compared to 46% of the general U.S. population.

- Top colleges like Stanford and Harvard accept homeschooled applicants at rates equal to (and sometimes nearly double) the rate of overall acceptance.

National Center for Education Statistics Issue Brief, NCES 2009-030, U.S. Department of Education, December 2008.

your curriculum each year for approval. Costs for this model can be as cheap (library books and free online materials) or expensive (new books and costly licenses and subscriptions) as you choose to make it.

Get *unschooled*. If you really want to free yourself from all limits on your learning, you can follow the model of "unschooling," and get rid of textbooks and tests altogether and simply follow what interests you at any given moment. You read, write, take field trips, do activities, and complete projects driven purely by your own passion for learning. A lot of people consider this practice pretty radical, but for a person who is motivated and disciplined enough, it has proven highly successful and many unschooled students have gone on to attain prestigious Ph.D.s and professional degrees. Again, costs vary greatly depending on what you choose to do—will you learn about Darwin and natural selection by watching a free webcast series about the Galapagos Islands? (*Tip:* Search for "Galapagos" in iTunes U!) . . . or will you book a plane ticket there?

Can You Homeschool Yourself?

What if you're sold on the idea of homeschooling, but your parents are not fully on board to be your teachers . . . can you school *yourself*? You might be shocked to hear this, but the answer is *yes*—depending on which state you live in. Most state laws require you to attend school until you're at least 16, so if you're 16 or older and you really want to finish your high school requirements at home, you probably can, if you have the necessary resources and motivation and your parents okay it. If you're under 16, it may be a bit trickier, especially if you live in a state with strict homeschooling laws.

For instance, if you're homeschooled in Minnesota, your parent must have teacher training and/or be supervised by a licensed teacher. And in Pennsylvania, your parent must file a notarized affidavit, evidence of your immunizations, formal outlines of all your educational objectives, and proof of English instruction, while also having your progress evaluated periodically by a teacher or psychologist and nationally normed tests.

Meanwhile . . . Alaska's statute simply requires that you are "equally well-served by an educational experience approved by the school board," following a written request for excuse from school attendance. And in Texas, not even curriculum approval is required: "Homeschools do not have to initiate contact with a school district, submit to home visits, have curriculum approved, or have any specific teacher certification. Homeschools need only have a written curriculum, conduct it in a bona fide manner and teach math, reading, spelling, grammar, and good citizenship." Likewise, Idaho requires no prior notification, teacher qualification, or standardized testing, and allows children to be instructed with minimal parent/guardian instruction, which may involve "another family member, relative, or individual."

A Few Famous Homeschooled People

Joining many old luminaries like Einstein, Edison, Whitman, and Mozart, more recent examples of people who were homeschooled include National Merit Scholars, MacArthur Fellows, Fulbright Scholars, Nobel Laureates, university presidents, Olympic athletes, and award-winning actors and artists. Here are just a few:

- *Fred Terman, Timothy Dwight, John Witherspoon, Jill Ker Conway*, and *William Samuel Johnson*, present and past presidents of Stanford, Yale, Princeton, Smith, and Columbia, respectively
- *Sandra Day O'Connor*, former U.S. Supreme Court Justice
- *Frank Lloyd Wright*, architect
- *Olivia Bennett*, painter, art prodigy
- *Margaret Atwood*, Booker Prize–winning author of *The Handmaid's Tale*
- *Christopher Paolini*, *New York Times* best-selling author of *Eragon*
- *Jimmy Wales*, founder of Wikipedia
- *Erik Demaine*, MIT professor and MacArthur Fellow, named "One of the Most Brilliant Scientists in America" by *Popular Science*
- *Willard Boyle*, winner of the 2009 Nobel Prize in Physics
- *Hilary Duff, Kristen Stewart*, and *Elijah Wood*, actors
- *Carly Patterson, Venus and Serena Williams*, and *Michelle Kwan*, Olympic athletes
- *Taylor Swift, The Jonas Brothers*, and *LeAnn Rimes*, singers

So, as you can see, the regulations vary greatly by locale. But if you're determined and resourceful enough and you live in a state with fairly relaxed guidelines, you can likely discover a way to meet your educational needs at home with minimal parental participation. Look up the homeschooling laws in your state at the Home School Legal Defense Association (hslda.org/laws). Also, check to see if your state or city has any homeschool organizations, which are often great sources of information. Finally, talk to your parents; you might be surprised how willing they are to go the extra mile for you and become your home educators—even if it means getting teacher training—especially if you're willing to do your homework.

Gifted People SPEAK OUT "A Homeschooling Success Story"

by Kelsey Ganes *

I have always described my education as a mosaic of classes, self-directed learning, opportunities, and luck. First, a brief curriculum vitae: my formal education included two years in a gifted program, five years of homeschooling, followed by a single grade skip into high school, and this is where things get interesting. I began high school as a normal freshman (well you know, all things considered), taking a few honors classes where available; I chose to participate in a dual-enrollment program (Running Start) and ultimately graduated in three years. At 16, I became a fully matriculated student at the University of Washington as a regular incoming freshman, living on campus and participating in residence life, including a brief flirtation with the Greek system and a developing love of the arts. I graduated from the University of Washington's Honors College with a Bachelor of Arts in art history and a minor in architecture. While my schooling experience has been incredible, homeschooling also provided my "real" education, so to speak.

As a homeschooler, and particularly as a student with multiple learning disabilities (dyslexia, dysgraphia, and central auditory processing disorder), homeschooling was more than class- or text-based learning: it was a process of self-directed investigation, discovery, and realization. (I feel

---

* This article is reproduced with the permission of Kelsey Ganes and the Gifted Homeschoolers Forum, from the July 2010 issue of *A Word from GHF*. Visit giftedhomeschoolers.org.

like I just described the path to Nirvana, and that's not far from the truth.) Homeschooling prepared me both for college (and soon, graduate school), but also the ever-mysterious future of life and the workplace. In addition to providing me with fundamental life skills such as managing my time, staying organized, working independently (and confidently), my time as a home-schooler allowed me to discover my passions—both in terms of academics (history, art, and architecture) and leisure (photography, writing, and cooking). Were it not for the many and varied experiences the flexibility of home-schooling allowed me (from youth theater to botany), and the skills acquired along the way, I know that my success in college would have been limited, and come at a much higher price.

As I have said, my future seems ever-mysterious, and to be quite candid, that is perfectly all right with me. I am taking off this coming year from academia, applying to graduate schools in the autumn (I am planning for a master's in education) and working in the meantime. This is not to say that I plan to jump into a 9 to 5 job just yet—not that this would be a bad thing!—but I am hoping to land an internship (or three) at local art museums, libraries, or universities. If possible, I also plan to audit a few classes in the coming year, keeping my toe in the academic world, so to speak.

Kelsey Ganes is a University of Washington graduate with a B.A. with honors in art history and a minor in architecture. She is currently taking a gap year before pursuing graduate studies and is employed at Glutenfreeda.com and Foodista, Inc. She is passionate about food and photography and wherever life may take her!

The Smorgasbord Approach

There's no rule that says you must try homeschooling, Model UN, enrichment classes, AP, early admission, or dual enrollment. If you can't make up your mind about which option is best for you, then perhaps you can decide *not* to decide. Don't do anything, or do a little bit of everything, trying bits and pieces of each program you find appealing. For example, you might register for two AP classes and, at the same time, contact colleges about transferring the credits you earn. Couple this request with a query about their summer enrollment policies for qualified high school students, and you may be on your way to designing an academic program that's ideal for you.

Which Options Are Available to You?

If you don't know or you're not sure—ask! If the option involves a specific academic area, go to the teacher who teaches that subject or to a department head. You might also check with your school counselor, if you have one. If you can't get answers from either of these sources, go straight to your school principal. Make an appointment to see him or her, and come prepared with questions about what your school offers to bright, motivated students.

If your school has requirements for participation in a program that you want to join, find out what they are. If you don't qualify, see what you can do to change your status. If the requirements seem unreasonable or unfair to you, list your reasons for feeling that way and share them with the person in charge. Request admission on probation if necessary. If, after a reasonable period of time, it becomes clear that the class or program isn't for you, be prepared to withdraw and move on to something else. What's important is to keep trying. Remember, it's *your* education and *your* future.

The following story of Alicia is a great example of someone who took the smorgasbord approach to explore her interests in-depth in many different ways—from homeschooling to online classes, AP courses, early college, special interest programs, and more. She is living proof of how being gifted and resourceful can open doors to you beyond your wildest dreams!

Gifted People SPEAK OUT "Following Dreams & Dinosaur Bones"

by Alicia Bierstedt

My interest in paleontology began at a really young age—two, to be exact. I could recite the names of several dozen dinosaurs, and would correct anyone who pronounced them wrong within earshot. My passion for the science, though, began when I went on a field trip sponsored by the Denver Museum of Nature and Science (DMNS). After talking with the field trip directors, Drs. Kirk Johnson and Bob Reynolds, they helped me get into the Paleontological Certification classes at DMNS, covering topics like geology, fossilization, plate tectonics, and topography. There was one problem, though: the minimum age to be in the certification program was 17—I was only 7. Kirk and Bob could see I was more than just a kid interested in dinosaurs, so they arranged for me to take these courses anyway. The only stipulation was that my mom had to complete the curriculum with me. So I started, mom in tow.

Things didn't always go smoothly. For one, the classes were designed for college students and most took place at night. I did my best to concentrate and take notes, but it wasn't easy for a kid my age to be in class until 9 p.m. a couple times a week. Fortunately, I was not a traditional student, so I didn't have the pressure of waking up for school at 7 a.m. every morning. Instead, I was homeschooled until seventh grade, and in an online school program, the Colorado Virtual Academy (COVA), after that. So as long as my homework was all in on time, my school day could begin and end whenever I wanted it to. This flexibility gave me the freedom to learn at my own pace, eventually accelerating through two grades, and to delve deeper into the subjects I really found interesting.

Kirk and Bob could see I was more than just a kid interested in dinosaurs.

By age 10, I completed all the basic certification courses and received my Paleontology Certification. That summer, my classmates and I camped out for a week at the Elbert County Fairgrounds where, every day, I experienced what it meant to be a field paleontologist and geologist, collecting and identifying rocks and fossils. Since I'd grown up taking classes at DMNS, it seemed like a logical next step to volunteer there, interacting with the public, telling and showing them what is beneath their feet in the Denver Basin. I also started volunteering in the Discovery Zone, a hands-on area geared toward children. There, I could share my love of science and learning with young kids, and maybe inspire them to engage their natural curiosity and discover how the world around them works. It was then that I discovered my passion for education. I no longer wanted to just do paleontology; instead, I wanted to share my knowledge with the general public, especially the next generation.

As my interest in paleontology and museum studies changed and grew, so did the track of my education. For my junior and senior years, I attended public high school in Sioux Falls, South Dakota. That was a new experience for me; the last time I'd been at a brick-and-mortar school, I was barely seven. It gave me some different opportunities. I was involved in concert and jazz band at school, and was on both the policy debate and oral interpretation teams. During the summers, I was able to travel back to Colorado and Wyoming to continue the museum and field work that wasn't available in South Dakota. I also was able to take even more AP classes, with the added benefit of having a teacher right there to answer questions or explain something I didn't understand. While I'd had teachers with COVA, I only talked with them via email or on conference websites. Most of what I learned I got from reading the course materials, doing the problem sets, and basically teaching myself. Attending public high school for that time was a good transition from my self-paced, self-directed schooling in Colorado to the highly rigorous environment at college.

For my 18th birthday, I received my first job offer. I was asked to be the student supervisor for the preparation lab of Dr. Paul Sereno, one of the most renowned paleontologists in the world. It's an incredible opportunity for any aspiring paleontologist. I get to do preparation work on important new discoveries, do some of my own research, give tours of the lab to the public, and train and supervise the other students who do prep work. It's a major step toward my eventual goal of being a curator of paleontology at a nature and science museum, and particularly exciting, considering my age and that I'm now only a second-year undergraduate at the University of Chicago.

Being at UChicago is itself a challenging new adventure. The courses I'm taking are among the most challenging I've ever had, but also the most interesting. Many of my professors are active researchers, and it quickly becomes evident what they are passionate about. I also have classmates with a diverse range of interests: I've become good friends with mathematicians,

I never felt like I was being pushed ahead too fast, or that I was socially alone.

economists, philosophers, musicians, pre-medical students, and other geologists. It's refreshing to be in an environment where everyone is interested in something.

In addition to courses, I'm currently volunteering in the Dinosaur Preparation lab on campus and at the Field Museum, again interacting with the youngest visitors. My fieldwork has also continued, and I have spent 10 summers assisting with the excavation of a *Diplodocus* skeleton in Wyoming. This specimen is very well preserved, but all tangled up with itself. There are ribs twisted in knots, feet stuck under legs, one femur standing on end and twisted a quarter-turn, and a plethora of bones. This whole project is really like a complex, often frustrating, jigsaw puzzle. Finally, on top of all that, I am still involved with my other interests: I'm in two University music ensembles, and in several student clubs and organizations. It's the ideal environment for me to continue as a student, as a budding paleontologist, and as an individual.

When I was younger, I was often told that I was taking life too fast, that I needed to "slow down" and "just be a kid." Looking back on it, however, I feel the track I took is the one that worked best for me. Through homeschooling, museum schooling, and online schooling, I learned to love learning and to enjoy the process of science and discovery, and I realized that I'd never know everything, but that it doesn't hurt to try. I never felt like I was being pushed ahead too fast, or that I was socially alone. So far, following my dream has taken me to places I'd never have predicted. I look forward to where it will take me next.

Alicia Bierstedt is a sophomore at the University of Chicago, majoring in geophysical sciences with a focus on geology and paleontology. She plans to become a curator at a science museum once she completes the next decade or so of schooling.

chapter 7

College, Careers & Beyond

"I'D LIKE TO GO TO A REALLY GOOD SCHOOL IN HOPES THAT THERE WILL BE OTHER GIFTED PEOPLE LIKE ME THERE. IF I DON'T GO TO COLLEGE, I MAY WORK IN CONSTRUCTION, OR PERHAPS TAKE UP A CRAFT OR TRADE. I'M REALLY NOT SURE. IF ALL ELSE FAILS, I WOULD LIKE TO BE A STREET POET IN SAN FRANCISCO." —Saalik, 17

College

Travel abroad

Write a Book

Earn a scholarship!

The Course to College

If you aim to go to college someday, it's never too soon to start planning. By "planning," we don't mean spending the rest of your pre-college years with your nose buried in a book, or hiring private tutors to supplement your schooling, or signing up for study courses that are "guaranteed" to improve your SAT scores. We perceive planning as a series of purposeful decisions that can improve your chances of being accepted by the college of your choice. Following are some suggestions to keep in mind as you face those decisions.

Accept the Challenge

Based on your performance in elementary school, you may be channeled into particular courses in middle school and high school. If you've been a strong student, you'll be guided into the more challenging classes; if not, you'll be steered toward the basic (easier) courses.

If this type of academic grouping of students takes place in your school, we advise you to do whatever you can to get into the more challenging classes. Many of the courses you may want to take in the future are based on completing "prerequisites" now. Taking lower-level courses in middle school makes it harder to get into upper-level courses in high school. It's kind of like trying to catch a train after it's already left the station; you have to do a lot of running to catch up to a place where you should have been anyway.

We don't suggest that you do this in every subject, but math and language arts would be our first choices. These courses offer the basic building blocks you need to succeed in other courses; also, schools are more likely to offer different levels for these subjects, less likely for social studies or health.

Note: Some middle schools are doing away with ability-grouped classes altogether. If this is the case in your school, you (and your parents) still have the right to ask how your high abilities will be challenged.

Tip: Take Algebra I, foreign language, and computer courses as early as possible to better prepare for state university admission requirements and Advanced Placement (AP), dual-enrollment, or International Baccalaureate (IB) courses in high school.

Explore the Liberal Arts

You may choose to take a high school course load that is strictly academic, squeezing in that one fine arts requirement credit only grudgingly during your last semester of senior year. If so, too bad for you. You've just limited yourself in unnecessary and unfortunate ways.

For too long, high school courses in music, art, film, and the social sciences (for example, psychology, sociology, economics, political science) have been considered the "fluff" rather than the "stuff" of learning. But as more colleges discover the benefits of an education that is well-rounded and well-grounded in the arts and sciences, they are actively seeking students who have done more than ace every trigonometry test. They want students who know that Manet and Monet are two different artists, that baroque is a style of both architecture and music, and that William Faulkner, Hermann Hesse, Willa Cather, and Amiri Baraka are all worth reading. So don't belittle or avoid courses in the liberal arts. If you take them seriously, they can help you in specific ways. Examples:

★ You'll be able to write erudite college admissions essays, with references to the impact of art and literature on your life and the lives of other educated people.

★ Teachers will love the literary and artistic allusions that pepper your writing.

★ You'll see the connections among specific periods in history and the art, music, design, and literature of each era. That makes both history and the arts more interesting and enjoyable.

★ You'll be a bigger hit at parties and with parents. It's embarrassing to have to admit that the last really great book you read was *The Very Hungry Caterpillar*.

While you're at it, learn about belief systems different from your own by taking a course in comparative religions. Shaping more of our world's political and economic structure than any other force, religions hold the key to understanding the world that did, does, or might exist. Don't worry about being manipulated or converted; these courses merely compare, contrast, and explain what different countries and cultures believe.

> "It has always seemed strange to me that in our endless discussions about education so little stress is ever laid on the pleasure of becoming an educated person, the enormous interest it adds to life."
> ★ EDITH HAMILTON, EDUCATOR AND AUTHOR

Gifted People SPEAK OUT

"Leave and Be You"

by Alec Bojalad

You are not you yet.

Well, you're close but you're not quite there. You're kind of like Gus Van Sant's remake of *Psycho*. Looks good, sounds good, but it's not *Psycho*. Yeah you're like that. Look good, sound good, but not quite *Psycho* . . . unless you're actually psycho. Savvy?

Probably not.

So here's what I'm saying: you're not you yet because you haven't been to college yet. I'm going to go ahead and assume that you have some preliminary plans to attend college. You're probably going to attend college because your intellectual capacity is high enough for it. You're probably going to attend college because that is just what people your age do. You're probably going to attend college because you're reading this book and the demographics for people who read books and who go to college correlate significantly. So I have little doubt that one year, two or three years from now you'll be in a 200-seat freshman seminar fighting the urge to claw out your eyes with a #2 pencil. But it is one thing to resolve yourself to go to college and another thing entirely to understand *why* you're going to college.

You're going to college, friend, to become *you*—to become the version of you that you've always wanted to be. Take a moment to wipe the tears away from your eyes (or the vomit away from your mouth) and let me explain.

You will meet people. Cool people. People who you fall in love with, people who vex you, people who you work with, people who you stay up till four in the morning with and share a pizza with. You will change these people and they will change you.

You know how there are only like 12 to 15 cool people in your entire school? Well that's because there are only like 12 to 15 cool people in every high school that's ever existed. But there are a lot of high schools—a lot more high schools than there are colleges. Consequently those 12 to 15 cool people from each high school all filter into the few number of colleges and give college one of the world's most impressive cool person to non-cool person ratio.

You will find out what you care about. Someone will pass you a flyer asking you to support a cause and you will roll your eyes. Then one day you will be passing out flyers yourself. You will meet people with hipster glasses and obnoxiously unkempt facial hair and you will argue with them about Proust or Tolstoy or *Finding Nemo*. Things will anger you and you won't quite know why. You'll find an organization to join and you'll consider it your life's work (for four years). You will be part of groups without feeling compromised personally.

You will begin to understand things within your area of study that you never thought you could. Something will make sense to you and you will be ecstatic. You will realize that your instructors view you as their equal . . . and this will not even seem strange. You will fight the urge to be pretentious, with varying levels of success.

You will listen to Asher Roth's "I Love College" and nod your head along to the music non-ironically.

You will have memories you cherish. You will wake up one morning and realize you have enough life-affirming memories stocked up to last you the rest of your presumably soul-crushing adult life. You will have stories to tell—stories you never realized you'd be able to. When you speak, not only will you sound interesting and appealing, you will *know* you sound interesting and appealing.

Most importantly, you will be you. You will be like that character in sitcoms who audience members cheer for every time they enter a scene. You will have an identity—but one that can't be described in only a couple of adjectives. You will feel wanted because you *are* wanted. And you will feel important and productive because you *are* important and productive.

That is why you are going to college. Getting good grades, getting good internships, getting good jobs—these are all reasons why *other people* need you to go to college. Because it's what someone your age does. But *you* need to go to have one last gasp of personal growth before you're booted into the real world. You need to be knocked on your butt by experience, and then step back onto the pavement with firmer footing than ever before.

So go.

Leave and be you.

Alec Bojalad is a journalism major at Ohio University. He speaks brashly and writes with great pretension.

Choosing a College

Over 7,000 accredited colleges are in the United States alone—and most of them would like you to be a student at theirs. There is a lot of hype about how difficult it is to get into the most elite schools, places like Harvard and Yale, but once you examine what you want from your college experience, Harvard and Yale may not even appear on your radar. In the following section, we want to give you some advice and ideas about selecting a college that fits the person you are and the one you hope to become after four years (or more) of living the undergraduate experience. Whether you are an intellectual who craves nonstop debates on issues—any issues; an environmentalist who seeks a school that respects the earth; an entrepreneur who wants to design her own curriculum; a late bloomer who anticipates college as being a place to start over with people who don't know you; or a shy high school senior who just awaits the chance to spread his wings wide open, you will find a college—many, in fact—that will suit your style.

The Survey Says . . .

46% want to know more about their education options after high school.

60% of respondents want to know more about selecting a career or field of study.

Nine Nagging Questions About College

1. Should I attend a large college, a small one, or something in between?
Accredited colleges in the United States range in size from 38 students (an environmental college in Arizona) to 50,000+ (Ohio State University). At smaller colleges (2,000 or fewer), you can expect more one-on-one contact with professors who know your name. Also, class sizes tend to be in the range you're probably used to in high school.

At a large university, your Introduction to Psychology class will most likely consist of hundreds of students in a large lecture hall. This mass of humanity will be moderated somewhat by weekly tutorials, study sessions, or labs, all of which translate into smaller groups of 15 to 30 students and a TA (teaching assistant), usually a graduate student, who answers questions and explains any concepts that the professor in the large group neglected to address. Even at the largest universities, courses tend to get smaller as you take classes in your major area of study, eventually approaching somewhere between 20

In order to ensure a basic level of quality, the practice of **accreditation** arose in the United States as a means of conducting unbiased peer evaluation of educational institutions and programs. It's better not to take a chance on a nonaccredited school—trust us. For a full list of accredited U.S. postsecondary institutions and programs, visit ope.ed.gov/accreditation.

and 35 students, especially if you're enrolled in the Honors College within the university, provided it has one (see page 172 for more information on Honors Colleges).

Initially, a large university can be as intimidating to a kid from a small town as a small college is to a kid from a big city. So don't rule out any college due to size alone. You'll be surprised how adaptable you can be when you're finally away from home. Also, even on a campus of 20,000 students, you "become a number" only if you choose to. A college of any size will offer many opportunities for your face and name to be known to others.

2. What's the deal with online degrees?

Attending college in person obviously has its benefits (live human interaction and fattening cafeteria food, for instance). However, if for some reason you wanted or needed to, could you obtain an undergraduate degree solely via the Internet? The answer is yes, but the pickings are slim—for now, anyway. The majority of colleges provide some kind of distance learning program in which students can complete some degree requirements virtually; among top colleges, Columbia, Stanford, Harvard, and Cornell currently have the most extensive for-credit online course catalogs. But only a small handful of schools offer full online undergraduate degree programs, and typically these programs are in engineering and technology fields. Most online degree programs are geared toward adults continuing their education. Accredited virtual universities, such as The University of Phoenix and Capella University, are gaining popularity, yet degrees from these institutions typically do not garner the esteem that degrees from established traditional colleges do.

3. Should I aim for a public or private college?

Public schools (state colleges and universities) are allocated money by their respective state governments. These subsidies lower the cost of tuition. Private schools don't have access to state dollars, so you pay a premium to attend these schools. As a general comparison, tuition at a public four-year university currently averages $7,500–$12,000 per year, depending on whether you're an in-state or out-of-state student, while a private school's tuition averages just over $27,000 per year, with some inching close to $60,000. Don't forget to add room and board costs, too—about $5,000 per year.

If your heart is set on a private school but your wallet is screaming poverty, don't despair. Most private colleges have money—more than public schools—to award in scholarships. So, when all is said and done, if you're a smart, achieving student, you may get enough financial aid from a private school to make it equivalent to (or cheaper than) the public alternative. Never rule out a private school because of cost alone. Most private colleges have both the wherewithal and the willingness to help capable students.

4. What about community colleges?

Public two-year community colleges charge, on average, just over $2,700 per year in tuition and fees. That's an attractive price if you're hurting for cash. An option gaining popularity among college goers—including high-achieving ones—is to enroll in a local community college for their first year or two to complete their "generals"—the general course requirements that nearly all liberal arts schools mandate, such as English composition or calculus. The reason for this is to save money on not just tuition, but also room and board and travel costs (students often choose to live at home while attending community colleges). Also, the academic pressure is not so great at most of these colleges, even though many do employ excellent teachers of introductory subjects (see page 178). And finally, many high-performing graduates of two-year colleges go on to complete the last two years of a four-year degree at prestigious universities.

Of course, you'll miss out on the prototypical college freshman experience if you take this route, forfeiting some campus involvement and networking opportunities, but that may be okay with you in order to save some serious money. Also, you can supplement your studies with online courses, or make use of your time outside of class by doing an internship or participating in any number of activities or programs in your community related to your fields of interest.

5. How can I find money for college?

Each year, hundreds of thousands of dollars in scholarships and grants (which never have to be paid back) aren't awarded because no one bothers to apply for them. Imagine—free money and no takers!

Your high school counselor should have ample information on available scholarships based on *need* (when you and your family can't afford to pay college costs) or *merit* (money given to you because of your academic record regardless of your family's income). Also, millions of dollars are available to highly able and motivated students from particular states, or those whose heritage is Hispanic, Native American, or whatever, or who happen to be female, or who plan to major in aerospace engineering or some other career of interest to a particular company or charity. Many books and websites describe the scholarships and grants available to you, such as these:

★ *College Board* (collegeboard.com/student/pay)

★ *Fastweb* (fastweb.com)

★ *Getting Financial Aid 2011* (College Board, 2010)

★ *How to Get Money for College 2011: Financing Your Future Beyond Federal Aid* (Peterson's, 2010)

★ *Paying for College Without Going Broke* (Princeton Review, 2010)

★ *The Ultimate Scholarship Book 2011: Billions of Dollars in Scholarships, Grants and Prizes* by Gen Tanabe and Kelly Tanabe (Supercollege, 2010)

Tuition-Free College? For Real?

If you're more than a little concerned about how to pay for college, in addition to applying for scholarships and grants you might consider applying to one of the small number of tuition-free colleges in the United States. The following four schools are all small in size, academically rigorous, and funded by generous endowments that make them able to provide all students with full tuition for their entire tenure.

Curtis Institute of Music in Philadelphia is just as prestigious as Julliard but totally free. The famous composer Leonard Bernstein was a graduate, which doesn't hurt its reputation any.

Cooper Union in Manhattan offers rich programs in art, architecture, and engineering, and boasts eminent alums such as graphic design icon Milton Glaser.

Olin College of Engineering in Needham, Massachusetts, ranks as one of the top engineering programs in the country and maintains a strong emphasis on philanthropy and entrepreneurship.

Deep Springs College is located in the middle of a remote cattle ranch in the California desert. It's an all-male two-year liberal arts college where students work on the ranch when they're not in class. Most graduates go on to complete their degrees at top-ranking universities.

6. Can I reasonably expect to finish college in four years?

The four-year college experience is rapidly becoming a relic of earlier, simpler, and less costly times. Today it's not unusual—and at many large public universities, it's becoming the norm—for a college degree to take four and a half to six or more years to complete. There are several reasons for this, including:

★ **Cost.** Tuition has become so expensive that many students must work while attending college. This cuts down on the number of courses you can take each term. Remember, in college you can decide how many courses you'll take each term. There's no guidance counselor or homeroom teacher breathing down your neck. (15 credit hours per term is typical.)

★ **Internships and co-op programs.** If your major requires or allows these options, you may find yourself at work in a real business, hospital, etc., while earning college credit for your efforts. Usually, though, this reduces the number of courses you can take at one time. Still, it can be worth trading the time for the experience. Many college graduates end up working for the firms where they interned.

★ **Cutbacks.** In recent years, colleges and universities have absorbed some major budget cuts. In response, many of them have eliminated courses that they would ordinarily offer. This may prevent you from taking a required course on schedule, throwing off your plan to graduate in four years.

★ **Life.** You want to spend a year abroad, you get married, your parents split up, you want a break from the college routine; none of these will necessarily prevent you from getting a degree in four years, but each of them might. Life's exigencies sometimes waylay even the best-laid plans.

If it's absolutely essential that you graduate within four years, make sure to ask your preferred colleges how many students finish within this time. If their answer is "less than 50 percent," ask for an honest explanation before you commit to that school. Also, remember those AP credits you earned in high school? They may help you finish college within a timeline that is more comfortable and cheaper than the "five-year plan" now endured by so many undergraduates.

7. How much academic pressure will I experience?

Almost any guide to colleges will include a section detailing whether the college is *noncompetitive* (all you need to get in is a high school diploma and a tuition deposit) or *highly selective* (admission is limited to no more than 20 percent of the applicants). Between these two extremes are *less competitive*, *competitive*, and *selective*—broad-based indicators of how much pushing and shoving goes on (figuratively speaking) to gain admission.

While getting in is probably three-fourths of the battle, especially at highly selective schools, staying in is another challenge. Suddenly you're competing with a more diverse student body than you've ever experienced before. You also may be competing with a much smarter group of students than you're accustomed to.

When it comes to pressure, you have three choices:

★ *If you want to be a big fish in a small pond,* attend a college with relatively low academic requirements. Your abilities and talents will rise to the top fairly quickly without much effort on your part.

★ *If you want to be a medium fish in a medium pond,* seek a college that fits your academic style and past performance. Most other freshmen will also have come from the top quarter of their high school graduating classes, excelling in ways that are obvious yet commonplace in this competitive setting.

★ *If you want to be a small fish in an ocean,* accept only the best. Soon after you arrive, you'll assume that everyone there is smarter than you. Don't panic! At least half of the entering freshmen will share the same fear.

As you consider a prospective college's academic qualities, keep these guidelines in mind:

★ Even noncompetitive schools have some strong programs, and even highly selective schools have some weaker ones. Don't just look at a university's reputation; look (closely) at the department that interests you (for example, history, education, biology, English, computer science).

★ Prestige doesn't matter when everyone has it. It may feel great to tell your high school friends, "I'm attending Highbrow University in September," but once you arrive at HBU, it's not news anymore. If you choose a school strictly on the basis of prestige, you may be in for a rude awakening.

★ Honors Colleges can give you a first-class education for a discount fare. Many large state universities offer a "college-within-a-college" for their most academically oriented students. For the same tuition you'd pay to attend mega-classes in lecture halls, you'll experience smaller classes, more personalized attention, dynamic professors, and a cohort of intelligent students who share your major and even your interests. Check out the Honors College route; it's like a gifted program at the university level, and the quality often rivals programs at more intense and expensive private schools.

★ Remember the transfer factor. More than 50 percent of entering college freshmen change their academic majors at least once during their college career, and up to 30 percent transfer from one university to another before attaining a bachelor's degree. So if you make a decision as a high school senior that you later regret, you'll be able to switch directions without losing any of the academic credits you've earned (at least through the end of your sophomore year). Your credits, like you, will move to a new department or a new home.

8. Are some colleges more unique than others?

When you think college, the first thing that comes to mind (. . . or should!) is academics: Do they offer your major? Are they reputed to have enthusiastic, knowledgeable professors? However, college is a lot like high school in one important way: it is as memorable for what happens *outside* of classrooms as *inside* of them. For this reason, you may want to consider a "catalytic college," a phrase used by Loren Pope, former education editor for the *New York*

Times, in her book *Colleges That Change Lives: 40 Schools That Will Change the Way You Think About Colleges* (visit the website at ctcl.org). The colleges Pope highlights are smallish in size (a few thousand students, primarily), and they share a common mission: the focus is on the students, not the faculty. They offer a sense of community and fellowship; learning is more collaborative than competitive; and the overall atmosphere is much more like a "family" than a "factory." In other words, the individual in you is valued and rewarded.

They may be highly intellectual campuses (like St. John's College in Santa Fe, New Mexico), greatly open to student input regarding curriculum and classes (Reed College in Portland, Oregon), or simply places that help you become the most confident and effective person you can be (Hendrix College in Conway, Arkansas, or Eckerd College in St. Petersburg, Florida). If you've been itching to get away to a place where your independent streak is cherished, take a look at one of these 40 college possibilities.

9. Essays and letters of recommendation? Help!

Many colleges require an essay as part of their application process. Even though the question you have to answer may be worded differently, the ultimate focus is the same: colleges want to discover *who you are and what makes you tick*. You've probably gotten advice from many an English teacher about effective writing techniques, so after you've written your essay (or essays), ask a teacher who knows you well to read it over and give you critical feedback. You'll need a thick skin if your essay comes up short in your teacher's eyes, but take this review in stride: if you revise the essay so that it captures your essence, admission to your college of choice is one step closer.

> ## Colleges want to discover who you are and what makes you tick.

Even though most colleges require an essay topic of their choice, you may luck out if you are applying to the more than 400 colleges that accept the Common Application. This is exactly as it sounds: you can submit the exact same application to any of these 400+ colleges. These colleges are in 44 states and Washington, D.C., as well as in Germany and Italy, and they even include "big guns" like Duke and Northwestern universities. Go to commonapp.org to determine which colleges participate. Also, if you need specific guidance in writing your essay, or you'd like to read some successful essays written by others in your position, get the most recent edition of *Accepted! 50 Successful College Admission Essays* by Gen Tanabe and Kelly Tanabe, or visit a consultant site such as College-Admission-Essay.com run by the Ivy League graduates of The Penn Group who will help you with your essay for a fee.

Top 10 Bizarre College Essay Questions

Read some of the wackier questions admissions officers have asked in recent years. Colleges that ask unusual questions like these are often connoisseurs of offbeat thinkers and this is their way of testing your originality. Usually they do not require an answer to these questions, and you won't be penalized for leaving them blank, but we advise you to always give them a shot, no matter how bizarre they are! (Well, within reason.) Try your hand at answering a few of the following questions, especially if you plan on applying to any of these or similar colleges.

1. *How do you feel about Wednesday?* (University of Chicago)

2. *In the year 2050, a movie is being made of your life. Please tell us the name of your movie and briefly summarize the story line.* (New York University)

3. *Are we alone?* (Tufts University)

4. *Please describe a daily routine or tradition of yours that may seem ordinary to others but holds special meaning for you. Why is this practice significant to you?* (Barnard College)

5. *Make a bold prediction about something in the year 2020 that no one else has made a bold prediction about.* (University of Virginia)

6. *You have just completed your 300-page autobiography. Please submit page 217.* (University of Pennsylvania)

7. *Can a toad hear? Prove it.* (Bennington College)

8. *If you were reduced to living on a flat plane, what would be your greatest problems? Opportunities?* (Hamilton College)

9. *Sartre said, "Hell is other people"; but Streisand sang, "People who need people / Are the luckiest people in the world." With whom do you agree and why?* (Amherst College)

10. *Analyze Seneca.* (Bard College)

As for teacher recommendations—ask for them early! Before your teachers are flooded with other requests. Approach teachers and counselors who know you as an individual, not just as a student. This personal touch will help the writers create a more complete picture of who you are. If recommendations aren't mandatory, get one or two anyway; they can only help your admission chances, especially if your academic record is somewhat spotty or your standardized test scores are a bit weak.

Do You Have What It Takes?
Insiders' Tips from Admissions Officers

Following are some valuable tips gathered from admissions officers at Stanford, Bowdoin College, Brown University, Massachusetts Institute of Technology (MIT), Haverford College, the University of Virginia, Penn State, and Loyola University[*]:

★ Start looking for scholarship and financial aid money *now*. The sooner you're able to establish some opportunities, the better. (See page 169 for more on this.)

★ Be realistic about what you and your family can afford when it comes to your college education. Too many students start out at the school of their dreams only to find out that after one semester or one year, the expense is more than they or their families can bear.

★ Do your research. What type of student are the schools of your interest looking for academically? What do you know about their institution and how can you be a great addition to their student body? What is the minimum admission criterion? What is the average criterion for current students? Sometimes these two things are different.

★ Keep in mind that many colleges compute their own GPAs for high school students, counting only "academically solid" courses and dropping grades for subjects like Drivers' Education and gym. (Stanford even drops all ninth-grade marks, assuming that long-ago year has little bearing on your collegiate ability.)

★ Demanding course loads are more impressive than high grades. As one admissions counselor observed, "We'd rather see a student take AP and honors courses and get B's than regular academic courses and get A's."

[*]Special thanks to Danita Salone, assistant director of admissions at Loyola University (and former gifted teen) for her tips!

★ Don't get lazy during your senior year of high school. First semester grades in particular remain important. Some students have even lost their tentative admission status because of a lackluster senior year.

★ The combination of high SAT/ACT scores and low course grades is a red flag to admissions officers. In the words of one, colleges generally avoid "the kind of person . . . whose teacher says he or she is gifted but is not using it."

★ Essays are very important. Not only do they highlight your writing talents; they also reveal your personality.

★ Teacher recommendations work in your favor only if they are specific.

★ Real talent—athletic, artistic, musical, or otherwise—is always noticed. But don't try to round out your résumé by suddenly signing up for every school activity. As one admissions official says, "You could play third trumpet for four years and by sticking it out, you'd still be showing loyalty, commitment, and dependability."

★ Volunteer work is looked upon very favorably, especially leadership roles: "Somebody who works in a soup kitchen is going to look good, but someone who got funding for a new center is going to be special," explains one admissions director.

★ Pay attention to deadlines. Every school you consider will have various deadlines to meet. Many are very strict about no second chances. You miss the deadline; you've missed your opportunity.

★ Establish communications with the colleges and universities you're interested in. Find out who your admissions counselor is (there's one assigned to every application that comes in) and contact him or her. Send an email, or call to check on your status. For some schools, your contact also measures the level of your interest.

In summary, while there's no magic formula for getting into the most prestigious colleges, it's obvious that it takes more than high grades alone. The good news is: the majority of all applicants are admitted to at least one of their top two college choices.

QUIZ Test Your College Knowledge

With so many politicians, pundits, and armchair professors out there spouting about the goals and costs of higher education, it's sometimes difficult to separate the fact from the fiction. See how well you do by answering the following seven questions *true* or *false*. Write your answers in a notebook.

1. Elite schools offer you more "bang for your buck" than nonelite schools.

2. Community colleges' undergraduate teachers aren't as good as elite colleges' because they aren't paid as much.

3. It is better to attend an Ivy League university and perform okay than to attend a small liberal arts college and perform well.

4. It matters less where you go to college than where you go to graduate school.

5. Most of today's top leaders in the United States are graduates of a large and diverse array of universities.

6. Graduating from an elite college pays off in high career income more often than graduating from a nonelite school.

7. You should attend the best college you can get into, even if you have to take out large loans to pay for it. After all, there's no better investment than your education.

Answers

1. *True.* Thanks to generous donations from wealthy alumni and other sources, the students at highly selective schools get a lot more benefits—in terms of quality facilities and services—and pay a lot less for those benefits. For those who can afford them, the Yales, Princetons, and Browns of the world are like education "value packs" where students pay as little as 20 cents for every dollar spent on them (which is an average $92,000 per pupil), while students at less selective universities and community colleges end up paying an average of 78 cents on every dollar spent on their education (which averages $12,000 per pupil).* Whether or not all of this increased spending on students in selective schools is vastly improving the quality of their education is not always clear. But you can be fairly sure that if you choose to attend a costly elite college, you *will* get your money's—or your scholarship money's—worth, one way or another.

*Richard D. Kahlenberg, editor, *Affirmative Action for the Rich: Legacy Preferences in College Admissions* (Century Foundation Press, 2010).

2. *False.* According to the annual Community College Survey of Student Engagement, the best community colleges do a better job than the average elite college at teaching—especially freshmen and sophomores. Why? Because the professors at highly ranked research universities tend to focus heavily on, well, *research.* That is how they are able to keep their jobs and build their academic reputations. Their second priority is graduate students (and some upper-level undergraduates) who can often help them with their research, and a distant third priority is first- and second-year undergraduates, who they must actually *teach.* In contrast, many community college professors specialize in instruction and are very good at employing the teaching practices that research shows lead to quality learning. That's not to say there aren't stellar teachers at top schools, it's just more difficult for them to prioritize teaching, no matter how much they are esteemed or paid—there are only so many hours in a day!

Check up on the quality of the community colleges in your area at ccsse.org. Most are two-year programs, but if you do well enough, you can often finish out your degree at a top university. (Plus that way, you'll garner a bit more of the esteemed professor's attention as a junior or senior, versus as a freshman or sophomore.)

3. *False.* As previously stated, the faculty at highly selective schools is often more focused on research than on teaching. If you're a very assertive person who knows exactly what you want, this might be fine for you, as you'll find ways to get your professors' attention. But if, like many freshmen, you're a little more reticent and unsure of yourself, you may get lost or overlooked in such a setting and not perform as well. A small liberal arts college with a focus squarely on *you*, the undergraduate, may be a better choice for you and elicit better performance. And performing well as an undergraduate is paramount—particularly if you plan to apply to graduate school later on.

4. *True.* Many professions nowadays require at least a master's degree in addition to a baccalaureate, which has made undergraduate schooling merely the first step on the ladder. The quality of graduate or professional school you attend will matter more in the long run to your career success than the ranking of your undergraduate college. And to get into a high-quality graduate school, you need to learn as much as you can and perform to your utmost ability as an undergraduate, at whichever institution you choose. For example, Johns Hopkins Medical School is most likely going to look more favorably on a *summa cum laude* graduate from a state university than a C-student from Duke.

5. *False.* As much as we'd like this to be true, it's simply not. Wealthy and selective colleges offer unparalleled access to leadership positions in the United States. In fact, about half of all of U.S. corporate and government leaders are graduates of just 12 universities. (You can guess which universities.) This certainly doesn't mean it's impossible to become CEO of Google or the next POTUS[*] without a prestigious diploma; it's just statistically less likely. Then again, it's also true that about half of all corporate and government leaders graduated from schools *other* than those 12. Plus, not everyone wants a high-pressure leadership role—which is a good thing! There are just as many smart, talented people needed in other roles, such as teachers, scientists, nonprofit managers, and union leaders, who can influence decision making in the leadership classes. A democracy requires depth and diversity to function—not just Stanford and Harvard MBAs.

6. *False.* A long-term study of nearly 6,500 college graduates[**] found that students graduating from an elite college (where entering students have high SAT scores) did not pay off in higher career income. In fact, the study showed that students who applied to several elite schools but didn't attend them—either because they were rejected or changed their minds—are *more* likely to earn more money later on than students who actually attended elite schools. Sound crazy? It's not.

Elite colleges admit students, in part, based on characteristics they deem predictive of the students' potential to earn lots of money. They're great at selecting for characteristics related to academic ability, which are reflected in test scores, grades, and other measures. But they aren't always good at selecting for other factors, such as motivation, ambition, and desire to learn—all of which have a much stronger effect on your career success than the average academic ability of your classmates. The researchers call this finding the "Spielberg Model" after the famous movie producer Steven Spielberg, who was rejected by both the prestigious USC and UCLA film schools before choosing to attend the less prestigious Cal State Long Beach instead. As you may have heard, Spielberg hasn't done half-bad for himself, along with plenty of others like him who were also rejected from elite colleges.

7. *False.* Just because you are offered a spot at an expensive elite school does not mean you should necessarily take it. If you are not well off financially and you're unable to secure ample scholarship and grant money, think twice before signing up for large federal student loans. These loans must be repaid as soon as you enter the workforce,[***] and even though the interest rate is generally low, if the principal loan balance is very high, your minimum monthly payment can be crushing, especially if you don't get a job that pays big (and we mean *big*) bucks. You may find your life choices—where you live, how much you travel or pursue hobbies, whether you attend graduate school or start your own company, and even whether you have a family—limited. So yes, your education is a wonderful investment, but keep in mind how long you want to be paying on this investment, and what other investments you'd *also* like to make in your life.

---

[*]President of the United States

[**]Stacy Berg Dale and Alan Krueger. "Estimating the Payoff to Attending a More Selective College: An Application of Selection on Observable and Unobservables." *National Bureau of Economic Research (NBER) Working Paper No. 7322*

[***]A few professions, such as teaching, medicine, and law, provide opportunities for certain types of loan forgiveness if you donate volunteer hours or work with disadvantaged populations.

The Envelope, Please

You've just been admitted to all three of your top college choices. Congratulations! Now what?

Once again, it's comparison time. After you've considered the factors most relevant to you—cost, distance, reputation, size, etc.—eliminate the *one* college that ends up at the bottom. This will be hard initially, but it will ultimately make your decision easier. Next, scour the websites and reread from cover to cover the catalogs from your remaining two options, keeping a running

Six Unusual College Majors

Not sure what you'll major in when you get to college? Many students already *in* college still aren't sure, which is totally okay. College is meant to be an exploration. And you can rest assured that for just about every interest you have, there's probably a way to major in it. For example, you can major in . . .

- **Ecogastronomy** at the University of New Hampshire

- **Bowling Industry Management and Technology** at Vincennes University

- **Packaging** at Michigan State University

- **Blacksmithing** at Southern Illinois University

- **Bakery Science** at Kansas State University

- **Underwater Basketweaving** at Reed College (Okay, so it's not exactly a major, but Reed truly has offered this outrageous class every year since 1980 as part of its annual *Paideia* festival of learning.)

- **[Insert Your Idea Here]** At many colleges, you're able to create your own major, provided there are enough courses available in relevant fields. Often called "Interdisciplinary," "Individualized Study," or simply "IS" majors, students combine courses from multiple departments to design a curriculum for themselves that does not adhere to any pre-planned package. For example, one student entered college caring deeply about animal rights, so she created a major in "Environmental Ethics," which combines politics, ethics, and science. Other examples of IS majors include "Genocide Studies, Human Rights, and International Relations," "Global Health and Poverty," and "Prelaw, Politics, and Critical Race Theory."

"[IS majors] generally fare better in the job market than do classmates with traditional majors. An individualized course of study allows students to market themselves as 'entrepreneurs and self-starters.'"
★TRUDY G. STEINFELD, HEAD OF NYU's WASSERMAN CENTER FOR CAREER DEVELOPMENT*

*Kowarski, Ilana. "Newly Customized Majors Suit Students with Passions All Their Own." *The Chronicle of Higher Education*. Sept. 5, 2010.

checklist of pluses and minuses. If the decision is still too close to call, visit the campuses again. If this isn't possible, call the admissions officials you've been dealing with and ask them to give you their best pitches one more time. Finally, after talking over your choices with other people whose opinions you value and respect, select the college that your heart, not your head, tells you is the best place for you.

College is so much more than classes and tests. During your four (or more) years there, you'll mature in ways you never thought possible, discover new interests and passions, encounter challenges you never knew existed, make new friends, establish contacts you'll draw on for years into the future, and perhaps even meet your life partner. All other things being equal, let emotion, intuition, gut feeling, your "sixth sense," or whatever you want to call it be your guide. And remember, there's always the transfer factor.

Alternatives to College: A Road Less Traveled

All this talk about college makes it appear that higher education is the only route that gifted teens take after high school. Not so. For multiple reasons, some gifted graduates take a different path once the cap and gown have been discarded. Maybe military service runs in your family or you've been intrigued by army life for years. Or, family and financial circumstances may be such that college just doesn't fit the budget, so you plan to enter the workforce right away. Or maybe you are inspired to start your own business or join a volunteer program such as AmeriCorps.* All of these options are legitimate and should be respected. As a wise colleague of ours once said, "The only thing worse than being denied opportunities is being forced to take them." College should always be a choice, not an obligation.

"COLLEGE IS NOT RIGHT FOR EVERYONE."
—Jennifer, 18

One alternative that has been common practice in Europe for years but is still rather rare in North America is something called a *gap year*. This is the year directly after high school graduation when most students head to college. You, however, do not. Instead, you fill in this gap with a set of planned

---

*The minimum age to join AmeriCorps is 17 and you must have a high school diploma.

experiences that takes you out of the grind you've been in since kindergarten: waking up each day and going to school. This may be especially attractive if you graduate early from high school and feel you can afford to take some time off before college. Some gaps are filled with travel or foreign exchanges with a family in another country (see Olivia's story on page 184). Others are more work-focused, whether it be in a job or internship that aligns with your career interest or just something mundane to pay the bills. The benefits of a gap year vary and, sad to say, some are neither productive nor fun. But you can make a gap year work for you:

1. **Have some idea of what you *will* do, not just what you *won't* do.** Merely saying, "College isn't for me right now," won't get you very far with parents or other adults who care about you. You need to have at least a semi-solid notion of what you'll do instead. Talk over your ideas with a trusted teacher or counselor, and present your parents with a clear rationale for choosing this direction. There's no guarantee they'll be keen on your idea, but you're better off with a well-defined plan than a loosely sketched one.

2. **Hedge your bets.** When the PSAT, SAT, and/or ACTs are offered, sign up for them. When "College and Career Night" rolls through your high school cafeteria, go and hear what these recruiters have to say. When you're able to enroll in honors-level or AP courses, take at least a few of them. And, most importantly, if you really do think you *will* attend college after your gap year is over, *apply and get accepted before you graduate high school.* Most colleges and universities will defer your admission for a year, understanding that a student like you is likely to be more serious about your studies if you can come to campus on your own timeline.

3. **Never say never.** When considering your future, it's tempting to talk in absolutes—as in "I'll never . . ." or "I'll always . . ." The problem with absolutes is that they eventually require retractions. As you mature, you see more clearly that the world has more shades of gray than it does stark blacks and whites. Also, when you say "never," you may not mean "forever," yet that's usually how adults interpret that word.

To avoid needless misunderstandings, try to avoid "I'll never" statements like "I'll never go to college. What's the point?" First of all, these are fighting words to any adult who has higher education on your horizon for you. Secondly, "I'll never . . ." is simply a naïve statement. You can't possibly know how your dreams and goals will change next year or next decade. Better that you say, "Right now, college is not my top priority. I'd rather do (fill in the blank) because (fill in the blank). I'm not sure if I'll feel this way next year, but it's what I'm feeling now. Please respect that." By using these words and this tone, you are opening doors instead of slamming them shut, and you are being sensitive to people whose dreams for you do not now coincide with your own.

4. Explain that your decision to explore a gap year is your choice, not someone else's fault. When relatives and educators hear of your nontraditional plans, their first response might be "Where did we go wrong?" Allay their anxiety by explaining that you've thought long and hard about your decision (you have, haven't you?); it is not a snap judgment. Relieve them of the "fault burden" by reminding them that the strength it took for you to make this choice is a direct result of the ways you were raised or taught: to be an independent thinker. Thank them for giving you the inner strength to pursue a course that seems best for you.

5. Show excitement about your gap year. Enthusiasm is infectious, so be sure to hype the benefits of your gap year's possibilities. By being as clear as you can about what you'll be doing, where you'll live, how you'll earn money, and how you'll stay safe, you are more likely to gain support for your ideas. You'll know you've succeeded when even one doubter says, "Well, this might not be such a bad choice after all." That might not be a ringing endorsement, but it's a step in the right direction.

Most adults yearn for the time when they had fewer responsibilities and more options, just as you do now. Use this nostalgia to your advantage. Since you'll be an adult for the rest of your life, you might as well squeeze as much out of your waning adolescence as you can. A gap year provides time to explore both who you are and who you hope to become. Don't mess it up by doing nothing.

Gifted People SPEAK OUT "My Gap Year"

by Olivia Fauland

In the fall of my senior year, I started the application process for college along with the rest of my class. As I wrote entrance essays, got letters of recommendation, and researched different schools and their many pros and cons, I began to feel lost within my applications. I didn't feel as if I was ready to make a solid decision about my occupation for the future and it did not feel right to me to spend a small fortune in college tuition for a degree in something I wasn't sure about. I couldn't seem to answer the most basic of questions; big school or small school? In state or out of state? Intended major? With every "I don't know" I began to feel a sense of panic and after a few simple applications to state schools I began considering other options.

Both of my parents are avid travelers and I had been fortunate enough to travel with them throughout my childhood; yet I had never fully understood another culture. Inspired by a friend of mine who went to Brazil on exchange our junior year, I applied to a study abroad program called American Field Service (AFS). Upon acceptance to the program I was assigned the country of Sweden and made my final decision to defer from college for a year and take a different route than the rest of my senior class.

I received support from my parents to go abroad and many of my closest friends, teachers, and mentors were excited for me and not particularly surprised by my decision to break the mold. But I did encounter some quizzical faces when I mentioned my post–high school plans and was often asked "why?" To this I responded by explaining my uncertainty and indecision. Even after my explanation some people, mainly my peers, were perplexed by my decision and skeptical about my ability to return to formal education after my year abroad. While I must admit neither the transition to Sweden, nor the transition back, was easy, my longing for new information and desire to learn made both decisions worthwhile for me.

My first few weeks in Sweden were among the hardest in my life. I felt out of place, confused, and above all overwhelmingly alone. The lack of familiarity was hard to cope with and yet made the smallest tasks—like going to the grocery store or riding the bus into town—huge adventures. As the year progressed I learned the language and experienced Swedish culture in its entirety. I made lifelong friends from all over the world and now have what I consider to be a second family in Sweden. In addition to new skills and new relationships, I gained invaluable knowledge about myself and my home.

I realized that I am capable of anything and have the ability to adapt to my surroundings without losing who I am. I learned to calm down and not be so hard on myself for making mistakes, because those are often the instances in which we learn the most. I assumed the responsibility of fending for myself and making informed decisions and judgments as an adult. My social and communication skills were taken to another level through the language barrier, allowing me to connect with people from diverse backgrounds and upbringings.

Along with an understanding of other people, I gained knowledge about the United States and the culture in which I was raised. Seeing the way another society functions allowed me insight into the societal structure of the United States—both the negative and positive aspects. Differences such as healthcare systems, the legal drinking age, consequences for driving under the influence, the education and public school systems, and the distribution of political power enlightened me and gave me insight that I do not feel I could have acquired in any other circumstance. I even found out that in Sweden it is extremely *un*common for a student to enter college directly after finishing high school.

A gap year is not simply a year off, but a year of discovery and growth.

For me, the benefit of a gap year was unparalleled. I learned in ways I never could have in a classroom, no matter the level of education. Even the ability to learn and take information from everyday situations was harnessed through my experience in Sweden. Upon returning to the United States and beginning college, I felt out of place once again, only this time it was for all the right reasons. Instead of feeling like I had lost a year or was in some way behind my graduating class, I felt wiser and more knowledgeable than the majority of my peers. Similarly in my classes, I connected more easily with the upperclassmen than with my fellow freshmen and upon hearing the perspectives and opinions of my classmates, I felt lucky to have had the experience and awareness that I did.

To anyone considering a gap year, I *highly* recommend it. I have to warn that a gap year is not simply a year off, but a year of discovery and growth. It was my personal experience that filling out applications, sending transcripts, etc., is much easier as a senior than during the gap year, and deferring from college is convenient and noncommittal. I would also recommend taking as many Advanced Placement or dual-enrollment classes as possible during high school, because it enables you to take a year off and, with enough credit, enter college as a sophomore. While planning and consideration are necessary, the benefits of taking a year to grow, mature, and learn in a different setting than a classroom is one of the best decisions I have made for my personal life, my education, and my future.

Olivia Fauland is a freshman at the University of Colorado in Denver, majoring in fine arts.

Internships: The Path to Passion

Whether or not you take a gap year or plan to attend college, doing an internship could be one of the most important steps you ever take toward your dream job or career.

For example, say you are really into movies and would love to get in on the production of one of them. You can apply for an internship at 40 Acres and a Mule Filmworks, a company founded by director Spike Lee.

Speaking of mules, perhaps animals are your passion and you'd love to educate others about the native habitats of ocelots. Check out the internship at the San Diego Zoo.

Or maybe you've been saving money and making interest-bearing loans to your friends who are short on cash for the prom. Finance is in your blood. There's an internship for people like you at the Bank of America.

Literally thousands of companies and organizations can help you take a dip in the world of work, often while you are still in high school. Lots of these internships are unpaid, but if you live at home you are probably still living off your parents' goodwill, so money may not be your prime consideration. Instead, an internship in an area of interest might lead you down a career path that you follow for years. Conversely, your internship may show you that a field that sounded intriguing is actually as bland as grits without salt. Both are valuable life lessons to learn.

So . . . where to start? Here are three suggestions:

1. Go to vault.com and click on "Internships," or check out the *Vault Guide to Top Internships* by Carolyn C. Wise. This website and book are filled with thousands of internship possibilities, including at places such as 3M, The American School for the Deaf, the Andy Warhol Museum, and the National Security Agency. The trick is that you have to live somewhere close to where these companies operate in order to take advantage of the internship. But with so many possibilities listed, that may be more likely than you think.

2. Visit your school's guidance office. Local employers are often looking for cheap or free labor (yes, that would be you), both during the school year and summer, and they frequently let school counselors know of these possibilities.

3. Or, simply check things out on your own: pop into a local veterinarian's office and offer to keep Fluffy and Fido company while they await their distemper shots. Stop in at a food co-op and volunteer to take on shifts to stack shelves or collect excess vegetables from nearby farms to distribute to local homeless shelters. Or give your teaching skills a run for their money while you work with struggling readers at the elementary school that dismisses two hours after your high school day is over.

Some of you might be skeptical, wondering if the benefits of an internship (especially an unpaid one) are worth it. Let's review why our answer is "yes":

★ The minute you enter a company or organization and work to improve it, you are now a professional, not a student. You will be respected as such.

★ You will be in close contact with people who are being paid to do something you might wish to pursue as a career. Who better to inform you of that field's pros and cons?

★ You will pick up skills you didn't even know you needed to learn, such as organization, conflict management, prioritization, and people skills.

★ When you complete your internship, you will have contacts and mentors you can connect with at a later time. They might even be ready to offer you a *real* job, if you've proven yourself to be an asset in their workplace.

★ Will you do "grunt work" that few others want to do? Probably, but somebody's got to fact-check book manuscripts—why not you? Plus, most professionals don't start off at the top; rather, their career ladder's first steps are the bottom rungs. Internships can provide that initial leg-up to a career worth exploring.

The Beauty of Not Being Sure

Unsure about what path you want to take after high school? You are certainly not alone among gifted teens. Consider this analogy...

Las Vegas is famous for a lot of reasons. One of them is the variety of all-you-can-eat buffets offered in many of the fanciest hotels. A typical dinner buffet would offer everything from prime rib to crab legs, hummus to guacamole, strawberry shortcake to chocolate torte. Literally, hundreds of foods are available for breakfast, lunch, or dinner.

"I THINK THAT THE MOST DIFFICULT THING GIFTED KIDS FACE IS CHOOSING A CAREER. WE CAN HAVE SO MANY TALENTS AND SO MANY HOBBIES, AND THEY CAN DIFFER SO MUCH THAT WE FIND IT MORE CHALLENGING THAN ANYTHING TO CHOOSE A SINGLE FIELD." —*Alexei, 14*

Imagine you pay your fee to eat and, as you are being seated, the maitre d' informs you of a buffet rule: you can eat as much as you want . . . of any one item. When you protest that the benefit of a buffet is to nibble and nosh your way through a variety of foods, you are informed that that is not allowed: one food and one food only can fill your plate.

Absurd, right? Well, that situation is analogous to what many gifted adolescents feel when they are asked to select a job, college major, career, or other pursuit: "How do I pick one when I am interested in and good at so many things?" This is such a common dilemma with gifted young adults that the situation has actually been given a name: *multipotential*. If you have it, you are not alone.

Thankfully, you do not have to know as a teenager what you want to do when you grow up. Many of your high school friends will have selected a college and/or a career path by their junior or senior year. They'll state with certainty that they are going to be an FBI agent or a neurologist or a freelance artist. They'll know, too, which path they will take—college, trade school, ROTC—and they will be convinced that they will never change their minds.

And many of them will be wrong. They *will* change their minds, or their career direction, between their high school graduation and the beginning of their chosen occupation. Why? Because when they leave the relatively provincial cocoon of high school and join the wider world that awaits them, they will be exposed to all manners of people and possibilities that they never knew existed. For example, if you are looking to attend a large university with a major in biology, one of the first questions you will have to answer is *what kind* of biology do you wish to study: marine? micro? forensic? neuro? The same is true for virtually every other college major. Layers and layers of divisions exist within the generic fields of chemistry or economics or English.

For some gifted students, this overexposure to the wider world is disheartening, as their surety in high school gets replaced with uncertainty just two years later. To others, it is exciting to consider possibilities that heretofore had been unknown. And to still more, this bountiful buffet of choices creates confusion and internal chaos, as they jump from one career direction or post–high school endeavor to another, with each new selection delaying their personal goals for another year or their college graduation for one more semester.

Our advice: b-r-e-a-t-h-e. You likely have 40 years or more of work ahead of you, so take your time in deciding what you want to do. Moreover, with the constant technological advances in today's workforce, even when you do decide what you want to do, chances are that you will change jobs—and possibly even careers—multiple times in your life. So bounce around as you learn about new options; if you enter college with an undeclared major, know that you are wiser than those who picked a particular major because it sounded like what a gifted young person should become. If some well-meaning adults pressure you to move in one direction—*their* direction—thank them for their concern as you continue to explore and meander through life's evolving adventures.

> "When I was growing up, I always wanted to be somebody. Now I see that I should've been more specific."
> ★LILY TOMLIN, ACTRESS

Or Not . . .

If you are one of those individuals who has known since an early age that you really want to spend your life as a travel writer, a programmer, a botanist, or a kindergarten teacher, more power to you. Some gifted people *just know.* If this is the case, multipotential won't become a huge issue for you. However, the opposite might occur: you could focus so intently on one area of study or work that you don't open yourself up to endeavors beyond the narrow path you have paved for yourself.

Now, it is not our goal to push you into things to try to make you unsure about your chosen endeavors, but we just want you to see the world without blinders. By broadening your scope's view even a little, you'll be more fun to talk with, you'll meet people who appear to have nothing in common with you (even though they probably do), and you'll use your fine mind to make connections among areas of study and fun that seemed totally separate at first glance.

The world *is* a buffet, and no maitre d' is standing guard to ensure that you sample only one thing from it. So taste away!

> "AS A GIFTED PERSON I FEEL THAT AS AN ADULT IN A WORK ENVIRONMENT I WILL BE MORE SUCCESSFUL BECAUSE I KNOW THE VALUE OF INFORMATION AND HOW TO FIND IT." —*Zach, 17*

Welcome to the 21st Century Job Market

No matter if you choose to go to college, do an internship, or take a year off to travel, eventually you'll find yourself on some sort of career path. And that career path will probably look a lot different from your parents'. Why? Today's careers demand a more sophisticated set of skills than did many jobs of the past. It's no longer enough to be well educated and able to recall and apply knowledge in a chosen field. Watch any old black-and-white movie and all those characters bustling around offices in sharp suits would likely be unemployed today, replaced by intelligent machines or workers in other countries.

Today, workers are expected to analyze, evaluate, and create *new* knowledge within and across fields. In this century—*your* century—the essential skills you'll need are things like adaptability, self-direction, cross-cultural

What exactly do we mean by **career**? In today's ever-changing world of constant opportunities, the terms *job* and *career* are becoming harder to pin down. We use the words interchangeably to mean any path that you choose to explore your interests, apply your talents, and earn your livelihood—be it as a freelance worker who completes short-term jobs as they arise, a part-time or full-time employee at a company or institution, a business owner, an author, an artist who relies on grants from foundations, or any number of other options. The possibilities are endless; if you can dream it, you can probably find a way to do it.

skills, leadership, and accountability.* You'll be immersed in a workforce that requires you to possess "literacy" in global issues, economics, government, healthcare, and the environment . . . not to mention technology. And you'll be competing for jobs with other very bright people who have these skills and literacies, some of whom may be hired before you and may *not* have your 4.0 GPA, prestigious internship, or relevant life experience. How can you prepare for such a daunting work world? Here are a few suggestions:

The Seven Routines of 21st Century Gifted Teens

1. Investigate STEM fields. The STEM fields are: **S**cience, **T**echnology, **E**ngineering, and **M**ath. The reasons they merit their own acronym are simple: they represent the majority of future careers and the United States is desperately lagging behind in them. Out of the 34 countries who measure standardized tests, the United States ranks just 17th in science and only 25th in math,** while China ranks first in both subjects. Needless to say, a big push is happening in the United States and other industrialized nations to educate and hire qualified workers in these fields. So do yourself a favor and stay on top of the major STEM developments and trends by taking relevant classes; reading books, periodicals, blogs, and newsfeeds; watching documentaries or webcasts; and talking to people in these professions.

> "WHEN YOU'RE OUT IN THE REAL WORLD, PEOPLE DON'T CARE IF YOU'RE GIFTED, THEY CARE IF YOU CAN GET YOUR JOB DONE."
> —*Celena, 13*

This may be a piece of cake if you happen to be a gifted techie, math nerd, or physics geek, but what if science, technology, engineering, and math just aren't your things? Not to worry. The workplaces that hire STEM professionals are often sophisticated companies and institutions that also are in need of talented employees in the arts and humanities. For example, if you're a word whiz, you might someday find yourself vying for a position as a communications manager at a medical foundation. Or say you're a talented visual artist—you may have a future opportunity to work in production design for a technology firm. In either case, it will be a huge asset when applying for the job if you already have at least a little background knowledge of medical science or technology.

---

*The Partnership for 21st Century Skills, www.p21.org.
**Based on the 2009 scores from OECD's (Organisation for Economic Co-operation and Development) Programme for International Student Assessment (PISA).

2. Master a foreign language (or three). Consider this: roughly 50,000 U.S. students are currently studying Mandarin Chinese, while roughly 300 *million* Chinese students are studying English.[*] Being fluent in another language is no longer a mere novelty or convenience, but fast becoming a necessity in the global workforce. Aside from English, the top five most widely spoken languages in the world are: Mandarin Chinese, Spanish, Arabic, Bengali, and Hindi. Obviously learning one or more of these would be advantageous to you. But don't limit yourself to only those, especially if you have a gift for words and language. Studies have shown that fluency in *any* language other than your own—including sign language and even computer programming languages like C++—increases adaptability, empathy, employability, and IQ. Meanwhile, each additional language you learn makes it that much easier for you to learn another language or system of knowledge.

3. Explore other cultures. This may seem like a no-brainer, but it's not. It can be very easy, especially if you live in a country as large as the United States—and especially as a gifted teen with your nose buried in books and Web research concerning your passions—to become somewhat oblivious about the rest of the world, even with all the global media and immigrant populations inhabiting the country. But cultural isolation will not help your career success, especially since virtually every company in the United States and Canada now has an increasingly diverse staff. The pressure to become more globally aware requires companies to look for employees who are, too.

Cultural sensitivity is not something you can easily fake. Travel internationally if you can. Also, make a habit of reading world news and literature, watching foreign films, sampling global music and food, and attending ethnic theater and dance performances. Visit the immigrant neighborhoods in your area, volunteer to be an English tutor, learn new languages, and connect with people online from all over the world. It's not only fun to explore your world in this way, it will give you a definite edge in your career and enable you to relate better to your diverse colleagues and community members in the future.

4. Learn to roll with it. It's no longer realistic to think that you just need to excel at one skill or in one field of knowledge to take you through years of a career. Your career, no matter how talented and well educated you may be at the outset, will likely throw many curveballs your way, given the rapid

[*]The American Council on the Teaching of Foreign Languages

pace of change in most industries. So your ability to flex and adapt—and not give in to perfectionism—will be extremely important. The key is to learn how to embrace change and use your problem-solving abilities to grow and learn. The more positive experiences you have with change in all areas of your life, the more adaptable you become. Moving, breakups, bombed tests, and sports injuries? Start seeing these curveball events as "career training" versus setbacks.

5. Create, create, create. As discussed in Chapter 2, creativity is a key component of overall intelligence. It's also a key to innovation—a necessary skill in many of the new jobs created as a result of all those smart machines that are replacing the old jobs. In large part, it's what distinguishes human ability from mechanical ability. Sure, IBM may be able to build a supercomputer that wins on *Jeopardy!*, but it still cannot build a computer to replace jobs like app developers, book editors, and clinical social workers that require innovative problem-solving and novel solutions, not to mention good old-fashioned people skills. So take our creativity tips on pages 57–58 and document your results in a portfolio to prove your creative thinking skills to potential employers, partners, or clients. We guarantee this will impress many people more than a 4.0 GPA or perfect SAT score.

6. Be a technology connoisseur. Invest some time to find the best devices, software programs, networking sites, and Web apps that can help you prepare for your future. For example, find out what software application the professionals in your fields of interest use and look for a similar cloud app or free trial version online. True, the programs and apps will probably change by the time you enter your chosen career, but it certainly won't hurt to already be familiar with the basic functions. Plus, just like learning a new language, learning a new technology makes it that much easier to learn another, perhaps similar, one in the future. Meanwhile, here are a few tips for improving your general technoliteracy[*]:

★ Find the minimum amount of technology that will maximize your options.

★ Get used to the fact that anything you buy is already obsolete.

★ Before you can master any technology, it will be replaced or updated; you will always be a beginner, so get good at beginning!

★ The proper response to a stupid technology is to make a better one. ☺

[*]Adapted from "Achieving Techno-Literacy" by Kevin Kelly, *The New York Times*, 9/16/2010.

What's Your Digital IQ?

Sure, you might be a digital native by virtue of your birth year, but are you a true technology whiz? How does your knowledge stack up of digital video formats, animation tools, emoticons, Web marketing, media branding, and computing history? What's the difference between Web 1.0 and 2.0 and 3.0? Test how wired your brain is here: apps.facebook.com/digitaliqtest. Sponsored by British-based nonprofit MediaTrust, the quiz doesn't just analyze your general knowledge but also your affinity for different types of digital media.

---

7. **Practice your elevator speech (and your Lincoln Center one!).** In addition to the more general social skills discussed in Chapter 2, you'll also need to know how to sell yourself. This can be daunting, to say the least, especially if, like many gifted people, you tend toward introversion, sensitivity, and emotional intensity. Some of the most seasoned business people, professors, doctors, lawyers, librarians, engineers, and CEOs still struggle (and sometimes sweat profusely) when presenting in public. In just about any job or profession you choose, there will be some expectation of presentation skills—be they used to woo a potential client in an elevator or to educate a room of several thousand at an industry conference.

So practice speaking about yourself and your interests and abilities—anytime, anywhere (in front of your computer video camera?), even if it feels silly. Speech and debate club, theater, poetry slams, karaoke, Toastmasters, or improv comedy classes are all great places to hone your skills, too. The more you ease yourself into public speaking now, the fewer panic attacks, sweat-stained shirts, and awkward interviews you'll have to endure in the future.

Meet 10 Teen Entrepreneurs

Why wait until you're out of college—or even out of high school—to start your career? Here are some young people who didn't:

1. **Lane Sutton**—age 14, *critic*—reviews books, films, activities, and restaurants from a teen's perspective on his acclaimed website. (kidcriticusa.com)

2. **Adam Horwitz**—age 18, *app developer*—launched Mobile Monopoly, a smartphone app that earned $1.5 million in its first three days. (adamhorwitz.tv)

3. **Lizzie Marie Likness**—age 12, *amateur chef*—is founder and creative culinary officer of Lizzie Marie Cuisine and has appeared on popular cooking shows such as *Rachael Ray*. (lizziemariecuisine.com)

4. Tavi Gevinson—age 13, *fashion blogger*—has made a stylish splash in the world of *haute couture* with her fresh and unapologetic insights and ideas. (thestylerookie.com)

5. Farrhad Acidwalla—age 17, *marketing agency manager*—is a college student in Mumbai, India, where he also manages Rockstah Media, a full-scale international marketing agency. (rockstahmedia.com)

6. Talia Leman—age 16, *philanthropist*—is founder and CEO of the nonprofit RandomKid, which seeks to empower ordinary kids to create extraordinary change in their worlds. (randomkid.org)

7. Adora Svitak—age 13, *author*—has published two books, been featured on *Good Morning America*, and presented at the annual TED (Technology, Entertainment, Design) conference. (adorasvitak.com)

8. Emil Motycka—age 18 (now 21), *small business owner*—began mowing lawns when he was nine. In his senior year of high school, his company Motycka Enterprises pulled in $135,000, offering everything from lawn care to Christmas light installation. (motyckalawns.com)

9. Catherine Cook—age 16 (now 22), *social networking website founder*—started My Yearbook with her brother while they were both still in high school. Today, the site has over 20 million members and $20 million in annual revenue. (myyearbook.com)

10. Michael Dunlop—age 16 (now 21), *finance blogger*—created a successful finance blog. He is dyslexic and has no high school diploma, but now makes six figures a year. (incomediary.com)

> "I'D LIKE TO LEARN MORE ABOUT HAVING A CAREER AT A YOUNG AGE. I HAVE BEEN WORKING PROFESSIONALLY FOR SEVERAL YEARS ALREADY." —*David, 17*

Do you have what it takes to be an entrepreneur?

According to several of these young self-starters, here are the key ingredients[*]:

★ A certain amount of *naïveté* (to even try it in the first place)

★ Tons of *support* from family, friends, and mentors

★ A distinct *passion* for your field

★ Endless *hard work*—this is unavoidable!

★ Dogged *perseverance*, even when the odds are stacked heavily against you

★ And finally, a healthy dose of *humility*

> "Young people really know what's going on and really are coming up with the best ideas and the best sites. If adults don't listen to them, they're fools." ★MICHAEL DUNLOP, YOUNG ENTREPRENEUR

[*]Adapted from "These 10 Pre-Teen Entrepreneurs Make Millions More Than Their Parents" by Matt Wilson, BusinessInsider.com.

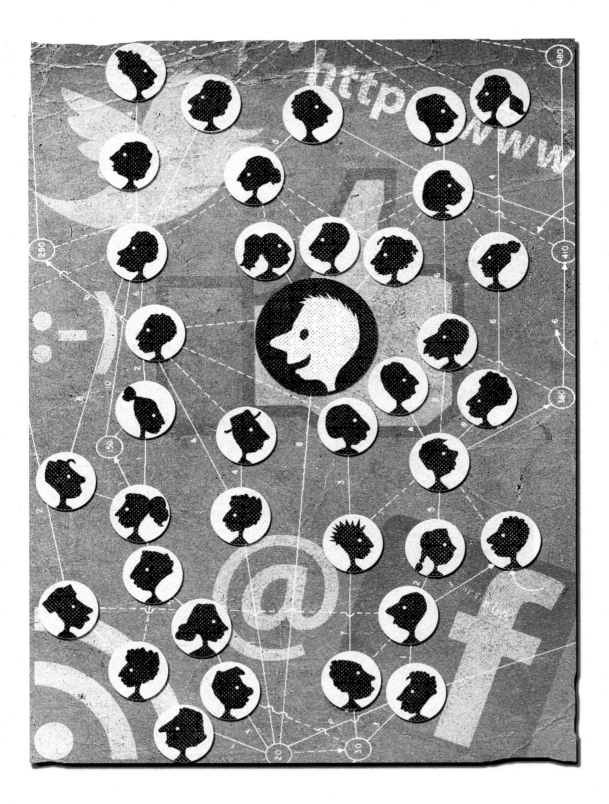

chapter 8

Social Smarts, Relationship Realities

To your parents, you may be the smart son or daughter they're always bragging about—or nagging. To your classmates, you may be the brain, the know-it-all, the one with the answers. Sometimes being gifted is a pain, especially when it affects your relationships with others. No matter how good you are at entertaining yourself, no matter how much time you spend inside your head solving problems, dreaming dreams, or thinking fascinating and creative thoughts, you need other people in your life,

"I TRY NOT TO LET THE FACT THAT PEOPLE THINK I AM GIFTED AFFECT MY SOCIAL LIFE. I WANT TO BE LIKE MY FRIENDS, JUST ANOTHER PERSON, BECAUSE BEING DIFFERENT SETS YOU APART. ANYONE WHO IS DIFFERENT GETS LAUGHED AT." —*Jayla, 14*

including age-mates and adults, both those who have been identified as gifted and those who have not. This chapter is about relationships—making new ones, reassessing some existing ones, and strengthening those that matter to you.

The Survey Says . . .

59% of respondents want to know more about how to improve their social skills.

55% want to know more about the importance of age in friendships.

46% want to know more about coping with peer pressure.

47% want to know more about how to get along better with parents.

Friendship 101

No one can argue about the importance of having friends. They support us in good times and bad; they enhance our enjoyment of many things, from athletic events to parties, special projects, even studying. Especially as your parents and teachers start exerting less influence over your actions and beliefs—a normal and natural part of your development that begins at around age 12—your friends assume greater influence and play a more central role in your life.

Gifted or not, we all need friends; gifted or not, we all sometimes have problems making and keeping friends. But being gifted can put a unique spin on social relationships and occasionally complicate them. Following are some questions about friends and friendship that gifted students have shared with us in surveys, interviews, letters, and conversations.

10 Common Questions About Friendship

1. Does everyone have trouble making friends, or is it just me? Relax; it's not just you. Some people seem to make friends effortlessly—they're in the right place at the right time with the right social skills. Other people find it difficult to connect because of shyness, circumstances, or whatever. But everyone—whether adept or awkward—has to work at forming and sustaining meaningful friendships. (For tips on making friends, see page 201.)

2. Do I have to conform to be accepted and have friends? It's not a bad thing to go along with the crowd—as long as the crowd is right for you. It's only when you compromise your own values, beliefs, and goals that conformity becomes a problem and can even be dangerous. On the other hand, if you always insist on doing things your way, be prepared for a lonely life. The key is to find a social group and some close friends who complement you, not contradict you. (For more about popularity, see pages 207–210.)

3. Is it normal to have just a few close friends? Yes. Gifted children and teens tend to be more adult-like in their relationships, favoring a few intense relationships over several more casual ones. What's important is to have at least one or two friends who you can rely on. When it comes to relationships, quality matters more than quantity.

4. Does it matter if my friends are two, three, or even four years older or younger than I am? No. Adults have friendships with people of all ages, so why shouldn't you? What matters is to cultivate friends you can count on and relate to. Sharing the same birth year isn't as important as sharing interests, goals, and values. (For more about breaking age barriers, see pages 204–206.)

5. I've just met someone I'd like to be friends with, and he asked me what *gifted* means. What can I say that won't alienate him or sound arrogant? You might begin by asking him what he thinks it means. If he really wants to know, this could lead to an interesting discussion about your individual points of view. Remember, there are no right or wrong answers about giftedness; even the experts can't agree on a single definition. By now you probably have your own ideas about giftedness. Share as much or as little as you want.

> "I DON'T ALWAYS KNOW HOW TO HANDLE MY GIFTEDNESS AROUND MY FRIENDS. WHO SHOULD I TELL, WHO SHOULDN'T I? WHEN AM I BRAGGING, AND WHEN AM I JUST TELLING THEM THE TRUTH?" —*Max, 13*

6. Some of my friends seem to resent me, or they're prejudiced against me because I'm gifted. Why is that? Usually people have prejudices when they don't understand something or someone. They may feel inferior if they don't have enough good things going on in their own lives. So putting you down may make them feel better about themselves (at least for the moment). Just be yourself, and they may come around—or you may need to start hanging out with other people.

7. How should I respond when my friends tease me about being smart? There's no single foolproof way to cope with teasing. If the teaser is someone you respect and care about, be honest and tell her how the teasing makes you feel. Ask her to stop being critical of you and explain that the teasing isn't helping your friendship. If the teaser is someone you don't respect or care about, ignore her and walk away. At first this may seem hard to do, and it may hurt, but if the teaser doesn't get a response from you, eventually she'll move on. (For more about teasing and how to handle it, see pages 211–218.)

8. How can I cope with "leech" friends—people who rely on me for homework help and want to copy my test answers? First, ask yourself, "Are they really my friends?" People who like you only for what they can get from you don't qualify as friends. So that's something you'll have to decide. Second, if you feel like helping (with homework, not with test answers), and if you have the time, then go ahead and do it. Otherwise, simply explain that you have your own work to do and you're not available this time around. Maybe the "leeches" will take the hint—or maybe not.

9. Do gifted students date less often than others? We're not aware of any formal studies that document an answer to this question. However, some of our survey respondents have told us—based on their own experience and that of their friends—that gifted kids are slower to date than others, and they might not date as often. Some feel that it's hard to be popular and intelligent at the same time; girls in particular believe that being smart intimidates boys and makes them less "dateable." Dating is stressful for everyone, regardless of gender or age. If you're ready to date but it's not happening, you may wonder if there's something wrong with you. Instead of worrying or blaming yourself, you might need to go beyond your regular circle of friends (at your school, place of worship, or wherever) to find other people with whom you share common interests.

"I THINK IT'S IMPORTANT FOR GIFTED TEENS TO FIND A BOY-FRIEND OR GIRLFRIEND WHO CAN MATCH THEM INTELLECTUALLY. AND IT'S GREAT TO BE SINGLE BECAUSE THAT MEANS YOU'RE WAITING FOR SOMEONE WHO'S RIGHT FOR YOU."
—Emily, 18

10. I don't have any trouble making friends, so why is there all this talk about gifted people being social misfits? It's true that many gifted children and teens make friends easily, but for others it's not so easy. They might perceive themselves as social misfits, which sabotages their self-confidence. Also, some people assume that because gifted kids are brighter and more intellectually advanced than their peers, they will automatically have problems relating to so-called "normal" kids.

If you are someone who doesn't have trouble forming friendships, count yourself lucky. Unfortunately, some people may still assume that if you're highly intelligent you must lack social graces and popularity, and vice versa. See Olivia's essay on page 209 for an example.

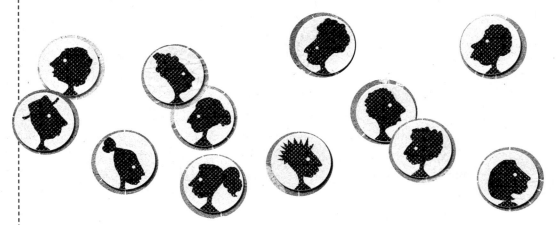

12 Tips for Making and Keeping Friends

1. Reach out. Don't always wait for someone else to make the first move. A simple "hi" and a smile go a long way. It may sound corny, but you'll be amazed at the response you'll receive when you extend a friendly greeting.

2. Get involved. Join clubs that interest you; take special classes inside or outside of school. Seek out neighborhood and community organizations and other opportunities to give service to others. And don't limit yourself to classes or organizations that are only for gifted people.

3. Let people know that you're interested in them. Don't just talk about yourself; ask questions about them and their interests. Make this a habit and you'll have mastered the art of conversation. It's amazing how many people haven't yet grasped this basic social skill.

4. Be a good listener. This means looking at people while they're talking to you and genuinely paying attention to what they're saying. (A long litany of "uh-huhs" is a dead giveaway that your mind is somewhere else.)

5. Risk telling people about yourself. When it feels right, let your interests and talents be known. For example, if you love science fiction and you'd like to know others who feel the same way, spread the word. If you're an expert on the history of science fiction, you might want to share your knowledge. BUT . . .

6. Don't be a show-off. Not everyone you meet will share your interests and abilities. (On the other hand, you shouldn't have to hide them—which you won't, once you find people who like and appreciate you.)

7. Be honest. Tell the truth about yourself and your convictions. When asked for your opinion, be sincere. Friends appreciate forthrightness in each other. BUT . . .

8. When necessary, temper your honesty with diplomacy. The truth doesn't have to hurt. It's better to say "Gee, your new haircut is interesting" than to exclaim "You actually paid money for *that*?" There are times when frankness is inappropriate and unnecessary.

9. Don't just use your friends as sounding boards for your problems and complaints. Include them in the good times, too.

10. Do your share of the work. That's right, work. Any relationship takes effort. Don't always depend on your friends to make the plans and carry the weight.

11. Be accepting. Not all of your friends have to think and act like you do. (Wouldn't it be boring if they did?)

12. Remember: Friendship is not about competition. You may have friends who are also gifted and perhaps you are driven to succeed in similar pursuits, which may lead to competition. A certain amount of competitiveness is normal and healthy among friends. However, don't let it prevent you from supporting one another through your challenges and celebrating your accomplishments together. Remind each other periodically that you are in this together, that life is not a race, and that having solid friendships is more important in the long run than winning any competition.

"AT MY SCHOOL AND IN MY COMMUNITY, I AM SURROUNDED BY GIFTED KIDS ALL THE TIME, VERY COMPETITIVE GIFTED KIDS." —*Jon, 12*

Gifted People SPEAK OUT

"Transatlantic Ping-Pong"

by Yuval Adler *

I've spent my school career in two countries, the United States and my native Israel. I am the youngest of three, and both of my older brothers are serving in the Israeli military, something that is required for both men and women. My name, Yuval, means "little river" in Hebrew. It's an uncommon name in America, but not where I live now, in Hod HaSharon, Israel.

I was like a transatlantic ping-pong ball for my education—attending school in Israel until second grade, coming to the United States for third through fourth grades, returning home for grades 5 through 10, and returning to America for grade 11 (such is the life of someone whose mom is a doctoral student in the States!). I'm back in Israel now, where I will finish my high school education. I'm not sure what I'll do next: perform my three-year obligation in the army or attend college first and then serve my military duty.

There are differences and similarities in the schools of both nations. One major difference is that in Israel extracurricular activities (like marching band) are not offered as part of school. One similarity is cliques: cliques exist in both countries.

Cliques have always been what they still are today: a social divide. It's almost like school cliques are one big pizza—one slice is "cheerleader," another is "jock," and yet another slice is "bookworm" or "nerd." I'm generally against this system, as I believe it makes people narrow their horizons and have very thin views on subjects and people. One of the things I liked most about moving between two countries was that my views on many subjects broadened greatly. When you hear, and actually listen, to many different views, you eventually have to make up your own mind. This helps make you a thinking person—an individual.

Before I moved to the United States for the first time, I unknowingly belonged to one of those cliques I claim to dislike! I was one of the "cool boys"

---

*Adapted from *More Than a Test Score* by Robert A. Schultz, Ph.D., and James R. Delisle, Ph.D. (Free Spirit Publishing, 2007).

in Israel, good at soccer and many other activities deemed to be popular. At age eight, I came to America, where I was an unknown, and I was able to see social divisions from an outsider's point of view. I learned firsthand that it is tough on the "new kid" to find his place when cliques are so, so present. And I did not speak English so, of course, things were difficult for me to understand at first—I would communicate my needs through gestures! (Still, I learned the language quickly and was fluent within a year.) I actually came to feel ashamed that I was once the "cool boy" who didn't want to talk to someone who couldn't play marbles well enough. After that I changed my ways.

Then, when I returned to Israel for the first time (for fifth grade), I found that the clique I had been in before no longer acknowledged me. My soccer skills had diminished in my years in America, and because soccer was such a big fad in Israel, I was instantly unpopular. Eventually I managed to fit in again, due to the fact that I wasn't quick to judge other people. But when I came back to America for the second time (for 11th grade) I had to start all over again! It was even harder than before to find new friends. In high school, especially, it is very hard to break the lines of social cliques.

However, one place I found that actually helped me break these social lines was my gifted program, in both the United States and Israel. In my gifted programs, I met new people I might not have met otherwise; intelligent people with interesting ways of thinking and open minds. I have met some of my best friends in gifted programs, and it would have been a shame if I had never met them because we didn't share the same social cliques.

One place I found that actually helped me break these social lines was my gifted program, in both the United States and Israel.

My frequent moves made some things difficult—it's hard to reestablish friendships after being away for a year or more—but they have also made me optimistic. My views have broadened, I have learned to adapt in academic and social situations, and I've overcome a lot. Those life lessons will serve me well in the years ahead.

Finding Friends Who Are Right for You

Many of the gifted students we've talked with over the years feel more strongly about world problems than their peers. They worry about hunger, war, global warming, the economy, poverty, overpopulation, human rights, the spread of AIDS, and other global issues. It's important to find friends who think as you do, because life gets lonely when you only have yourself to talk to. And it's easy to start thinking that there's something wrong with you if there isn't someone around who can relate on the same level.

Gifted students need to spend at least part of each day with others of similar interests and abilities. One way to accomplish this is by taking gifted, accelerated, or honors classes. Students who do this have told us that these classes are places where they can really be themselves. They don't have to worry about using certain vocabulary for fear that other students will accuse them of showing off; they don't have to concern themselves with whether the rest of the class understands what they are saying because it sounds "too complicated or philosophical." They can brainstorm freely, ask sophisticated questions, and contribute to discussions without being belittled or teased. Some gifted students have said that their gifted class was *the* most important time of the day or the week for them.

But what if your school doesn't offer these classes? Where else can you go to find people who are like you? Fortunately, you have several options to choose from.

"WHY DO I HAVE A HARDER TIME CONNECTING SOCIALLY TO THE REST OF MY GRADE?" —*Abbey, 14*

Breaking Age Barriers

For a 10-year-old whose mind grasps the theory of relativity, or the 15-year-old whose goal is to discover a cure for cancer, friendship—*true* friendship that involves sharing, understanding, and mutual respect—may seem rare or even unattainable. For this reason (among others), some gifted students often seek relationships with adults or older students.

Some gifted students form close friendships with parents, teachers, and neighbors—adults whose interests are in keeping with theirs. The adults don't accuse them of showing off their intellectual abilities; they don't chide them because they are different. Adult friends can be wiser, more objective, and less judgmental than peers.

Other gifted students have found that the people they most enjoy are several years older or younger than they are. In fact, either is common for bright, creative young people. Here are a couple of reasons why:

★ If you prefer older friends—for example, you're 13 and they're 16—it may be because they are more at your level mentally and socially than people your age. You may have outgrown your 13-year-old classmates several years ago.

★ If you prefer younger friends—for example, you're 12 and they're 10—it may be because you appreciate their open-minded acceptance of you. They don't seem as interested in competing with you or pointing out that you're not as smart as you think you are. You feel safe in their company, plus they're more playful and fun to be around than people your age.

When you're an adult, you'll probably have friends, colleagues, and coworkers who are old enough to be your grandparents or young enough to be your children. About the only time in life when friendships are determined primarily by age is from kindergarten through 12th grade. After that, years matter less and other things matter more—compatibility, common interests, mutual respect, and the countless other factors that bring people together.

Just because you happen to have been born in the same year as 90 percent of your classmates doesn't mean that you must look only to them for social gratification and acceptance.

Oddly, the social worlds of children and teenagers operate under a set of more stringent and complex rules than the adult world. For example, it's no big deal for a 30-year-old person to be dating someone who's 25, but a five-year disparity is significant if you're 15 and the person you're dating is 20.

Most people don't understand that there's a big difference between *age-mates* and *peers*. Just because you happen to have been born in the same year as 90 percent of your classmates doesn't mean that you must look only to them for social gratification and acceptance. If you prefer alliances with older or younger people, then that's who you should seek out. There may be a few raised eyebrows or expressions of concern by those who care about you, so you'll need to be mature enough to accept these comments. Even better, talk these concerns over with the people you enjoy spending time with. They will probably understand perfectly why some people have questions about your relationship.

How can you meet people who are likely to be your peers? It's difficult to do this at school, where grade levels still function as social hurdles. It may be easier if you're in an open or nontraditional school, where students from different grades are grouped in homerooms and take classes together. (Actually, this isn't such a modern notion after all; it happened in the one-room schools our grandparents and great-grandparents attended.)

You may have better luck if you look outside of school for opportunities to meet and make friends. Examples:

★ Take a class through a university extension or adult education program that attracts people of all ages. Or see what's available at your local community college, neighborhood recreation center, or online.

★ If your interests lie in the arts, volunteer to work at a museum or usher at a concert hall or theater. Find out about special projects or activities that use volunteers, then get involved.

★ Join a hobby club or other special interest group. If you're into computer programming, try finding a local coding club. If you play a musical instrument, look into a community orchestra or band, or start a small ensemble of your own. If you're passionate about Victorian novels, beat poetry, or the plays of Tennessee Williams, check out a book discussion group, or start one of your own.

CAUTION

If you prefer the company of older peers, their chronological ages may have made them eligible for certain privileges that are still taboo for you—for example, drinking, driving, or overnight stays. The surest way to lose the right to hang out with older peers is to abuse the rules that your parents (or society) have established for you. Enjoy your friends, whatever their ages, but remember the legal limits of your youth.

Also, some adults might try to take advantage of younger people. We're not suggesting that you live your life being constantly suspicious and on your guard, but don't be naïve, either. If you feel uncomfortable around someone, trust your instincts. When something doesn't feel right, it usually isn't.

Friendship vs. Popularity

There's a big difference between having friends and being popular. It may be hard to recognize at times when you seem to be the only person not surrounded by a crowd of admirers and acquaintances, but the distinction is real and significant. *Friendship* implies acceptance of you at all times, while *popularity* means that you're accepted only when it's convenient or fashionable. As one Canadian college student explained:

"It is only in the last year and a half that I've discovered the delights of belonging in a group of real friends. We are an odd, sometimes ridiculous crew who are accepted as such by others. . . . Many kids who have social problems in high school discover that things get better by the second or third year of university—maybe earlier, depending on how quickly they learn the rules. It's no fun to go through bad social times, but I know now that I wouldn't trade popularity and 'ordinariness' for the solid friendships and ability to function on my own that I have now."

> *Friendship* **implies acceptance of you at all times, while** *popularity* **means that you're accepted only when it's convenient or fashionable.**

Things *will* get better if you're willing to be patient and make the effort. You might try these survival tips gleaned from the experiences of people who have been there:

★ Be content with one or two solid friendships; they're worth more than you realize.

★ Don't expect everyone to like you. (Do you like everyone you meet?)

★ Seek out activities and groups that form around a common interest. Don't let your relationships be determined by age alone.

★ Talk to your parents—sometimes to get advice and sometimes just to sound off. Problems seem less daunting and more manageable if you share them.

★ Be yourself. It's too tiring to maintain a facade for someone else's sake, especially if it means compromising your gifts and talents. Besides, you're bound to be found out sooner or later. Friendships work best when they're based on honesty, sincerity, and WYSIWYG (what you see is what you get).

The Survey Says . . .

Q: Do you sometimes dumb yourself down to get along or fit in?

66% said "No."   **34%** said "Yes."

"Yes. I don't usually tell my friends I'm in the gifted program. Sometimes I also act stupid, or I usually try my best on all my work, but sometimes if a friend says they got a bad grade and I got a good grade, I might not say my score." —*Kendal, 13*

"Yes. I purposely act as if I don't know the material, so people won't make fun of me. I don't want to have the pressure of everybody expecting me to know the answer." —*Sam, 17*

"Yes. When hanging out with friends in a social setting, I'll often pretend I don't understand something because I feel like I need to act a certain way so that we can relate more to each other." —*Pamela, 15*

"No. Even though people sometimes make fun of me for answering questions, I know that what they do or say won't make a difference in my education. Not answering that question or asking questions could make a difference in my future." —*Travis, 14*

"No. I know that being smart is just part of me, as much as my eye color, hair color, name, etc. There is no reason for me to hide my intelligence." —*Megan, 15*

"No. If being dumb or acting dumb makes you fit in better, then I'd rather not fit in at all." —*Cole, 13*

"No. I am proud of the way I am. I feel like I already fit in with my peers." —*Paige, 15*

"No. I learned a long time ago that most people wouldn't understand certain things I talk about, so I tend to talk about other things with them instead. But I am myself, 100 percent, because I feel that's important. It took me a long time to learn that it's better to be liked for myself by a few than liked by many for being someone I'm not." —*Lauren, 17*

"Sometimes 'dumbing down' is a misnomer for a life-skill strategy. It is time to recognize how 'smart' it is to adjust your communication style to your audience in order to socialize." —*Desirae, 17*

Gifted People SPEAK OUT "Between Two Worlds"

by Olivia Patrick

As difficult as it is to be gifted in a high school setting regardless of gender, being a female of exceptional intelligence presents a very unique set of challenges. However, my personal struggles are vastly different than those associated with the stereotypical "smart girl." My IQ falls well within the range that distinguishes someone as highly gifted, but I do not display any of the social ineptness that frequently goes hand-in-hand with that designation. Thus, I find myself being misunderstood by pretty much everyone—both the "smart kids" and the "popular kids," for lack of better categorizations.

Unfortunately, most highly gifted teens are viewed as socially awkward. I have witnessed this as my friends—who I have known since we were geeky little elementary school students together in the "smart class"—navigate the social land mines of high school. As we began to mature, I began to find that I operate on different emotional and interpersonal wavelengths than nearly all of my highly gifted peers. I don't derive my energy from solitude, facts, numbers, or reading a story that transports me into a fictional world. Instead, I'm inspired and motivated by individuals, history, culture, and humanity primarily from an interpersonal and empathic perspective—not a highly quantitative and fact-based one. I thrive on socialization, networking, and communication. I *need* those things to get out of my own head and maintain my sanity.

Sometimes, the so-called "popular" kids are the people who enable me to be melancholy and shallow (I disdain that I occasionally crave unproductive conversation); they allow me to be emotionally and socially who I am. This is where the fun-loving person I am most comfortable being emerges. But while I am socially comfortable here, I become intellectually uneasy and disinterested. I can only take so many conversations about how someone (heaven forbid!) weighs four pounds more than they did two weeks ago. Small talk can become positively tiring after a certain point, especially when you filter everything you say so you don't unintentionally alienate anyone. Constantly transitioning between proving my intelligence to my intellectual peers, who doubt it, and concealing my intelligence around my social peers, who are intimidated by it, is an exhausting exercise. Remaining relevant in high school is all about maintaining the status quo—and this attitude, as I can state from experience, will play all sorts of games with your mind.

The simple answer here is balance, but that is far easier said than done. Being highly social and "popular" and being highly gifted and "nerdy" are two vastly different worlds in high school; it's truly sad that they do not coexist. I can count on my fingers how many people I know who have "dual citizenship," with me being one of very few girls. I feel as if I stick out like a sore thumb at conferences with other gifted high school students. The other gifted girls look at me like I don't belong, as if I have sold out to the people who most of them often feel ridiculed by. I am not at all one of those people; if someone sits down and has a conversation with me it is quite blatant that I celebrate my intellect and encourage others to do the same—*especially* other girls.

All the while, I don't remember the last time a male really took me seriously from square one and paid attention to me solely for what I was saying. I have no problem commanding the attention of a room predominated by males, which I have found most of my academic arenas are, but to get them to really listen to me is an uphill battle. If I employ the level of aggression, confidence, sarcasm, and gumption it requires to accomplish that feat, I am essentially stamping an expletive beginning with a "B" across my forehead. The quest for intellectual gender equality is analogous to Sisyphus and his rock—each time I nearly summit the mountain of respect, the big sexist boulder comes plummeting downhill because in the land of intellectuals it is a sin to be brilliant and ambitious if you are unwilling to mask every last little ounce of sex appeal. Regardless of intention, this pesky age-old injustice is a reality.

I feel as if I am the only one who truly exists in both the social and intellectual realms of high school. Though my ability to exist in both worlds is very much a gift, existing is vastly different than belonging. I long for the place where the entire me can thrive. It seems that my true niche should lie somewhere between the two worlds, but I have yet to find anything more than inhabitable space.

Olivia Patrick plans on majoring in some form of international development and hopes to be accepted to the Naval ROTC program. She feels it important to note that, contrary to what is assumed of those with military aspirations, her primary news sources are National Public Radio and the Daily Show, *not* Fox News.

The Truth About Teasing

Long before there was even such a thing as gifted programs, bright students have been called everything from "bookies" and "schoolies" to "dweebs," "nerds," "geeks," and "dorks"—along with an endless list of other odious labels.

Why? Take a look at our culture and the way it depicts gifted people. Consider Margaret, the brilliant, bespectacled classmate of *Dennis the Menace*; Milhouse and Lisa from *The Simpsons*; or Sheldon Cooper from the TV show *The Big Bang Theory*, among countless others. The media have long portrayed intelligent young people as stereotypes—awkward, unathletic, out-of-sync individuals with bad clothes, thick glasses, and pocket protectors. These goofy images of gifted kids may make us laugh, but when they're applied to you, they're not funny anymore.

> "I'M MOSTLY THE SAME AS OTHER KIDS MY AGE IN THAT I LIKE THE SAME CLOTHES, CLUBBING, ROCK MUSIC, BOYS, AND THE REST OF THAT TEENAGE FOLDEROL. SOMETIMES, THOUGH, I FEEL I'M SEEN AS A POSER OR NERD, IN LIEU OF THE COOL KID WHOSE PERSONA I AFFECT. MY FRIENDS TELL ME I NEED TO CHILL OUT, THAT I AM PARANOID. IT'S A FEELING I CAN'T SHAKE—THE FEELING OF BEING A STRANGER IN A STRANGE LAND."
> —*Nellie, 17*

The truth is that many people are uncomfortable with the idea of giftedness. After all, we're all supposed to be equal, so when some people (especially kids) seem more equal than others in the brainpower department, others look for ways to artificially equalize them. When the highly intelligent boy is portrayed as a basketball team reject, or the gifted girl sits home alone on prom night, this knocks them down a rung on the social ladder, making them appear more average and less special.

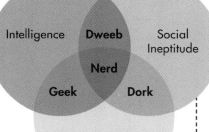

This Venn diagram (which has gone viral on the Web), shows a humorous way to view the goofy images of gifted people in our society—and what traits their particular "labels" specifically refer to.

How to Handle Teasing

We all need to feel as if we belong somewhere. As a gifted person, you want to be part of the crowd, accepted, and admired. While you may get a laugh out of the diagram, you don't necessarily want to be included on it, or to be perceived as different. Teasing sets you apart so you feel even *more* different and disconnected. Eventually, you may start to question whether being gifted is such a great thing after all. And you may begin to wish that you *weren't* gifted.

In order to handle teasing, it's important to recognize that the problem comes from the outside *and* the inside. First, you need to understand that as a gifted person, it's absolutely okay for you to:

* study a lot
* enjoy reading
* get high grades
* worry about world problems
* seek out and savor challenges
* pursue demanding goals
* have a wide variety of interests
* solve complex problems
* have an advanced vocabulary
* spend large amounts of time in front of your computer
* learn and know about many things
* achieve great things

And it's *also* absolutely okay for you to:

* go to parties
* goof off
* date
* dance
* go shopping
* play video games (even noneducational ones)
* watch TV (even reality TV)
* surf the Web
* play around on Facebook
* text and IM your friends
* listen to loud music
* sleep late
* take part in other activities that have nothing to do with school, learning, books, and grades
* swim, skateboard, bike, sail, surf, rock climb, play street hockey, and/or shoot hoops

If you enjoy some, most, or a few things from both lists, you're not so different after all. If you feel that you're especially susceptible or vulnerable to teasing, maybe you need to take a closer look at yourself. Nothing attracts a teaser more than someone who lacks self-confidence and self-esteem. Many teasers seek out targets who can't or won't fight back.

Why Teasing Works

Effective teasing depends on three things:

1. who's doing the teasing
2. the reason why they're teasing
3. whether you accept or reject the teasing

Who's doing the teasing?

Suppose someone calls you a "loser nerd." It makes a difference whether the teaser is 1) your mother or father, 2) someone you barely know, 3) a close friend, 4) a teacher, 5) your grandmother, or 6) the class bully who has been making your life miserable since kindergarten. Obviously it matters whether the teaser is someone you care about, feel close to, trust, and respect. The person behind the words can determine whether you feel 1) embarrassed, 2) annoyed, 3) amused, 4) elated, 5) proud, or 6) homicidal. You'll need to tell the person how you feel about the teasing. Chances are that he or she didn't mean to hurt you and was just trying to be funny. Or perhaps you took the teasing too seriously. Either way, real friends can usually reach an agreement about acceptable vs. unacceptable teasing.

> "I ENJOY PLAYING A LOT OF SPORTS, AND I FEEL THERE ARE STEREOTYPES AGAINST KIDS WHO ARE CONSIDERED GIFTED. WHEN SOMEONE THINKS OF A GIFTED PERSON, MOST KIDS IMAGINE THEM BEING GEEKY, HAVING NO SOCIAL LIFE, AND NOT DOING ANYTHING OTHER THAN SCHOOLWORK AND I BLAME A LOT OF THIS ON HOW THE MEDIA PORTRAYS GIFTED KIDS IN MOVIES AND TV SHOWS. HOWEVER, I HAVE MET A LOT OF PEOPLE WHO ARE NOT ONLY GIFTED, BUT THEY ARE GREAT ATHLETES, MUSICIANS, AND ALL-AROUND PEOPLE." —*Todd, 15*

Why are they teasing?

There are several reasons why people you know (including your friends) might tease you:

★ They may be jealous of you and your accomplishments.

★ They may not know a better way to tell you that they're proud of you and happy to be your friend. Strange as it seems, teasing can sometimes mean "I like and admire you."

★ Some teenagers regard genuine compliments as sappy or mushy or lame. Teasing is more acceptable. (Think about football players who pound each other on the back and/or knock each other down, and this starts to make sense.)

★ Consciously or unconsciously, they may feel inferior to you because they don't have enough good things going on in their own lives. Teasing is a way to bring you down a notch.

★ They just may not like you.

★ They may feel defensive around you. Check your own behaviors—what you do and what you say. Observations like, "If you weren't so stupid, you'd know the answer," are not going to win any diplomacy awards.

★ Peer pressure.

Of course, you may never learn the reason behind the teasing, but you can still appreciate the importance of the question. Depending on how well you know the teaser, you may want to try the direct approach. Asking "Why did you just call me that?" or "Why would you say such a thing?" might elicit a shrug and an "I don't know," but it might also cause the teaser to think twice before teasing you in the future.

Should you accept or reject the teasing?

That's entirely up to you. No one can *make* you feel bad or sad or weird. Depending on the source of the teasing, it may be worth pondering whether the teasing was warranted. Is it possible that you've been studying so hard that your friends feel neglected? Has your third blue ribbon in the annual art fair given you a fat head? Are you a little too full of yourself, too focused on your own interests? The teasing could be a mini wake-up call.

> "I have endured a great deal of ridicule without much malice; and have received a great deal of kindness, not quite free from ridicule. I am used to it."
> ★ ABRAHAM LINCOLN

On the other hand, it could be an attempt to hurt you or "get back at you" simply because you're gifted and talented, qualities that threaten and intimidate some people. The point is, only you can choose whether you accept or reject the teasing.

If you automatically accept the teasing that comes your way, you relinquish control of your own feelings, which is not a good idea if you plan to stay mentally healthy. Instead, consider the source, try to figure out the reason for the teasing, and choose to believe it or not. You *always* have a choice.

For example: You got a C on a very tough biology test. Your friend finds out and immediately starts giving you a hard time: "What? The genius got a C? How the mighty have fallen!" You can either think and respond like this: "I got a C on the test, and my friend is making fun of me for not getting an A, therefore I say, 'You're right. I'm an idiot. I can't believe I let everyone down—myself, my parents, the biology teacher, even you.'"

Or you can think and respond like this:

"I got a C on the test, and my friend is making fun of me for not getting an A, therefore (*choose one*):

★ "You're right, I didn't get the grade I was hoping for. But I can afford to blow a test once in a while."

★ "Oh well, nobody's perfect."

★ "You don't think I'm a genius anymore? I can live with that."

★ "I certainly did bomb that test. So what?"

★ "Actually, I deserved an A on that test, and I'm going to find out why I didn't get one."

★ "Where is it written that I must get A's at all times?"

★ "Yes, I got a C. I guess they'll be arresting me along with all the other C students."

★ "Yes, I got a C, which is exactly what I deserved, since I didn't study."

★ "Thank you for your support. Can we change the subject now?"

★ "_____" (*your response here*)

When Teasing Becomes Bullying

Now imagine the same scenario involving your grade on the biology test, but with a few key differences. This time, your friend doesn't just tease you about your grade, she also decides it's funny to spread a rumor throughout the school that you are planning to sue your biology teacher over it because you're scared of it lowering your GPA.

And she doesn't stop there. She proceeds to print out a bunch of fake tests, score them with big red Cs, Ds, and Fs, and post them on your locker for all to see. Then, she enlists others to hand you litigation lawyers' business cards in the hallway, slip them in your book bag, and tape them to your locker. Soon it feels like you're the laughing stock of the entire school, thanks to this "friend" who thinks of the whole thing as a hilarious practical joke. Only you're not laughing. The line has now been crossed from being teased to being bullied.

People used to think of bullying mainly as teasing that turns physically violent. But in truth it's much more than that, and often does not involve any physical contact at all. In addition to the more obvious pushing and hitting, bullying also includes incessant teasing and name-calling, ongoing harassment, rumor spreading, threats of harm, and social exclusion. And sometimes the person bullying you may even be someone you thought was a friend or at least a friendly acquaintance. People bully for many of the same reasons they tease, but bullying is intentionally hurtful, not simply a clumsy compliment or harmless joke. It can be very painful for the person being bullied and can lead to severe anxiety, depression, or worse.

Mean Behind the Screen

An especially common form of bullying today is called *cyberbullying* and involves many of the behaviors listed previously, but instead of being done face-to-face or through handwritten notes, it's done through emails, voice-mails, videos, digital photos, texts, IMs, or online posts. Cyberbullying can also involve stealing passwords, hacking into computer systems, creating a false identity to threaten others, and building a website to harass someone. Because cyberbullies can hide behind their computers or phones, they often feel less accountable and are less sensitive to how they're affecting others. Teens who normally would not think of bullying someone in person may find themselves tempted to do so in the seemingly anonymous world of cyberspace—which explains why cyberbullying has become such a hot-button issue.

But Most *Gifted* Teens Aren't Involved in Bullying . . . Right?

A common misperception among teens and teachers alike is that academically gifted students are unlikely targets or perpetrators of bullying in school—that somehow as a gifted teen, you're above it all. But that's oh-so-wrong. Not only are you singled out more often than other kids for being

Can Bullying Scar Your Brain?

Several new studies have shown that bullying can throw your hormones even more out of whack than they already are (particularly one called *cortisol*, which is the stress hormone), reduce connectivity between your neurons (mostly in your *corpus callosum*, which connects your two brain hemispheres), and lower your rate of *neurogenesis*, the growth of new brain cells (especially in a part of your brain called the *hippocampus*, which is your memory-maker). All of these brain changes may lead to:

- higher rates of depression
- memory problems, especially verbal memory
- weakened immune system

Are these changes permanent? More research still needs to be done, but the hypothesis is that yes, they can be, especially if the bullying persists over a long period of time.[*]

---

[*]Teicher, M., et al. "Hurtful Words: Association of Exposure to Peer Verbal Abuse with Elevated Psychiatric Symptom Scores and Corpus Callosum Abnormalities." *American Journal of Psychiatry* 2010; 167: 1464–1471.

According to a recent Purdue University study, 67 percent of gifted students reported experiencing bullying by the time they entered eighth grade, and nearly a third of gifted students had bullied someone at some time in the past.[*]

[*]Peterson, Jean S., and Karen E. Ray. "Bullying and the Gifted: Victims, Perpetrators, Prevalence, and Effects." *Gifted Child Quarterly,* Spring 2006; 50 (2): 148–168.

different, you are no more able to deal with bullying than other teens; in fact, you might even be *more* vulnerable to it, especially if you experience any of the intensities that often accompany giftedness (see Chapter 3).

Gifted teens are also not immune to bullying others, particularly if it means a chance to showcase their often unusually sharp wit. For this reason, as a gifted teen you may be especially susceptible to bullying behaviors. You may not always recognize how your witty words affect those around you and may be unknowingly condescending at times. Smart words can often "smart" just as badly as (or worse than) run-of-the-mill insults. Also, if you're being bullied, you may, in turn, bully others to take the focus off of yourself, fit in with a particular crowd, or retaliate against your bullies.

> "A FEW OF MY FRIENDS HAVE DESERTED AND OPENLY RIDICULED ME. THE MORE AMBITIOUS AND SUCCESSFUL I'VE BECOME, THE MORE THEY TAUNT ME. STILL, I'VE MADE A CONSCIOUS DECISION THAT MY LIFE'S WORK IS MORE IMPORTANT THAN A FEW BULLIES. BUT THE PAIN I FEEL IS REAL." —*Jason, 18*

Chances are high that you've either been the target of bullying or cyberbulling and/or the perpetrator of it, or that you're close to someone who fits into one or both camps. You may even know someone who has harmed himself or herself due to bully-ing. Phoebe Prince, Tyler Clementi, Billy Lucas, Megan Meier—maybe you've heard their names and many more—were teens who were bullied to the point of deciding to take their own lives. Sometimes, bullying can get under your skin so deeply that it may feel like there's no way out and no hope for the future. But there is *always* a way out. Always!

What Can You Do?

If you or someone you know is currently being bullied, harassed, or otherwise treated badly, take the following action **immediately**:

1. Tell an adult you trust—a teacher, counselor, parent, mentor, or some-one else. If you're uncomfortable doing this right away, talk it over with a close friend first or connect with one of the many online resources such as those on page 253. Don't wait. Take positive action now.

2. If you're being cyberbullied, *never* respond to harassing messages—you'll only fuel the flame by giving the bully exactly what he or she wants: a response. Also, save all messages in case you need them as evidence later on.

3. If the bullying is happening at school, make sure that you or someone else tells a school official about it. Then, if you are comfortable doing so, suggest that the school also notifies the parents of the student doing the bullying. (Some schools require this already; some do not.)

4. After reporting the bullying to a school official, ask if you can have an appointment with a school counselor or psychologist to talk over the causes and effects of the bullying. Also, if you're comfortable doing so, ask if a counselor can talk to the person who bullied you. (Again, some schools already practice this; but many do not.)

5. Check to see if your school or community has a peer support group for teens involved in bullying. If not, consider starting one. You might even start a group that is specifically for gifted teens.

How to Be Net Smart & Web Wise

Although cyberbullying is a very real challenge, you don't want it to scare you offline completely. There's danger, too, in being a technophobe. The fact is, to be successful in today's world, you need to be researching and networking

Cases of Gifted Teens & Cyberbullying*

Justin Swidler, now a lawyer after graduating from Duke Law School at age 22, was expelled from school in eighth grade and his family was sued for over $500,000 in damages after he created a website criticizing his teacher and principal.

James Ancheta, a gifted computer whiz, began hacking when he was a young teen and succeeded in taking control of 400,000 online computers and renting access to them to spammers and other hackers, while making more than $100,000. At age 20, he was arrested and sentenced to five years in prison.

Sixteen-year-old Ricky Alatorre's classmates created a fake online profile of him called The Rictionary that claimed he was gay and loved dictionaries, and that made fun of his high grades in school. Ricky was devastated and considered suicide. He later was successful in getting the profile removed and gained support from his family and school.

*Adapted from *Teen Cyberbullying Investigated* by Judge Tom Jacobs (Free Spirit Publishing, 2010).

online, and frequently. We've already extolled the many obvious virtues of social networking and Internet use and provided tips on how to manage your time online (see pages 105–111). Now, we offer some advice on how to handle your virtual identity and relationships in the smartest way possible. Just as the best swimmers are often the ones in danger of drowning because they think they're invincible, the smartest and most technologically adept teens are often the ones who are caught with their guards down online (as evidenced from the box on page 218). But with enough net smarts and Web wisdom, navigating the virtual world should be as smooth sailing for you as navigating Beginning Algebra or Intro to Biology. It should also provide you with opportunities to hone, advance, and display your gifts in some of the best ways possible.

For starters, here's a list of ways to stay safe and make the most of your online presence. Some of these things may already be second nature to you, but if they're not, jump—or click or tap—to it!

Eight Trusted Tips for Being Brilliant Online

1. **Change your passwords often** and don't share them with *anyone*. (Well, except for maybe your parents, if they ask.)

2. **Set your profiles to private** and never list your address, phone number, or name of your school online. Also, ask your friends' permission before posting any photos or personal info about them, too.

3. **Don't lie about your age** in order to gain access to a site. Age requirements are in place for your protection.

4. **Avoid in-person meetings.** If you do choose to meet someone you met online, be sure to meet during the day in a public place, bring someone with you, and tell an adult about your plans beforehand.

5. **Google your name frequently,** especially before applying for a job or to college. If you find any embarrassing photos or postings, have them removed immediately by writing to the person who owns or manages the website or profile page. Then, fill your profiles with positive information about yourself.

6. **Stay skeptical.** Keep in mind that people online aren't always who they seem to be, not everything you read online can be accepted as fact, and any offer that sounds too good to be true probably is.

7. Avoid sites with "inappropriate content." This is, of course, a euphemism that covers everything from pornography to live sex chats, bomb-building instructions to blogs run by hate groups. Don't give your parents (or anyone else who may gain access to your browsing history) reason to doubt your responsible use of the Internet; it's a far too precious tool to lose access to.

8. Think before you click. Remember that everything you post or write online or via cell phone is ultimately public, regardless of your privacy settings or how often you delete your messages, clear your cache, and empty your trash. If people—such as parents, teachers, authorities, employers, or college admissions officers—really want to, they *can* trace any content that you create back to you.

To Blog or Not to Blog?

Blogging isn't for everyone. It can be very time and energy consuming, especially for a gifted teen (such as you) who may already be stretched to the max with other endeavors. However, if you're considering a career in any kind of communications field, such as journalism, graphic design, advertising, or any one of the plentiful careers that prize good writing or design skills—a well-written, beautifully designed blog or website showcasing your experience, personality, and talents is a huge asset. It will also help you continually improve your writing and communication skills. And it's a bonus to list such sites on college and job applications to help you stand out from other highly accomplished applicants without an online presence.

Blog for College Bucks

If you're an avid blogger in search of money for college, visit collegenet.com where you can write on a variety of topics and have other readers vote on your entries. CollegeNET gives out *weekly* tuition awards of up to $5,000 to the student with the most votes on his or her blog.

Pleasing (and *Not* Pleasing) Your Parents

As a gifted kid, you likely have a unique relationship with your parents. As we discussed in Chapter 5, sometimes your successes in school might lead a parent into forming expectations of perpetual perfection, or your talents in an activity might inspire parents to put undue pressure on you to reach greater heights than you may care to. Why?

One reason may be that one or both of your parents may also be gifted, since above-average intelligence and other traits associated with giftedness can run in families. If you were identified as gifted at some point in your life, you may have asked your dad or mom, "Were you gifted?" Oddly, this question is generally asked in the *past* tense, not the *present* tense, for kids often assume that giftedness is something you outgrow after high school graduation. Not so. Parents of gifted teens, whether identified formally as gifted or not, generally share many of the same characteristics as their kids: intensity, a strive for perfection, high expectations in all aspects of life, and the ability to learn things quicker and sooner than most. So if you stare in the mirror and see a reflection of your mom or dad looking back, physically or metaphorically, know that the same is probably true for your parent, and this can be the main reason for both your conflicts and your connections.

As they say: the apple often does not fall far from the tree.

In addition, parents sometimes make demands on you in an effort to fulfill their own unrealized hopes and dreams, especially if they are gifted, too. On the face of it, this sounds like a bad thing: parents living life vicariously through their kids. And, if taken to an extreme—where their expectations are way out of whack in relation to your own wishes and wants—it can be. However, there are times when their unfulfilled goals can be a springboard for launching your own successes. For instance, if your parents never attended college but they just assume that you will enroll, hear them out. Or, if your mom gave up piano after two years of lessons and has regretted it ever since, she may insist that you stick it out longer than you would like; in this case, give it another six months.

What Can You Do?

Now that you know some reasons why your parents might be the way they are, what can you do about it? You can take positive steps to cope with and perhaps even change your parents' great expectations. *Examples:*

Talk to them

According to gifted teenagers we've spoken with, surveyed, and interviewed over the years, the most effective way to get your parents to have realistic expectations for you is to talk to them. (For specific strategies, see pages 223–224.)

Trust yourself

Don't let your parents' expectations control you. After all, you're the one who ultimately has to live with your choices. Obviously, this doesn't mean that you should ignore your parents' counsel; they do have more life experiences than you, probably tempered with real wisdom, and we all have to abide by some rules. But whenever possible, try to make your own decisions and take responsibility for the consequences.

Pick and choose the times when you'll do your best

Contrary to popular opinion (and parental pressure), you don't have to put 100 percent effort into everything you do. Sometimes it's impossible; sometimes it's impractical. When your parents encourage you to do your best and it doesn't seem feasible for whatever reason, talk it over with them. Evaluate and explain why you may not want to strive for perfection in this particular instance.

Encourage your parents to learn more about giftedness and what it means

Gather information for them, if you must, and review it before you give it to them. You might even give them this book to read, and maybe you can read it together. If they aren't interested in knowing more, at least you'll have learned something new.

Seek support from other adults you trust and respect

If there's absolutely no way you can get through to your parents, find another adult you can talk to who will give you the support you need. Not everyone is blessed with attentive, cooperative parents who are willing to listen to their children and take them seriously. Some teens have to look elsewhere for role models and advocates, and that's okay.

Strategies for Successful Parent Conversations

As a little kid, you probably found it easy to talk to your parents. When the topics were Friday's math quiz or Tuesday's Little League game, there wasn't a lot of room for conflict. Your conversations were more informational and informal. As you mature, though, so do your interactions with your parents. Topics now may include dating and driving and all the responsibilities that go along with both activities. Or, you might discuss the realities of life after high school, or the existential drama of life after death. In any case, talking honestly with your parents is essential if your relationship is to flourish as you become an adult.

For many teens, the hardest part of talking to their parents about sensitive or important topics is getting started. And, depending on your history of openness with your mom and dad, you might choose to approach them in different ways. Let's examine three scenarios:

SCENARIO 1: **You and your parents have a long history of talking to each other about big issues**

Maybe your parents have already talked to you about heavy-duty topics like sex and drugs. If so, it should be fairly easy for you to open a conversation about almost anything else. Your opening salvo? "There's something I would like to talk with you about. I respect your opinions and I know that you respect mine. When would be a good time to talk?" With this approach, you are paving the way for a mature, focused discussion.

SCENARIO 2: **You and your parents have limited experience talking with each other about big issues**

If you haven't formed the habit of talking to your parents about meaningful matters, beginning a conversation might be awkward—for you *and* for them. Try starting your conversation with this: "I've been thinking really hard about something and I wonder if I could get your angle on it." With this statement, you are not making demands, you are merely asking for help. Few parents would turn down such a request.

SCENARIO 3: You and your parents have almost no experience talking with each other about big issues

Some parents find it hard to see their children as maturing young adults. Reluctant to acknowledge that their "kids" are now biologically capable of being parents themselves, moms and dads who live in this permanent limbo where you will *always* be a child may be hard to approach about sensitive topics. If this is your situation, it's time to bring in the reinforcements: another adult you trust who can act as your go-between with your parents. Approach this person (perhaps an aunt, uncle, teacher, counselor, coach, or spiritual advisor) and say, "There is something I need to talk to my parents about and I'm not sure that we can do it on our own. Would you be willing to participate if I can get my parents to agree to meet?" If that person agrees, go to one or both of your parents and say, "There's something that's been bothering me. It's been on my mind a lot. I was wondering if we could go to someone else and talk about it together."

"IF I WERE A PARENT OF A GIFTED TEEN, I'D HELP THEM IF THEY NEED IT AND MAKE SURE THAT THEY ARE REACHING THE TOP OF THEIR CAPABILITIES. I WOULD ALSO DO THEIR LAUNDRY FOR THEM." —*Austin, 14*

Your parents might not agree right away. In fact, they might even get angry because you took a family matter to an outsider. If this happens, say: "This is really hard for me, too. I don't want to fight, I just want to talk. I trust this other person and I thought that she (or he) could help keep the conversation flowing."

If this sounds uncomfortable, that's because it is. But even *more* uncomfortable is letting an important topic go undiscussed because it is awkward to bring up. Take the risk; communication has to start somewhere. If you can communicate with your parents now about both life's ups and downs, you are setting the stage for a future filled with honesty and sharing.

The Survey Says . . .

Q. If you were a parent of a gifted teen right now, what's the most important thing you would make sure to do for him or her?

"Basically, I'd make sure he or she was living life to the fullest and creating a balance between learning and social activities." —*Elle, 16*

"I would make sure that they knew they were smart, but not pressure them into trying to be perfect." —*Jacob, 15*

"I would make sure that they didn't have too much stress on them, and let them know how special they truly are—but making sure not to get their head too big." —*Jacquie, 13*

"I would make sure that they had an excellent education and I would fight to achieve this for them." —*Adam, 15*

"I would make sure to tell them they should not sacrifice friendships or love in pursuit of their talent . . . but also not to sacrifice their talent in pursuit of friendships or love." —*Kamron, 15*

"I would try to instill a passion for something in them. It doesn't matter what, but they need to know what they love in life." —*Tata, 17*

"I'd make sure they know that it doesn't matter what the societal norms are and that 'fitting in' is not necessarily a good thing." —*Willow, 16*

"Let them have their space. Let them be messy and unorganized. We know where everything is." —*Jared, 12*

"Make sure the child has a large supply of Legos nearby at all times . . . or other creative outlets." —*Ben, 12*

"Make sure they understand that being gifted doesn't mean that you're weird or supposed to be making straight A's, it just means you approach the world a little different than others." —*Bhavana, 18*

"I would be there to support them, because being a gifted teen is a lot harder than it seems." —*Sydney, 17*

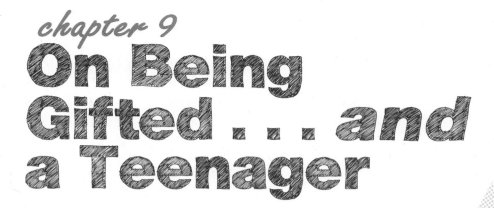

chapter 9
On Being Gifted . . . and a Teenager

It's no news to you that being a teenager is like riding an emotional roller coaster that lasts for several years. Just when everything is on the rise—school is okay, friends are there for you, parents respect your growing independence—you start careening down a huge hill that takes your breath away. On these days, it seems that life is one problem after another—a steady stream of hassles too overwhelming to solve or an unending series of quandaries that makes you doubt yourself and the validity of some beliefs you never questioned before.

> "I AM ON THE BRINK OF INDEPENDENCE AND STRUGGLING WITH MY PLACE IN THE WORLD, JUST AS MY CLASSMATES ARE, EVEN IF WE COPE WITH IT IN DIFFERENT WAYS. IN SHORT, WE ARE ADOLESCENTS, AND AS SUCH, MUST BIND TOGETHER, SINCE THE REST OF SOCIETY HAS JUST CAUSE TO AVOID US."
> —*Crist, 15*

Maybe you've wondered about stuff like this:

★ "Am I (*choose one or more*): pretty, tall, thin, popular, smart, athletic, or talented enough?"

★ "Am I living up to the expectations of my (*choose one or more*): parents, teachers, siblings, or teammates?"

★ "Will anyone ever want to (*choose one or more*): date, have sex with, love, or marry me?"

★ "If I'm supposed to be so smart and gifted, then why don't I (*choose one or more*): feel smart, have all the answers to life's questions, know where I want my life to go beyond high school, have a boyfriend/girlfriend, feel respected?"

These questions and many more arise in the minds of most teenagers, not just the gifted ones. However, your intensities as a gifted adolescent can make you more vulnerable to the worries of teenagedom. (See Chapter 3.)

The Survey Says . . .

45% of respondents want to know more about how to define success for themselves.

30% want to know more about how to develop a philosophy of life.

Understanding Adolescence (or Trying To)

One reason why it's tough being a teenager is that you have to be an adolescent at the same time. It would be nice to be able to postpone adolescence until you were ready for it, but unfortunately that's not possible. Actually, adolescence is a 20th-century invention. In the 1800s, a person went directly from childhood to adult responsibilities like work and family. A mere three generations later, a person might spend the years between 13 and 24 going to high school, then college, then graduate school without dipping more than a toe into the real world. There's no social track record for what's supposed to happen during this long and often tumultuous period.

Why do some people sail through adolescence seemingly effortlessly, while others fall apart at the first hint of hormones? Why do some have good looks and energy to spare, while others lurch around like Quasimodo in a semicoma? Why do some later think back on their teenage years as "the best years of my life," while others compare theirs to an extended stay in Motel Hell?

Experts who study adolescents have discovered some similarities among this group of very different individuals. The most obvious are the physical changes that pave the road from childhood to young adulthood. Who doesn't know about growth spurts, cracking voices, pimples, the sudden compelling and confusing interest in sex, and the myriad other burdens of puberty? These combine to create the feeling of being out of control and overwhelmed by strange and powerful forces from within. Add to this the expectations the world lays on you just because you're growing up, and it's no wonder teenagers get cranky.

Then there are the social and emotional issues. On the one hand, you're learning that you're different from everyone else, an individual, unique. On the other, you're finding out fast how important it is to fit into society and the world. Just as you're starting to figure out your family, you're preparing to leave it and go off on your own. One day you're getting your act together, and the next you're taking it on the road.

In addition to the issues we've already discussed in previous chapters—like conformity, expectations, and risk taking—following are a few key issues that are often of special relevance to gifted adolescents.

Dissonance

"If I'm so smart, why can't I do everything right?"
Prone to perfectionism from an early age, some gifted kids have an especially hard time during adolescence. Already off balance because of the physical, social, and emotional changes going on, they feel a dissonance between how well they *do* and how well they *think* they should do.

Your talents and abilities are growing, but even you have limitations. Becoming aware of them and learning to live with them doesn't mean you're giving up. It means you're growing up.

Impatience

"I want it NOW!"
Gifted teenagers don't hold the patent on impatience; it's a universal adolescent trait. They can, however, carry it too far. They tend to want clear-cut answers to everything—from complex problems to career choices and personal relationships.

Sometimes those clear-cut answers don't exist. Sometimes they take a long time to emerge and make themselves known. Impatience can lead to hasty resolutions that leave you feeling angry and disappointed.

This doesn't mean that you should spend hours each day agonizing over which socks to wear (if any). But when it comes to the Big Issues—like what to be when you grow up or how to resolve a difference with a friend—it makes sense to go slow, be patient, and ask for help when you need it.

Identity

"I know who I am and what I want to be!"

Competing expectations and impatience can propel gifted adolescents toward deciding their futures too soon. The 14-year-old who declares that she's going to be a doctor is closing the door to other opportunities. And the 16-year-old who's determined to be a dancer may never discover his talents in science or math.

One man in his late 20s recalls an argument he had with his father at age 13: *"I had decided that I wanted to be an English teacher. My dad wanted me to take more science courses. I told him that those didn't have anything to do with teaching English. 'Take them anyway,' he suggested. 'Why narrow your options?' 'I know what I want to be,' I shouted, 'and I'LL NEVER CHANGE!' Today I remember that as one of the dumbest things I ever said."*

Narrowing your interests too early can sometimes prevent you from exploring life's myriad possibilities. It can keep you from the satisfying, integrated careers and relationships that make the most of your abilities. Besides, whoever said you have to decide now what you'll be for the rest of your life?

Gifted & Gay

Another issue that can be a very real struggle for some gifted teens is that of sexual identity. On top of all the other challenges, this one has a way of making others pale in comparison—often bringing with it intense confusion, anxiety, self-loathing, depression, or worse, because of environmental pressure.

Do you identify as GLBTQ (gay, lesbian, bisexual, transgender, or questioning) or simply as gay? Do you know of someone who does? Chances are very good that you answered "yes" to at least one of these questions given that: 1 in 10 people in the world is GLBTQ, and 1 in 4 families has an immediate relative who is. And it's also possible that you know (or you are) someone who is both gay and gifted.

Some interesting similarities exist between GLBTQ people and gifted people. GLBTQ individuals, like gifted ones, tend to score higher than the norm (the norm in this case being heterosexuals) across the first five intensities discussed in Chapter 3.[*] They also lean toward creative pursuits

---

[*]"Beyond Analysis by Gender: Overexcitability Dimensions of Sexually Diverse Populations and Implications for Gifted Education" by Alena R. Treat, Ph.D., dissertation, Indiana University, 2008.

more often than their peers, maybe because the creative world is usually pretty accepting of differences. And some GLBTQ teens have a tendency toward overachievement, perhaps because they may feel shameful about being gay and are trying to somehow compensate for it.[*] For example, she or he might think: "Well, I may be gay, but at least I get good grades/play five sports/am an accomplished musician/etc." These affinities between being gay and being gifted mean that teens who are both gifted *and* gay are often hit with a double whammy of challenges to deal with.

Not surprisingly, the biggest whammy these teens encounter is harassment. Echoing the issues faced by twice-exceptional teens (see page 21), gifted gay teens must deal with being different on two counts. Teens who are both gifted and gay, lesbian, bisexual, transgender, or questioning experience unusually high rates of teasing, bullying, social alienation, substance abuse, depression, anxiety, suicide, dropping out of school, and homelessness. And while most gifted teens who are bullied can usually talk to their parents about it, many gifted gay teens do not feel comfortable reporting bullying to their parents—or to anyone, for that matter—either because they are not ready to discuss being gay or because their parents do not accept that they're gay. Even if other kids and adults are not openly hostile toward them, GLBTQ teens report sometimes feeling uncomfortable in social settings.

Gifted gay teens must deal with being different on two counts.

This must change. Whether you identify as straight or gay (or you're not sure which), and whether you're "out" or not, one thing is certain: you deserve to learn in an environment that is safe, accepting, and productive for all students. Do you have this environment? If not, you can work to get it. Check out the resources on page 254 for ideas of where to begin.

You don't need to be gay to support gay people, just like you don't have to be gifted to support gifted people. After all, you wouldn't want *only* other gifted individuals to support you, right? Just like you, gay teens—including those who are also gifted—need everyone's support to help them deal with and value their differences. Following are a few things you can do to be an ally and help

---

[*]Peterson, Jean Sunde. "Gifted and Gay: A Study of the Adolescent Experience." *Gifted Child Quarterly*, Fall 2000, vol. 44, no. 4: 231–246.

support your gifted GLBTQ friends and peers. (If you're GLBTQ, share this list with others so they know how to support you.)

★ A lot is going on in their heads, so treat them with compassion.

★ Talk openly about GLBTQ topics and GLBTQ people in the world.

★ Support them when they're ready to come out as GLBTQ to their friends and family.

★ Let them know they are okay, and not "bad," "evil," "wrong," or "sick."

★ Let them know they're not alone in their differences.

★ Speak out if you see them being harassed and encourage others to do the same.

★ Engage them in philosophical discussions about sexuality and identity—put your gifted brains together and marvel at the astounding complexities of being human.

Famously Gay

You may know of many current gifted GLBTQ celebrities, such as Adam Lambert, Jane Lynch, Ani DiFranco, Clay Aiken, Elton John, k.d. lang, Ellen DeGeneres, and Calvin Klein. But you may not know about the following notable people throughout history who are confirmed or widely believed to have been gay, lesbian, or bisexual. (*Note: As long and illustrious as this list may be, it's nowhere near comprehensive!*)

Alexander the Great, Socrates, Julius Caesar, Sir Francis Bacon, Michelangelo, Leonardo da Vinci, Lord Byron, Ludwig Wittgenstein, Pyotr Ilyich Tchaikovsky, Walt Whitman, Oscar Wilde, Marcel Proust, Gertrude Stein, Virginia Woolf, Jean Cocteau, Rainer Maria Rilke, Tennessee Williams, Herman Melville, Willa Cather, Hans Christian Andersen, Anaïs Nin, Ralph Waldo Emerson, E.M. Forster, Noël Coward, James Baldwin, Langston Hughes, June Jordan, Alan Turing, Eleanor Roosevelt, John M. Keynes, J. Edgar Hoover, Andy Warhol, Frida Kahlo, Rudolf Nureyev, Leonard Bernstein, Cole Porter, Bessie Smith, Janis Joplin, James Dean, and many, many others. *

Needless to say, being both gifted and gay puts a person among rare company—so if you fit this description, it's yet another reason for you to appreciate your uniqueness, not despair. But it also may present additional challenges in your life that you must cope with. Just remember: you don't have to do it alone—not the coping, *or* the appreciating. Reach out and connect. You'll be surprised how many others out there can relate and be supportive.

*From LAMBDA GLBT Community Services (www.lambda.org).

Gifted People
SPEAK OUT

"Accept the Confusion"

by Alex Menrisky

Pimples and hair aren't the only terrifying things about growing up. For me, the most terrifying thing was the confusion. Identity is something very important to me; *control* of identity is even more important. The loss of control is something I found very hard to cope with . . . and there is no greater loss of control than emotional and sexual confusion.

Homosexuality is gaining ground. People have been carving footholds for years, and while they're still shallow footholds, they exist; little grooves in society that allow for diversity to emerge. I've watched friends struggle, fight, and die to find just one little foothold. And I remember my own confusion as I developed, the questions that arose about my sexuality, and how terrible I felt. It wasn't because I couldn't find a foothold. It was because of the confusion itself—a threatening storm that battered my steely control—control I was terrified of losing.

I won't lie. I still don't know who I am.
No one really does.

Emotion scares me more than anything in the physical world. It means a loss of my control. And when something so powerful as sexual uncertainty gets jammed in the gears of your brain, suddenly that well-oiled machine starts to falter, and control collapses. For me, nothing was more frightening than this uncertainty, especially while being surrounded by friends—both homosexual and straight—who seemed so sure of themselves. To me, it was a kind of failure: uncertainty in the face of a friend base that was so full of conviction. It was enough to cause a dwindling spiral of shame and self-loathing—both for my feelings and my apparent ineptitude at being able to figure out who I was.

I won't lie. I still don't know who I am. No one really does. But I've found that ignoring the confusing questions, or abusing yourself because of them, harms much more than it helps. I went through too much self-harm because I felt I was failing to identify myself sexually.

Am I gay or bisexual? No. But I thought I was, and yet thought I wasn't, all at once. And that hurt me almost as much as feelings of persecution have hurt my gay friends. I can't speak for them. I don't know how it feels to be hunted or hated. But I know how it feels to hate myself, when you keep it quiet, when you shove confusing thoughts and emotions down to the bottom of your brain. Confusion is the first hurdle you face when falling into the shoes of your sexuality. And I overcame my confusion only after I stopped hiding it.

I introduced myself to questions of sexuality. Shook their hands. Sat down with them and talked our issues out. I acknowledged their existence, and that is ultimately what lifted a burden that had weighed on me for years. Oftentimes, regardless of the pressure you feel from the outside, your greatest enemy can be yourself, and the fear of change or loss of control. Ignoring the questions doesn't help. You have to be active in your search for your sexuality. You have to think about it, otherwise you'll start acting without thinking, sometimes with disastrous and painful results.

I have often marveled at the pain my gay friends feel in the face of ridicule, but I admire them for more than their steadfast stand against hatred. I admire them because they were able to accept themselves, to get past that initial confusion. And that is half the battle. You can be more harmful to yourself than any bigot can. And let's face it: who should know us the best but ourselves?

Alex Menrisky is a college senior studying journalism, English, and French at Ohio University.

Depressed, Me?

One of the most insidious myths out there about giftedness is that "smart people don't have problems." Because of your superior mind, you're supposed to be able to handle even the most emotionally draining and/or tumultuous times without help from others. In other words, you're supposed to be immune from depression.

But gifted people get depressed, too. And left unacknowledged, unchecked, and untreated, depression can be very dangerous. The signs of depression are remarkably similar to the warning signs of suicide, which shouldn't be surprising, since suicide is an extreme reaction to extreme depression. Here are some of depression's calling cards:

* change in appetite
* low (or lower) grades in school
* the constant desire to be alone instead of with others
* negative views of the future
* focusing on mistakes you've made in the past instead of on your successes
* an overall lack of initiative; you're almost always tired or bored
* lack of concern (or less concern) about physical appearance
* frequent arguments with others
* change in sleep habits
* an overall attitude that everything is hopeless
* loneliness and a sense that you've lost some part of yourself

Of course, you will have the occasional bad day, when all you want to do is pull the covers over your head and sleep for a week. That's not depression, it's a natural reaction to stress or boredom. Depression, in contrast, is long-term (lasting more than a couple of weeks) and intense. Each day, the pit you're in gets deeper, the wall you've built around yourself gets taller, shutting people out becomes easier, and although you can't say you enjoy your isolation, there is a predictability about it that you find comforting. When this happens, it's time to get help.

Depression is an illness, just like strep throat or diabetes. And you wouldn't *not* seek help for those things, right? While you may feel shameful or frustrated that, especially as a gifted person, you can't simply "think yourself through it"—the truth is you can't. Just like you can't "think yourself through" pneumonia. Talk to someone *now*—a parent, friend, teacher, counselor, nurse, or other trusted person. Don't wait for it to get worse.

Too Smart to Die . . . or Not

A few topics are so taboo and painful to discuss that many people choose to ignore them entirely. Suicide is one of them. Working under the misguided assumption that "If you don't talk about suicide, it will go away" (or "If you do talk about it, more suicides will occur"), many teens and adults dismiss teen suicide as something that happens to *other* families in *other* towns. And a lot of people believe that gifted adolescents are too smart to even consider ending their own lives.

Although no firm evidence suggests that gifted teenagers are more likely to attempt or commit suicide than less able adolescents, some aspects of being gifted may, in some cases, contribute to suicidal behavior. (We have deliberately qualified this statement with "may" and "in some cases" because it is simply not true that being gifted makes one more prone to suicide.) *Examples:*

★ A perception of failure that differs from others' perceptions of failure. (For example, feeling that a B is equivalent to an F if your personal standard of success calls for an A or above.)

★ External pressures to always be number one and a life orientation that identifies one as a future leader or a "mover and shaker of the next generation."

★ The frustration that comes when one's intellectual talents outpace his or her social or physical development. ("For being so smart, I'm awfully dumb at making friends," or "Starting school early and skipping second grade was fine, but now I'm the freak of the locker room—I'm so puny!")

★ The ability to understand adult situations and world events while feeling powerless to effect positive change.

If you read your local newspaper or watch your local news, you've probably seen stories about teens who have killed themselves. If you went online, you could easily find many more. A large number will describe teens who were "bright," "top students," "successful," "attractive," "college-bound," and so on. Perhaps you know someone who attempted suicide or committed suicide. We do. Following are some recent examples:

★ Katy was 17 when she killed herself. She was an A-student and a regular member of her school's Honor Society for academic achievement. She was also a cheerleader, a model, a beauty contestant, and a driven perfectionist who battled both anorexia and bulimia. One February afternoon, she drove to a state park, poured two cans of gasoline over herself and lit a match.

★ Steven, 13 years old, shot himself in the head during reading class. Steven was an A-student who had been identified as gifted. He was also a star player on his school basketball team.

★ David learned one month before graduating from high school that he had missed being valedictorian by a third of a grade point. Fearing that he had disappointed his parents, he took a shotgun from his dad's closet and killed himself.

★ Jackson, a senior mechanical engineering student at Cal Tech, died in his dorm room less than 48 hours before he was to collect his college diploma. Described by many as one of the smartest, most well-liked people they knew—"the best of the best."

Sadly, we could fill this book with stories as tragic as these. Depression and suicidal thoughts don't plague all (or even most) gifted teenagers, and you may not identify with any of them. But if any of these things do concern you, please do not delay: seek help *now*. Tell someone—a friend, parent, teacher, mentor, counselor, or at least someone on a telephone hotline or website. See page 254 for resources.

Developing Wisdom

We've said a lot in this book about being gifted, intelligent, social, creative, sensitive, emotional, assertive, and successful. But what about being *wise*? Wisdom is not something that can be easily measured, as it has to do with learning from experience, amassing practical knowledge, and gaining patience, balance, self-awareness, and humility. It usually takes years to form; for many people it takes a lifetime. Who is someone in your life who you consider to be very wise? Chances are this person is not young.

Is it possible to develop true wisdom as a teenager? Given the fact that your brain is still rapidly forming, and that you probably haven't had a large number of varied experiences yet in your life, the answer is: probably not. But, as someone who is already thinking at advanced levels and living with heightened sensitivities, you're in a very good position to *begin* developing wisdom. And beginning this process now will make your present-day life more bearable, even joyful, by helping you value ordinary everyday existence and also develop self-confidence (which is, by the way, routinely rated by both males and females as the single most attractive trait in a person—above looks, smarts, popularity, and even sense of humor).

The first step on the road to wisdom is to look beyond your grades, trophies, medals, awards, and especially your test scores. In his book *What Intelligence*

Tests Miss, professor Keith Stanovich lists the following important cognitive abilities—all associated with wisdom—that IQ tests fail to measure:

1. **Rationality.** How well can you realistically manage your available resources and behaviors in order to achieve success?

2. **Practicality.** Can you tell the difference between mere brain processing power and practical knowledge (or common sense)?

3. **Open-mindedness.** Do you make it a point to gather all conflicting information before making up your mind about something?

4. **Sound judgment.** Do you base your level of certainty on the strength of available evidence and *not* on fixed beliefs or prejudices?

5. **Tolerance for uncertainty.** Are you able to go for long periods of time waiting for an answer to become clear?

6. **Correction of bias.** Are you aware of your personal biases and do you actively try to correct them?

Don't worry if you feel a little less-than-brilliant in these areas right now. We're pretty sure not many teenagers have mastered them—and also not many adults! So how can you improve your ability to be rational, practical, patient, sound of judgment, open-minded, and unbiased? Here are a few fairly basic suggestions to get you started:

★ **Think the unthinkable.** Contemplate at least one complex and seemingly unsolvable problem every month, be it global warming or the Riemann Hypothesis. You might even hold regular "Deep Thought Sessions" with a couple of friends where you choose such a topic to discuss over pizza and challenge each other to think as broadly and deeply as you can . . . without giving yourselves serious headaches, that is.

★ **Make it matter.** At the end of every school day, decide which single fact or idea is the most intriguing to you and come up with two or three ways it applies to your life or to the lives of your family members and friends. Then, share your list with a friend or family member.

★ **Solve a common problem.** Every week or so, think of one nagging problem in your life that has absolutely nothing to do with your GPA, test scores, IQ, résumé, or college application. The more mundane the better. For example, do you always misplace your keys or cell phone? Is your locker a mess? Do you miss your bus every other day? Then, focus all of your considerable wits and available resources on coming up with the absolute best solution to this problem that has ever been devised.

- **Keep a manifesto.** Create a personal manifesto—a document of your top five or 10 strongest opinions, on anything from religion to politics. Then, plan to either read a book, watch a movie, or see a play that directly conflicts with each opinion. Record your thoughts about it afterward in your manifesto.

- ★ **Seek disagreement.** Think of the one person in your life who you tend to disagree with the most. Then, make it a point to have regular conversations with this person—and listen as closely as you can to his or her arguments. Instead of debating viewpoints, ask the person questions to help clarify his or her viewpoint for you. The point is not for either of you to win, but to examine topics from different perspectives. *Note:* If any of these disagreements do turn into heated arguments, you can always put an end to them by simply resolving to "agree to disagree" for now.

> "The test of a first-rate intelligence is the ability to hold two opposed ideas in the mind at the same time, and still retain the ability to function."
> ★F. SCOTT FITZGERALD, AUTHOR

- ★ **Volunteer.** There may be no better, easier way to develop wisdom than to use your gifts to help improve the lives of those around you—without expectation of compensation. Why? Because when you do something for nothing, you are not motivated by extrinsic rewards like money, food, prizes, or scholarships. Instead, you learn to seek out intrinsic rewards like self-confidence, a sense of accomplishment, and feelings of compassion and altruism—which in the long run will be far more valuable to you in your future than will any monetary award, college acceptance letter, or job offer.

Not to mention, study after study confirm that people often learn *more* from and perform *better* on tasks that they voluntarily participate in versus on tasks that they are doing to satisfy a requirement or achieve a specific reward. There you have it: volunteering will make you both wiser *and* smarter. You simply can't lose.

Gifted People SPEAK OUT

"The Sky Is Not the Limit"

by Jalil Bishop

I never got much higher than a 3.0 GPA. I never went a year without going to the principal's office. I never could stop crying out for something better. This was my life throughout my education until I reached eighth grade and was able to understand the identity that I had created for myself. People saw my grades and knew I had the ability to succeed, but they also saw that I refused to apply myself. They thought I was a "bad" child because I was always in the principal's office, and to my peers that also made me a "dumb" child. They never understood that my frustrations were due to my inability to believe in myself, which made me a "lonely" child. When I realized that people thought I was dumb, bad, and incapable, I was infuriated that I had picked these labels for myself. I could no longer blame my image on poverty, on teachers, or on other students; I had created it. This revelation led to the decision that changed the course of my life—the decision to run for class president.

Running for president was an attempt to prove that I was capable, no matter what circumstances I came from. I could be a role model, a leader, an advocate. I knew I was a popular student in school, but for none of the reasons that would convince students I could be their class president. I had to start my eighth-grade year with no visits to the office, nothing but A's on my report card, and no one viewing me as a troublemaker. I was aiming to transform myself *into* myself—to become the person I envisioned I could be, not simply a victim of circumstance. I accomplished this by forcing drastic changes in my thought process, actions, and beliefs. I won the presidency by showing the real me that I had kept hidden for so long. For the first time in my life, I got top grades. For the first time in my life, I did not get sent to the principal's office. For the first time in my life, I proved to myself that every goal, dream, and ambition I had were there for me to realize.

I am proud of what I did then for myself, but I would not be able to tell this story if not for those people—my parents, teachers, and friends—who gave me a chance to change. They saw in me a greatness that I denied, and they did everything they could to open my eyes to it. My father indoctrinated me with the importance of my education and how I had to make a better reality for myself than he made for himself. My mother inspired me daily as I watched her hold together our household of six children with a powerful confidence and a mighty compassion. Numerous teachers sensed my desire to reach beyond my circumstances and provided whatever tools they had to help me. My friends supported me however they could, even when I had little to give back to them but a "thank you."

These people are why I graduated high school as an honor student, captain of my track team, and class president all four years. It has been startling to know that people—many from completely unrelated backgrounds—thought I deserved a chance: a poor African-American male from a single-parent household who was not formally identified as a gifted student. But I soon realized they were giving me a chance to do better because they saw I was giving *myself* a chance. I learned that self-betterment allowed my need for help to transcend race, social class, or any limiting labels.

I now attend an Ivy League college and am dedicating my life to reaching out and giving others a chance. I started this mission back in eighth grade by raising $5,000 for Hurricane Katrina victims, moved on to form a club at my high school to help underachieving black males, and continue it now by speaking to younger students from similar backgrounds as mine about the power of their stories. I do not have money, a big house, or a new car, but I do have something to offer and I am obligated to share that with whomever I can. I only want to give others a chance to help them learn to give themselves a chance, because I understand that although our individual struggles are what make us uniquely great, those struggles can also hinder us from tapping into that greatness. From my perspective: life is just a series of chances, and those who succeed are the ones who are prepared and audacious enough to seize them.

> I do not have money, a big house, or a new car, but I do have something to offer and I am obligated to share that with whomever I can.

I've never subscribed to the old saying "the sky is the limit," because once upon a time my "sky" was the low-income city of Twinsburg Heights, Ohio. Living in the Heights exposed me to people who worked relentlessly just to stay afloat against all odds. That exposure gave me the idea that if I could take that same work ethic and apply it not just to getting by, but to getting what I truly wanted out of life, my barriers would crumble. Now, my sky is the thriving campus of Dartmouth College in Hanover, New Hampshire. I make my own limits. I keep going because I have to, and I hope that shows others they have to also. We cannot wait until we are older, better established, or more comfortable; today has to be the day we decide to make our lives—and the lives of those around us—better.

Jalil Bishop is majoring in government with a minor in public policy at Dartmouth College in Hanover, New Hampshire. His mind is open to any career path that is able to captivate his passions—everything from becoming a teacher to a civil rights lawyer. The sky will never be his limit.

The Meaning of Life (or Something Like That)

Closely related to developing wisdom is developing your philosophy of life, or what we call your POL. Your POL is determined by how you answer questions such as: *What really matters? How should we live our lives? What is our purpose on this planet? Do we even have a purpose? What is real? What is time? What is the meaning of truth, beauty, love, and freedom? Is there such a thing as good and evil? Is pure altruism possible? Does God exist? What happens when we die?*

"ALL OF MY FRIENDS ARE HIGHLY GIFTED THEMSELVES. WE HANG OUT AT A COFFEE SHOP DRINKING ICED TEA, DISCUSSING PHILOSOPHY, AND PLAYING BRIDGE. THIS ISN'T ELITISM; IT'S JUST HOW WE RELATE TO EACH OTHER."—*Nick, 17*

These questions, even though some seem deceptively simple, have no easy answers—whether you're 18 or 80. And your answers to them will change often throughout your life, depending on your level of wisdom and experience. But it's almost certain that you *will* ask them, and ask them often; in fact, you probably already have been for a few years. As a gifted teen with a large cognitive capacity and intellectual intensity, you may be more likely to sit at home on a Saturday night reading Steven Pinker or Friedrich Nietzsche and contemplating the nature of existence, while your peers attend a football game or shop at the mall. (Or maybe you're the one reading Nietzsche to your friends *at* the football game.) The key is to learn how to think about big questions in a systematic way. Read on.

What's Your Big Question?

To begin building your POL, it helps to start with a central question. It can be huge and metaphysical, such as "What is reality?" or more quirky, such as "Is Schrödinger's cat alive or dead?" (*Hint:* Google it!) Crafting your question and investigating how others throughout history have attempted to define and answer it can be a fascinating process. And contrary to what many believe, thinking philosophically can be *just* as satisfying as winning a race or buying a new outfit at the mall. So take out a journal and start questioning.

The next part is a little trickier: learning how to philosophize about your question—to evaluate claims based on reason and analysis rather than on fixed beliefs and prejudice. Here is where classes, conversations, websites, and books come in handy (see resources on page 254). It takes some time and effort to learn the basics of philosophical reasoning, but it's well worth the investment. It will teach you truly to think for yourself, and will inform your attitudes and opinions about everything from books and movies to the environment, animal rights, economics, and even giftedness.

Rest assured that just because you might enjoy philosophizing doesn't mean you must major in philosophy in college and become a professor. An ability to think, reflect, wonder, and puzzle deeply about abstract questions will serve you in any class, job, or career you choose and enrich your life in endless ways.

> "The real questions are the ones that obtrude upon your consciousness whether you like it or not, the ones that make your mind start vibrating like a jackhammer, the ones that you 'come to terms with' only to discover that they are still there. The real questions refuse to be placated."
> ★INGRID BENGIS, AUTHOR

> "PSYCHOLOGY, SOCIOLOGY, ETHICS, EXISTENTIAL QUESTIONS . . . I CAN SPEND HOURS AT NIGHT THINKING ABOUT THIS KIND OF STUFF WITHOUT EVER FINDING ANSWERS THAT SATISFY ME."
> —*Ana Lucia, 18*

Existential Crises 101

While you may have a knack for contemplating the great questions of life, you may also be more likely, as a gifted teen, to experience what is called an existential crisis, existential dread, or existential depression.[*] An existential crisis occurs when your mind gets overwhelmed attempting to wrap itself around the infinite and unknowable. You may become fixated on the essential futility and meaninglessness of existence. Perhaps you've experienced a crisis like this already, or are in the middle of one now. These crises can be very painful and troubling and can last for some time. They can be paired with clinical depression, anxiety, and other mental health issues, or can be triggered by a major loss or change in your life, but they don't have to be. In fact, existential crises more often occur spontaneously in gifted people—for instance, on a random Tuesday afternoon during a rain shower.

Why might you be more prone to existential crises? Because as a gifted person you're able to see possibilities where some people do not—possibilities of how the world *might* be—which can tend to make you an idealist. When you're an idealist, you may be more likely to encounter major disappointment when you spot inconsistencies, arbitrariness, unfairness, absurdities, hypocrisy, indifference, and dishonesty in society . . . in other words, when the world does not match up to your ideals.

"I'M INTERESTED IN DEPRESSION, PARTICULARLY ENDURING APATHETIC EXPERIENCES. ALTHOUGH COMMON, I'VE NOTICED THIS TYPE OF DEPRESSION IS USUALLY MORE DIFFICULT FOR MY PEERS TO LABEL FOR THEMSELVES. THIS TENDS TO BE QUITE UNSETTLING FOR THEM."
—*Tate, 18*

In addition, with your multipotentialities, you may grow frustrated with the existential limitations of space and time, and wonder: *How can I possibly find enough hours in the day—or in my entire life—to pursue all of my talents and passions? Where do I begin narrowing down my goals and interests, and why should I have to?* This disappointment and frustration can lead to strong feelings of sadness, fear, worry, apathy, and possibly anger, especially if you find that other teens (and even many adults) do not share your concerns and are focused instead on mindless TV shows or consumerism.

But the truth is, it's totally healthy and normal to experience existential crises. In fact, many middle-aged adults can relate to what you're experiencing;

[*] *Misdiagnosis and Dual Diagnoses of Gifted Children and Adults: ADHD, Bipolar, OCD, Asperger's, Depression, and Other Disorders* by James T. Webb (Great Potential Press, 2005).

only in their world it's called a *midlife crisis*. You just happen to be experiencing an earlylife crisis, as do some other gifted young people. See the following tips on how to deal with these crises.

10 Tips for Taming an Existential Crisis*

1. Do not isolate. Connect with an adult or another teen who has experienced an existential crisis and share your concerns. You might start by saying, "I've been feeling really sad about all the violence around the world and how powerless I am to stop it. Has this ever happened to you?"

2. Educate yourself about existential issues. Understand they are not issues that can be dealt with only once, but ones that will need frequent revisiting.

3. Seek physical touch. Just like babies need to be held and touched so they feel secure, people experiencing existential dread do, too. Hugs, shoulder rubs, and even pats on the back can help diffuse feelings of aloneness and insignificance.

4. Build your personal POL to help infuse your life with meaning and wonder. (See previous section.)

5. Avoid burying yourself in causes. When in the midst of an existential crisis, it can be tempting to throw yourself into a bunch of political, academic, or social issues in a desperate attempt to belong and create meaning. Unfortunately, this usually does not help and can even make things worse. Obviously, it's good to support a few causes, but in moderation.

6. Explore how others have meaningfully structured their lives. Read about people who have chosen specific paths to greatness and made real differences in their worlds. Try not to compare yourself with them, simply observe their choices. If you need book suggestions, talk to your school or community librarian, or search online.

7. Commune with nature. Spending time in nature can be very healing and life-affirming during times of existential distress, especially when accompanied with a close friend or family member.

8. Meditate. Making conscious efforts to quiet your very active brain and practice "mindfulness" can go a long way in quelling existential dread. Look into classes or meditation centers in your area to learn about how to get started if you don't already practice.

---

*Parts of this list are based on "Existential Depression in Gifted Individuals" by James T. Webb, Ph.D., greatpotentialpress.wordpress.com, "Author Articles," Great Potential Press, 2011.

"What I need is the dandelion of spring. The bright yellow that means rebirth instead of destruction. The promise that life can go on, no matter how bad our losses. That it can be good again."

★KATNISS EVERDEEN IN MOCKINGJAY BY SUZANNE COLLINS (BOOK 3 OF THE HUNGER GAMES TRILOGY)

9. Get immediate help if you are depressed. If you grow frustrated and isolated enough with your own powerlessness to change or comprehend existence, it can lead to a very serious depression and even thoughts of suicide. If this happens, tell an adult you trust *immediately*. (See page 254 for a list of other resources.)

10. Stay hopeful and optimistic. This goes without saying, and is probably the most important defense you have when faced with an existential crisis. You can never, ever have enough hope that things will improve.

Expert Essay
"Five Life Lessons in a Flat World"
by Thomas Friedman*

The following advice is taken from a college commencement address given by Thomas Friedman, *New York Times* columnist and Pulitzer Prize–winning author of *The World Is Flat: A Brief History of the Twenty-First Century*.

Lesson #1: Do what you love. Whatever you plan to do, whether you plan to travel the world next year, go to graduate school, join the workforce, or take some time to think, don't just listen to your head. Listen to your heart. It is the best career counselor there is. Do what you really love to do and if you don't know quite what that is yet, well, keep searching, because if you find it, you'll bring that something extra to your work that will help ensure you will not be automated or outsourced. It'll help make you an untouchable radiologist, an untouchable engineer, or an untouchable teacher.

Lesson #2: Be a good listener. The ability to be a good listener is one of the most underappreciated talents a person can have. . . . You can get away with really disagreeing with people as long as you show them the respect of really listening to what they have to say and taking it into account when and if it makes sense. . . . Never underestimate how much people just want to feel that they have been heard, and once you have given them that chance they will hear you.

Lesson #3: Learn how to learn. The most enduring skill you can bring to the workplace is the ability to learn how to learn. . . . It is what enables you to adapt and stay special or specialized. . . . Go around and ask all your friends who are the best teachers in your school and then just take their classes,

*Excerpted from "Journalism as Life" by Thomas Friedman, Williams College, July 5, 2005. Used with permission.

whether it is Greek Mythology or physics. Because I think probably the best way to learn how to learn is to love learning. When I think back on my favorite teachers, I am not sure I remember much anymore of what they taught me, but I sure remember enjoying learning it.

Lesson #4: Don't get carried away with the gadgets. In this age of laptops and PDAs, the Internet and Google, MP3s and iPods, remember one thing: all these tools might make you smarter, but they won't make you smart; they might extend your reach, but they will never tell you what to say to your neighbor over the fence, or how to comfort a friend in need, or how to write a lead that sings or how to imagine a breakthrough in science or literature. You cannot download passion, imagination, zest, and creativity— all that stuff that will make you untouchable. You have to upload it the old-fashioned way, under the olive tree, with reading, writing and arithmetic, travel, study, reflection, museum visits, and human interaction.

Lesson #5: Be a skeptic, not a cynic. Skepticism is about asking questions, being dubious, being wary, not being gullible, but always being open to being persuaded of a new fact or angle. Cynicism is about already having the answers—or thinking you do— about a person or an event. The skeptic says, "I don't think that's true; I'm going to check it out." The cynic says: "I know that's not true. It couldn't be. I'm going to slam him."

So be a skeptic, not a cynic. We have more than enough of those in our country already, and so much more creative juice comes from skepticism, not cynicism.

In summary: I guess what I have been trying to say can be summed up by the old adage that "happiness is a journey, not a destination." Bringing joy and passion and optimism to your work is not what you get to do when you get to the top. It is *how* you get to the top. If I have had any success as a journalist since I was sitting down there where you are 30 years ago, it's because I found a way to enjoy the journey as much as the destination. . . . Oh yes, I have had my dull moments and bad seasons—believe me, I have. But more often than not I found ways to learn from, and enjoy, some part of each job. You can't bet your whole life on some destination. You've got to make the journey work, too. And that is why I leave you with some wit and wisdom attributed to Mark Twain:

> Always work like you don't need the money. Always fall in love like you've never been hurt. Always dance like nobody is watching. And always— *always*—live like it's heaven on earth.

You can't bet your whole life on some destination. You've got to make the journey work, too.

What's Next?

We hope that you now have some of the knowledge you'll need to understand, accept, and celebrate your giftedness. We hope that you'll be able to carve a bigger, more delectable and challenging slice of life for yourself. And we wish you the very best as you continue on your journey . . . wherever it leads you.

"Cheshire Puss," [said Alice], "Would you tell me, please, which way I ought to go from here?"

"That depends a good deal on where you want to get to," said the Cat.

"I don't much care where—" said Alice.

"Then it doesn't matter which way you go," said the Cat.

"—so long as I get somewhere," Alice added as an explanation.

"Oh, you're sure to do that," said the Cat, "if you only walk long enough."

Lewis Carroll, *Alice's Adventures in Wonderland*

Recommended Resources

Giftedness

Hoagies' Kids and Teens (hoagieskids.org). A virtual cornucopia of gifted resources, including links, magazines, and reading lists, as well as "nerd" shirts, contests and awards, smart toys, and more.

Imagine magazine, published by Johns Hopkins University Center for Talented Youth (cty.jhu.edu/imagine). Written by both students and professionals, this award-winning magazine is full of advice on planning for college, profiles of careers, and information about summer programs and extracurricular activities.

More Than a Test Score: Teens Talk About Being Gifted, Talented, or Otherwise Extra-Ordinary by Robert A. Schultz and Jim Delisle (Free Spirit Publishing, 2007). What do other teens think about being gifted? With hundreds of quotes from gifted teens, this book tells it like it is, and you may find yourself knowingly nodding along. *Note:* This title is out of print but worth finding a copy online or at your library.

Outliers: The Story of Success by Malcolm Gladwell (Little, Brown and Company, 2008). Does a high IQ guarantee success? Have all successful people worked hard, or have they been afforded unique advantages? Gladwell takes a close look at the relationship between potential and achievement and challenges the notion of the self-made person.

Intellectual, Social, Emotional & Creative Intelligence

Emotional Intelligence by Linda Wasmer Andrews (Children's Press, 2005). This succinct guide to EQ defines both basic and complex emotions and includes a brief Myers-Briggs-style personality test to help facilitate young readers' self-examination.

Future Problem Solving Program International (fpspi.org). Founded by Dr. E. Paul Torrance, FPSPI stimulates creative thinking skills, encourages students to develop a vision for the future, and prepares students for leadership roles. Visit this site to enter the Torrance Creative Writing Awards and Torrance Legacy Visual Arts Awards.

Manners Made Easy for Teens: 10 Steps to a Life of Confidence, Poise, and Respect by June Hines Moore (B&H Publishing Group, 2007). Boost your social IQ by mastering these simple rules of etiquette in a variety of key social interactions, from dating to job interviews.

Mensa (mensa.org) is the International High IQ Society, with more than 110,000 members worldwide. A score of 130 on the Stanford-Binet qualifies you for membership. Challenge your mind with the Mensa workout, found on this site.

MindHabits (mindhabits.com). Develop social and emotional intelligence by playing these simple, scientifically based games developed by researchers at McGill University in Montreal.

Teen Ink (teenink.com) is a magazine, book publisher, and website devoted entirely to writing, art, photos, and forums for creative young people.

Young Composers (youngcomposers.com) is a one-stop resource for anyone interested in music composition. Upload your music to the site, and an insightful review team will help you hone your craft.

Intensities & Personality Types

Gifts Differing: Understanding Personality Type by Isabel Briggs Myers (Nicholas Brealey Publishing, 1995). Written by a cocreator of the Myers-Briggs Type Indicator, this gives you the lowdown on the 16 major personality types identified by the MBTI instrument.

Jung Typology Test (humanmetrics.com/cgi-win/jtypes2.asp). Take a free online test based on the Myers-Briggs Type Indicator (MBTI) to get an idea of which of the 16 types fits you best.

The Smart Teens' Guide to Living with Intensity: How to Get More Out of Life and Learning by Lisa Rivero (Great Potential Press, 2010). Learn how to deal with perfectionism, your parents, and school while keeping your intensity and creativity in mind.

Brain Development

How the Gifted Brain Learns by David Sousa (Corwin, 2009). The brain may work in mysterious ways, but *yours* needn't be a mystery any longer. Sousa's book translates the latest neuroscientific findings into practical strategies for understanding and engaging gifted minds. Share it with your teachers and parents.

Neuroscience for Kids (faculty.washington.edu/chudler/neurok.html). Learn (almost) everything there is to know about the nervous system—the spinal cord, neurons, sensory systems, why most people use only 10 percent of their brains, and more.

Perfectionism, Success & Stress

The Stress Reduction Workbook for Teens by Gina M. Biegel (New Harbinger Publications, 2009). This book will help you learn how to relax, prioritize your schedule, and stay calm, even when you're super-stressed.

The Success Principles for Teens: How to Get From Where You Are to Where You Want to Be by Jack Canfield and Kent Healy (HCI, 2008). Achieve your goals with these 23 strategies that have been tried and proven effective by exceptional teens.

What to Do When Good Enough Isn't Good Enough by Thomas S. Greenspon, Ph.D. (Free Spirit Publishing, 2007). Find out if you are a perfectionist, read about the effect perfectionism has on one's life, and learn how to accept "good enough" as good enough. Although written with tweens in mind, this book has proven equally as helpful for older teens and young adults.

Study Skills & Online Habits

Becoming a Master Student (13th edition) by Dave Ellis (Cengage Learning, 2011). Get tips on everything from choosing a major to overcoming a fear of public speaking.

Cyber Junkie: Escape the Gaming and Internet Trap by Kevin Roberts (Hazelden Publishing, 2010). Hooked on gaming, or know someone who is? This book offers steps and strategies for helping friends and family members overcome their cyber addiction.

Hamlet's BlackBerry: A Practical Philosophy for Building a Good Life in the Digital Age by William Powers (Harper, 2010). This book takes a look at thought leaders throughout history and shares how they dealt with their own changing times.

Virtual Learning & Homeschooling

Consumer's Guide to Online AP Courses (apguide.edutools.info). This resource can help you find the online AP courses that are right for you.

Gifted Homeschoolers Forum (GHF) (giftedhomeschoolers.org) is the hub for information related to homeschooling gifted students. Share it with your parents and browse for ideas to enrich your off-campus education.

Institute for Educational Advancement (educationaladvancement.org). Click on "Gifted Resource Center" to search their extensive database for distance learning options and other resources.

Real Lives: Eleven Teenagers Who Don't Go to School Tell Their Own Stories edited by Grace Llewellyn (Lowry House Publishers, 2005). This updated classic features an eclectic group of homeschooled students and shares the college and career paths they followed.

College & Beyond

College Planning for Gifted Students: Choosing and Getting into the Right College by Sandra Berger (Prufrock Press, 2006). Get advice on writing college application essays, requesting recommendation letters, visiting colleges, and successfully getting through college entrance interviews—all presented with the gifted learner in mind.

Considering Your Options: A Guidebook for Investigating Gap Year Opportunities. Get a free download of this valuable gap year guidebook from The Davidson Institute for Talent Development at davidsongifted.org.

The Insider's Guide to the Colleges, 2012: Students on Campus Tell You What You Really Want to Know by the staff of *Yale Daily News* (St. Martin's Griffin, 2011). College students share inside information on what their college is really like. This book doesn't just cover the academic side of college; you will also read about nightlife, dorms, and student organizations.

Renegade CEOs (teenentrepreneurblog.com). Check out this blog written for and by teen entrepreneurs, intended to inspire and empower "renegade CEOs." Parental approval advised for ages 13 and under.

What It Takes to Make More Money Than Your Parents by Nick Sheidies and Nick Tart (Wise Media Group, 2010). Get inspired by the 50 interviews of young people who have blazed their own trails and succeeded.

Cyberbullying

A Thin Line (athinline.org) is a site hosted by MTV that provides facts about sexting, constant text messaging, spying, and more; tips on how to take control of your digital domain and support others; and enlightening quizzes.

Teen Cyberbullying Investigated by Judge Tom Jacobs (Free Spirit Publishing, 2010). Learn about your First Amendment rights online and read the gritty details of court cases involving teens who have used cell phones and the Internet to harass others, including teachers, and the legal ramifications they faced.

That's Not Cool (thatsnotcool.com). Cyberbullying, sexting, and cyberstalking are not cool, but this site is. Download funky "callout cards" to stand up for yourself if you are being harassed, get advice on how to solve cyber-conflicts, and play fun animated games.

Social Networking

Cogito (cogito.org). If you're into math and science, visit this site hosted by the Johns Hopkins University Center for Talented Youth, and connect with other kids like you across the world. Participate in forums, research educational programs, and read essays, editorials, and more.

Davidson Young Scholars (davidsongifted.org/youngscholars) is a program of the Davidson Institute for Talent Development. Check out the free services provided for gifted students, including consulting services, an online community, annual get-togethers, and more.

Hoagies' Gifted Education Page on Facebook (facebook.com/HoagiesGifted) is a great place to connect with like minds and share links and comments. You must be at least 13 to join Facebook.

GT World (gtworld.org) is an online community for gifted and talented individuals and those who support and nurture them. We recommend subscribing to the "GT-Families" list for discussions appropriate for kids and teens.

GLBTQ

Campus Pride (campusclimateindex.org) includes reviews, ratings, and other info on gay-friendly college environments. Get the scoop on your top choices!

Gay-Straight Alliance Network (gsanetwork.org). Is there a GSA (gay-straight alliance) in your school? If not, consider forming one, maybe even specifically for gifted GLBTQ teens.

GLBTQ by Kelly Huegel (Free Spirit Publishing, 2011). This cutting-edge teen guide includes the most recent news and legislation regarding gay marriage and Don't Ask, Don't Tell, as well as a wealth of information on everything from making friends and dating to coming out.

It Gets Better Project (itgetsbetter.org) is a worldwide movement to provide support and encouragement for GLBTQ teens, inspiring over 10,000 user-created videos viewed over 35 million times. Watch videos from celebrities, organizations, activists, and leaders, including U.S. President Barack Obama.

Depression & Suicide

National Suicide Prevention Lifeline; (suicidepreventionlifeline.org; 1-800-273-TALK). If you are ever considering suicide, get help right away. Call the toll-free number and a caring person will be on the receiving end.

When Nothing Matters Anymore: A Survival Guide for Depressed Teens by Bev Cobain (Free Spirit Publishing, 2007). If you've ever been depressed or suicidal, you are not alone. This book, written by a relative of deceased rock singer Kurt Cobain, is a testament to that fact. Find out what other teens have to say about depression, suicide, and coping.

Wisdom & Philosophy

Philosopher's Playground (philosophersplayground.blogspot.com). Follow this blog about extraordinary artists, fascinating books, politics, ethics, and, as the blogger notes, "all topics philosophical."

Philosophy for Teens: Questioning Life's Big Ideas by Sharon Kaye and Paul Thomson (Prufrock Press, 2007). Read this 14-lesson guide and muse philosophical about lying, cheating, love, beauty, government, hate, and prejudice.

Index

About the Authors

Judy Galbraith, M.A., has a master's degree in guidance and counseling of the gifted. She has worked with and taught gifted children and teens, their parents, and their teachers for more than 30 years. In 1983, she started Free Spirit Publishing, which specializes in Self-Help for Kids® and Self-Help for Teens® books and other learning resources. She is the author of numerous books, including *The Gifted Kids' Survival Guide: For Ages 10 & Under.* Judy lives with her partner Gary in Minneapolis, along with their rescue dogs Twiggy and Sally, two spirited black terriers. Judy's hobbies include sailing, traveling, reading, scuba diving, biking, and hiking.

Jim Delisle, Ph.D., has taught gifted children and those who work on their behalf for over three decades as a professor of education at Kent State University and a gifted education teacher in the Twinsburg, Ohio, Public Schools. Jim has written 16 books on various topics related to children and education, and his frequent consulting with schools has allowed him to visit each of the 50 states as well as nations as diverse as England, China, Saudi Arabia, and Turkey. Jim and his wife Deb live in South Carolina, exploring beaches on a daily basis. Their son, Matt, is a special effects editor in California, making money while playing with technology.

Other Great Books from Free Spirit

Fighting Invisible Tigers
Stress Management for Teens
(Revised & Updated Third Edition)
by Earl Hipp
Research suggests that adolescents are affected by stress in unique ways that can increase impulsivity and risky behaviors. This book offers proven techniques that teens can use to deal with stressful situations in school, at home, and among friends. They'll find current information on how stress affects health and decision making and learn stress-management skills to handle stress in positive ways. Filled with interesting facts, student quotes, and fun activities, this book is a great resource for any teen who's said, "I'm stressed out!" For ages 11 & up. *144 pp.; softcover; 2-color; illust.; 6" x 9"*

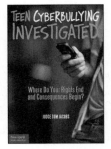

Teen Cyberbullying Investigated
When Do Your Rights End and Consequences Begin?
by Thomas A. Jacobs, J.D.
Teen Cyberbullying Investigated presents a powerful collection of landmark court cases involving teens and charges of cyberbullying, which includes: sending insulting or threatening emails, text, or instant messages directly to someone; spreading hateful comments about someone through emails, blogs, or chat rooms; stealing passwords and sending out threatening messages using a false identity; and building a website to target specific people. Each chapter features the seminal case and resulting decision, asks readers whether they agree with the decision, and urges them to think about how the decision affects their lives. For ages 12 & up. *208 pp.; softcover; 6" x 9"*